ROAD BIKING™
North Carolina

Judi Lawson Wallace

FALCONGUIDES ®

GUILFORD, CONNECTICUT
HELENA, MONTANA
AN IMPRINT OF THE GLOBE PEQUOT PRESS

For Bruce—still the world's best "sagwaggie"
and my favorite dining companion
And
For Elizabeth—you make me so proud

FALCONGUIDES®

Copyright © 2003 Morris Book Publishing, LLC

Road Biking is a trademark and Falcon and FalconGuides are registered trademarks of Morris Book Publishing, LLC

All photos by Judi Lawson Wallace unless otherwise noted.
Project Editor: David Singleton
Text design by Lesley Weissman-Cook
Maps created by Trailhead Graphics © Morris Book Publishing, LLC

Library of Congress Cataloging-in-Publication Data
Wallace, Judi Lawson.
   Road biking North Carolina / Judi Lawson Wallace.— 1st. ed
      p. cm. — (A Falcon guide) (Road biking series)
   ISBN 978-0-7627-1191-8
      1. Cycling—North Carolina—Guidebooks. 2. North Carolina—Guidebooks.
I. Title. II. Series. III. Series: Road biking series

GV1045.5.N64W35 2003
796.6'09756—dc21   2003044908

Printed in the United States of America
First Edition/Second Printing

Contents

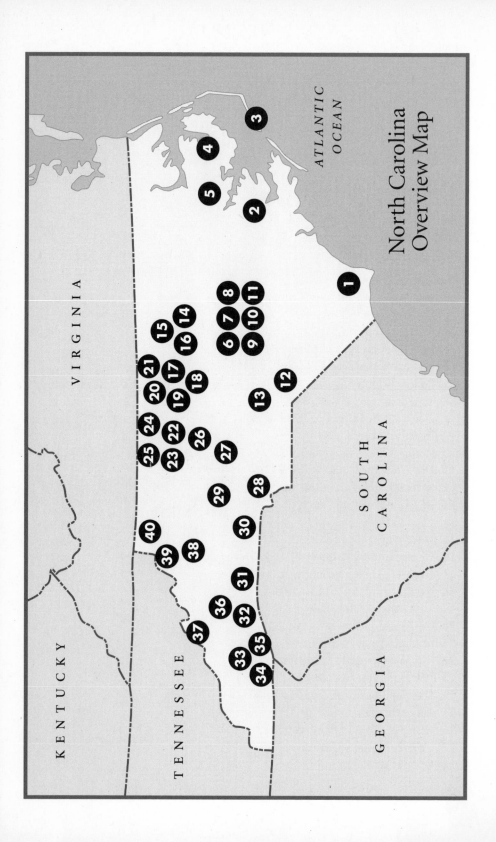

North Carolina
Overview Map

Preface

What a difficult task—selecting only forty rides for this book! There could easily have been twice that many. Fortunately I had the privilege of scouting the state for interesting sights, challenging routes, beautiful scenery. This book is the result of months of research and years of cycling experience. I also had some great recommendations from other cyclists across the state. All of the state's major regions and largest cities are represented here. Wherever possible, the routes use less traveled roads. Some of the state's more scenic areas have several routes because they have made special efforts to welcome cyclists and encourage their motorists to share the road.

Many people helped behind the scenes with this book by providing suggestions, contributions, encouragement, and support as I worked intensely for four months to meet the publication deadline. This book would not have been completed on time without the invaluable support of Bruce Heye, my special guy, who chauffeured me around, double-checked the mileage, loaded and unloaded my bike a thousand times, provided sage advice, and lifted my spirits—all without a word of complaint, even when we had to leave at an ungodly hour. Immeasurable thanks, Bruce!

Thanks also to: Mary Meletiou of the Division of Bicycle and Pedestrian Transportation in the North Carolina Department of Transportation for making available route maps for these areas, which her office had produced: Cabarrus County, Randolph County, Henderson County, Pamlico/Beaufort Counties, Transylvania County, Moore County, Richmond County, and the Lincoln County portion of the North Carolina Bike Route System, Raleigh, High Point, and Southport.

Greer Beaty, Jim Robertson, and Mariann Dellerba at the North Carolina Division of Travel and Tourism for making arrangements for accommodations in all the areas I toured. The following people in local areas provided valued assistance and hospitable accommodations during our research: Kay at the Laurinburg Chamber; Norma Faulk at Comfort Inn in Laurinburg; Lorraine Amlot at Hampton Inn in Southern Pines; Margaret Skinner at the Carolina Inn in Chapel Hill; Patty Griffin at Chapel Hill/Orange County Visitors Bureau; Kate Russell-Cobb of MountainSouth USA; Marla Tambellini of the Asheville Convention & Visitors Bureau; Mark and Vicky Mauer at The Wright Inn & Carriage House in Asheville; Jim Wooten at the Best Western Inn in Boone; Reg Poteat at the Comfort Suites Riverfront Park in New Bern; Pat and Bob Holz at the Thistle Dew Bed & Breakfast in Belhaven; Tarshi McCoy at the

Craven County CVB; Margie Brooks at the Hyde County Chamber; Judy Dale at the Best Western Hendersonville Inn; Karen Baker with Henderson County Travel & Tourism; and my friend Robert Attaway at Berkley Manor on Ocracoke.

Other thanks are due to these people and organizations for their help:

♦ My daughter Elizabeth for assisting with route research for Pilot Mountain and Durham and my niece Jessica Lawson, who accompanied us and assisted with Pilot Mountain.

♦ My friends Penny Ender; Stephan Dragisic; and Kris, Benton, and Stroud Dinkins for kindly making themselves available for photographs.

♦ The other cyclists who allowed themselves to be photographed on the spur of the moment as they were out on their bikes.

♦ Owen D. Young of the Triad Wheelers Bicycle Club for his recommendations of two routes in Guilford and Rockingham Counties.

♦ Claudia Nix and the Blue Ridge Bike Club for their suggestions and information for the ride in Burnsville.

♦ Ken Putnam of Ken's Bicycle Shop in Winston-Salem for introducing me to the Fleetwood to Todd ride more than twenty-five years ago and then supplying maps and information regarding the Pilot Mountain and Hanging Rock rides. He also kept my bike tuned up for the duration of the tours.

♦ Mike Boone of Magic Cycles in Boone for recommending the route in Valle Crucis.

♦ Shelly Green and Zenda Douglas of the Durham Convention and Visitors Bureau for the wealth of information they provided, including photographs of sites in the city.

♦ Kenneth J. Tippette of the Down East Cycling Club for his recommendations and accurate detailed directions for the tours in Bath and around Lake Mattamuskeet.

♦ Rooney Coffman, my fellow classmate at St. Andrews, for his research and route recommendations for Scotland County.

♦ Chris Lawrence of Cabella Bicycles in Landrum, South Carolina, for his recommendations for routes in the Polk County area.

♦ Jacquie Ziller, director of travel and tourism for Polk County, for the maps, information, and photographs.

♦ My mother and stepfather, Doris and Harold Lewis, for their encouragement and support.

♦ My brother Jim Lawson for gathering maps and information on the Salisbury area for me.

I apologize in advance in case there's anyone I've overlooked. My poor memory in no way detracts from my appreciation of your efforts.

Introduction

Lots of sunshine, moderate temperatures even in winter, four gorgeous seasons, beautiful scenery, and varied terrain make North Carolina a perfect place for bicycling. Historic and cultural attractions complement its natural beauty and offer something for everyone. From stock car racing to opera, Carowinds to Old Salem, lounging on the beach or hiking in the mountains, you'll find lots to enjoy in the Old North State.

Frequently called the Variety Vacationland, the Tar Heel State stretches several hundred miles from the Blue Ridge Mountains and the Great Smoky Mountains of the Appalachian chain through the Piedmont and the Sandhills to the Coastal Plain. Its highest point, Mount Mitchell (north of Asheville), rises to 6,684 feet, the tallest peak in the eastern United States. Sea level at the coast is its lowest. With 52,586 square miles, North Carolina ranks twenty-eighth in size but tenth in population, which is more than 7 million.

Since the establishment of the North Carolina Bicycle Program in 1974, the state has developed many wonderful routes and programs to attract cyclists to its well-maintained highway system. The first of these was the Murphy to Manteo route for the Mountains to Sea System. With the assistance and oversight of the state office, many local areas have also produced maps and guides for bicycle tourists. Some of these served as the basis for tours in this book.

Getting ready to ride.

North Carolina has also invested in improving roadways for cyclists, especially along the coast where alternate routes aren't available. There you'll frequently find paved shoulders and bridges with extra room for cyclists. Some bridges even have higher railings as a protection for bicycles and their riders.

North Carolina's climate is almost ideal for

Cycling is popular around Carr Mill Mall in Carrboro.

cycling year-round. Humid and hot summer days make it prudent to start very early to avoid the hottest times of the day. But spring and fall are spectacular anywhere in the state. Except for the mountains, the winters are generally mild enough for cyclists to get in some miles.

In North Carolina you can find just about anything you'd like to see: sand dunes, rugged mountain peaks, lush valleys, historic towns, quiet forests, islands, lakes, and red clay. You can start in the east where the flat terrain makes pedaling easy—although the winds are sometimes very strong—move inland to the Sandhills and Piedmont for more rolling terrain, then to the mountains for some real challenges. But believe it or not, even the mountains have their share of lovely, flat rides beside rivers.

For more information on North Carolina, you should contact the Division of Film, Tourism, and Sports Development at 430 North Salisbury Street, Raleigh, NC 27611; (919) 733–4171 in Raleigh or (800) 847–4862 outside Raleigh; or check out their Web site at www. visitnc.com.

For more about cycling in the state, the North Carolina Department of Transportation's Division of Bicycle and Pedestrian Transportation offers a wealth of information on its Web site: www.dot.state.nc.us/transit/bicycle. Or you can write to 1552 Mail Service Center, Raleigh, NC 27699-1552, or call (919) 733–2804.

ROAD AND TRAFFIC CONDITIONS

Wherever possible, these routes use quiet back roads and neighborhood streets. In North Carolina all the rural roads have been given names to help emergency services more quickly find those who need help. In addition, the state's secondary roads continue to use SR and a four-digit number. In some locations, these state road numbers may be difficult to find. They are frequently—but not always—placed on green-and-white road signs along with the road's name. In some highway divisions and counties, however, you may have to look for black-and-white numbers shown vertically on the posts for stop signs or other directional signs at intersections.

Most highways in North Carolina are in good repair, although railroad crossings can sometimes be rough. Take care to slow down and cross the tracks at a ninety-degree angle to avoid getting your wheel caught or sliding off a rail.

In some places it is necessary to use busier streets and highways. For example, on the Pamlico Sound Classic ride, the only way to get from New Bern into Pamlico County is on a four-lane highway that crosses the only bridge over the river. Fortunately there is a wide shoulder for bikes. In other (rare) cases, you'll need to use your best judgment and experience in negotiating with motorists. Every effort was made to keep the distances on these major roads as short as possible.

♦ *A Bike Is a Vehicle.* In North Carolina, as in many other states, bicycles are considered vehicles and must obey the same rules of the road. That means cyclists have the same rights but also the same responsibilities as motor vehicles when sharing the road. However, even being right doesn't mean you'll win if you tangle with a two-ton car. So courtesy and prudently giving way to others is your safest bet.

Many of North Carolina's secondary roadways are designated as either local or state bike routes. These bike route signs help alert motorists to the presence of cyclists. North Carolina was also the first state to develop a SHARE THE ROAD caution sign with a small bicycle emblem under it. You're likely to see these on highways with more motorized traffic.

As a vehicle, you're entitled to a full lane—but be considerate of motorists behind you. Remember the Golden Rule!

♦ *The Roadway.* These routes have been selected because they usually have less traffic than alternatives. However, conditions change. It's up to you to be alert for potholes, debris on the road, construction projects, and other road hazards. Especially in the summer months, you might want to call ahead to find out about road construction and conditions before starting your ride. You can also check traffic conditions on the North Carolina Department of Transportation Web site at www.ncdot.org.

♦ *Look Around You.* Always be conscious of your surroundings, particularly if you're riding alone. I've done a lot of cycling by myself and use my rearview mirror and check ahead to anticipate problem situations or conditions. Consider carrying a cell phone and/or riding with a friend or a group.

♦ *Be Visible.* One reason for brightly patterned clothing for cyclists is to make us stand out in traffic. Especially in town, myriad signs and other traffic can distract drivers. So wear bright, contrasting colors to make you visible. While I don't recommend riding at night, if you choose to do so, you should wear retroreflective clothing or vests and equip your bike with a bright front light and effective red rear reflector. Some cyclists place a flashing strobe on the back of the bike to alert drivers.

Cyclists can be really hard to see in the very-early-morning and late-evening hours, when shadows and the angle of the sun can keep drivers from seeing us. Take special care at these times. At all times remember that drivers are looking for other vehicles, so act like one. If you need to do so for safety, ride farther out into the lane so you're more visible for drivers. This is especially true on the few sections of these routes where there are four lanes. Always signal your intention to turn or change lanes so that drivers can react properly.

While cyclists are expected to ride as far to the right as practicable, on curvy roads it's important to position yourself far enough into the lane so that motorists approaching from behind will see you in time to react appropriately.

Two Chicago cyclists ride the Ocracoke ferry with their fully loaded bikes after cycling from Maine to North Carolina.

One of the best things about cycling is that you don't need a lot of fancy gear. Still, some basics will make your tours safer and more enjoyable.

♦ *Helmet.* Absolutely essential for your safety. Make sure you wear one that fits properly with a secure strap. You should wear it so the front of the helmet comes almost to your eyebrows, to really protect your brain if you have an accident. In 2001 North Carolina passed a helmet law requiring children under the age of sixteen to wear a bike helmet when cycling or being carried on an adult's bike. Children under 40 inches or forty pounds must be carried in an approved restraint.

♦ *A Bike That Fits.* Make sure you and any companions are riding the right-sized bike and that your seat is positioned properly. If the seat is too low, your legs will tire too quickly; if it's too high, you might injure your knees. Also, you'll have difficulty handling the bike properly in either case.

♦ *Check Out Your Bike.* Check your tire pressure, brakes, handlebars, cables, and reflectors before you start riding to make sure that everything works properly before you get 10 miles out into the country.

♦ *Water.* This liquid is a must any time of year but particularly in the hot, humid summer months. Always drink before you're thirsty and consume at least a pint of water every hour. Bike shops carry water bottles and holders that can attach to your bike frame.

♦ *Bike Lock.* A strong lock is essential if you plan to leave your bike for sightseeing or other stops. It's important to secure both wheels and the frame to an immovable object.

♦ *Clothing.* You can wear just about anything to ride a bike as long as it won't get caught in the chain or other bike parts and throw you off. However, for longer rides, padded cycling shorts or tights prevent chafing and won't bunch up while you ride. Jerseys and jackets of lightweight materials that wick water away from your skin are especially helpful when you ride in colder weather. Padded gloves also protect your hands from numbness or scrapes if you should fall.

♦ *Bike Computer.* These neat gizmos that clip to your handlebars will help you measure mileage and help keep you on track with the directions. They're available in bike shops and by mail order.

♦ *Cellular Phone/Repair Kit.* If you do run into problems, a lightweight cell phone in your bike bag can be a big help. Of course, you'll need numbers with you so you know who to call. If you don't have a cell phone, I suggest carrying a small repair kit or at least a spare tube, tire irons, and a frame pump.

♦ *Bike Bags.* Speaking of carrying things, you'll also need a small seatbag—ideal for tools and pocket change. A handlebar bag with a clear pocket on top is handy for keeping your map and directions right in front of you as you ride.

♦ *Glasses/Sunglasses.* Good eye protection can be important to keep bugs and other debris out of your eyes while you're riding. Preventing harm from ultraviolet rays is a consideration, too, especially if you'll be riding for several hours.

FOR MORE BICYCLE INFORMATION

Division of Bicycle and Pedestrian Transportation
North Carolina Department of Transportation
1552 Mail Service Center
Raleigh, NC 27699-1552
(919) 733–2804
www.dot.state.nc.us/transit/bicycle

Touring Information
League of American Bicyclists
1612 K Street, NW, Suite 401
Washington, DC 20006
(202) 822–1333
www.bikeleague.org

HOW TO USE THIS BOOK

The forty routes in *Road Biking North Carolina* are divided into four categories according to degree of difficulty. These classifications are based principally on distance; the summary at the beginning of each will guide you as to the terrain and difficulty of the ride. Here's a description of each category:

♦ *Rambles* are the shortest and usually the easiest of the rides in the book, accessible to almost all riders, and should be easily completed in one day. They are 25 miles long or less and are generally on flat to slightly rolling terrain, although some may have steeper climbs.

♦ *Cruises* are intermediate in distance and difficulty, ranging from 26 to 40 miles long, and may include some moderate climbs. Cruises can generally be completed easily by an experienced rider in one day, but inexperienced or out-of-shape riders may want to take two days with an overnight stop.

♦ *Challenges* are more difficult and are designed for experienced riders in good physical condition. Their distances, at 40 to 60 miles, should be a challenge even for fairly fit riders attempting to complete them in one day. Less experienced or fit riders should expect to take two days.

♦ *Classics* are long and hard. They are more than 60 miles—and may be more than 100. They can include steep climbs and high-speed downhills. Even fit and experienced riders may want to take two days. These rides are not recommended for less fit and experienced riders unless they are done in shorter stages.

Most of these rides were selected because of interesting or historically significant sights along the way. The rides within the state's largest cities offer a physically healthy way to see the city's points of interest and get a feel for the overall ambience, although the city rides do involve more frequent turns. If your goal focuses more on a physical workout, you'll want to choose one of the rural routes where you can cut loose.

Many of these rides tie in with local bike routes or are part of the network of Bicycling Highways that crisscross North Carolina. Use the routes in this book as a starting point in combination with these state and local routes for creating your own tours.

Fort Fisher to Southport Cruise

The 27.1-mile Fort Fisher to Southport Cruise explores a small coastal town at the mouth of the Cape Fear River and then crosses by ferry to the coastal island across the river where Fort Fisher is located. The sea breezes will cool you as you pedal along these flat roads; however, the seeming ease of the route can be offset by strong coastal winds. This route links the town of Southport with Fort Fisher State Historic Site, the North Carolina Aquarium, and Carolina Beach State Park. Since the starting point is in the middle of the route, you have the choice of which section to do first. You'll probably want to base your decision on the ferry schedule.

Starting at the Southport–Fort Fisher ferry terminal, you can ride either the Southport or the Fort Fisher portion first. The city of Southport, established in 1792, has been both a military town and a fishing village, which it clearly continues to be. The Southport part of the tour winds around the small town to give you a look at some of the historic houses and buildings, each with an interesting story. For example, at the corner of Atlantic Avenue and Brown Street (319 Atlantic Avenue), you'll see the three-story house that A. E. Stevens built in 1894 for his bride-to-be. She said "No" and married his best friend. The newlyweds built a house across the street from Mr. Stevens, who never married.

At the corner of Atlantic Avenue and Bay Street stands the Brunswick Inn, which was built in 1859 as a resort hotel. It supposedly is home to Tony the Ghost, referring to Antonio Caseletta, an Italian harpist who went sailing and drowned in 1882. The next morning guests reported that his harp's strings had been ripped out. His spirit roams the building, and mysterious sounds are still heard. You may want to stay there and see for yourself.

As you pedal along the waterfront, you can look across the water to see the lighthouses on Oak Island and Bald Head Island. The route follows the waterfront, winding along Yacht Basin and Brunswick Street to the Southport marina. West Street is a lovely divided street under a canopy of live oaks. You'll see Franklin Square Park on the right at the intersection with Howe Street. One humorist in Southport likes to joke that three of Southport's streets are Howe, Drye, Iam. Look out for these street signs as you pedal along West Street.

For the Fort Fisher portion of the ride, take the thirty-minute ferry ride from Southport to Fort Fisher (the cost is $1.00 per bike rider and $3.00 per car). The paved shoulders along U.S. Highway 421 make the pedaling more enjoyable since this is the main highway on the island. The first attraction you'll pass is the North Carolina Aquarium at Fort Fisher, one of three along the North Carolina coast. Besides the exhibits, they have all sorts of programs and activities to teach people about the coastal environment and wildlife.

The next point of interest is the Fort Fisher State Historic Site on the river side of the island, called the last major stronghold of the Confederacy. Once one of the largest and most important earthwork fortifications in the South, much of it was destroyed; only about 10 percent of the fort remains, along with a restored palisade fence. You can still see the impressive work that was done and how important it would have been during the Civil War.

From Fort Fisher you'll continue up the island through the towns of Kure Beach, Wilmington Beach, and Carolina Beach with glimpses of the ocean on your right between the beach houses and buildings. North of Carolina Beach is a state park of the same name. Besides offering a vista over the Cape Fear River, the park has several nature trails of varying lengths and a visitor center with exhibits about the different coastal ecosystems present in the park. Several interesting carnivorous plants thrive in the park by trapping and digesting insects: pitcher plants, bladderworts, and—the most spectacular—the Venus's-flytrap, which is native only within 60 to 75 miles of Wilmington. Destruction of habitat has threatened these unique plants, so the park is designed to help preserve them. After your visit to the park, you'll turn around and pedal south to the ferry to return to the Southport side.

LOCAL INFORMATION

♦ Southport Visitors Center, 107 East Nash Street, Southport, NC 28461; (910) 457–7927.
♦ Cape Fear Coast Convention & Visitors Bureau, 24 North Third Street, Wilmington, NC 28401; (910) 341–4030 or (800) 222–4757; www.cape-fear. nc.us.
♦ North Carolina Division of Transportation, Ferry Division, 113 Arendell Street, Morehead City, NC 28557; (252) 726–6446 or (800) BY–FERRY; www. ncferry.org.

LOCAL EVENTS/ATTRACTIONS

♦ North Carolina Aquarium at Fort Fisher offers exhibits, programs, and activities designed to promote awareness, understanding, appreciation, and

Trees frame a view of the defensive mounds at Fort Fisher.

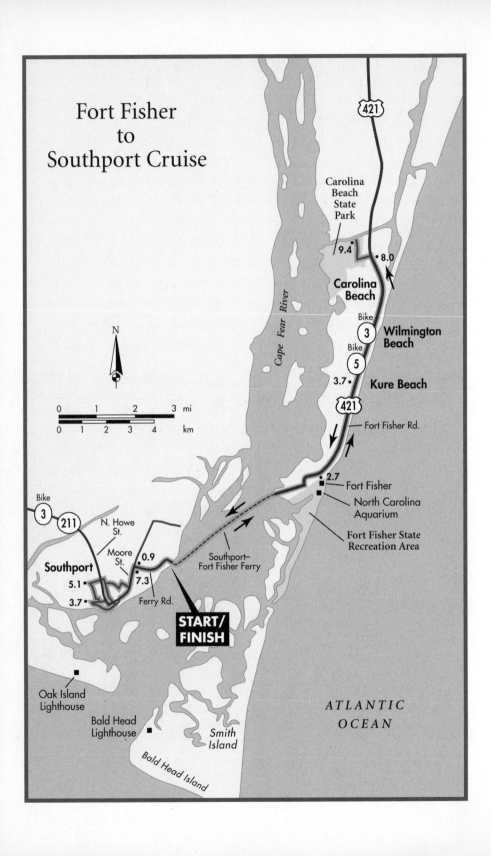

Fort Fisher
to
Southport Cruise

421

Carolina Beach State Park

9.4 • • 8.0

Carolina Beach

Bike **3** **Wilmington Beach**

Bike **5**

3.7 • **Kure Beach**

421

Fort Fisher Rd.

2.7 • Fort Fisher

North Carolina Aquarium

Fort Fisher State Recreation Area

Cape Fear River

N

0   1   2   3 mi
0   1   2   3   4 km

Bike **3** **211**

N. Howe St.

Moore St.

0.9 •

Southport

5.1 •

3.7 •

7.3 •

Ferry Rd.

Southport–Fort Fisher Ferry

START/FINISH

Oak Island Lighthouse

Bald Head Lighthouse

Smith Island

Bald Head Island

ATLANTIC OCEAN

You have a choice of the direction in which to start this ride; you can either take the ferry and do the Fort Fisher section first or you can do the Southport section and then take the ferry. You'll probably want to base your decision on the ferry schedule.

Southport Section

0.0 From the Southport–Fort Fisher ferry terminal, take Ferry Road toward Southport, following the signs for North Carolina Bike Routes 3 and 5. Ferry Road has bike lanes.

0.9 Turn left onto Moore Street.

1.5 Turn right onto Fodale Drive.

1.7 Turn left onto Longleaf Drive.

1.8 Turn right onto Herring Street. Jog left at Leonard Street to stay on Herring Street.

2.2 Turn left onto Atlantic Avenue.

2.9 Turn right onto Bay Street toward Southport Marina.

3.3 The street curves right around the marina.

3.4 Turn left onto Yacht Basin and then make an immediate right to follow the street.

3.5 Turn left onto Brunswick Street, which winds along the waterfront marsh, then bear right to the stop sign.

3.7 Turn right onto West Street.

4.2 Turn left onto Atlantic Avenue.

4.7 Turn left onto Ninth Street.

5.1 Turn left onto Burrington Avenue.

5.5 Turn left onto Brown Street.

5.6 Turn right onto Clarendon Avenue.

5.7 Turn left onto West Street.

5.9 Turn right onto Howe Street.

6.0 Turn left onto Moore Street.

7.3 Turn right onto Ferry Road toward the ferry terminal.

8.1 Arrive at the Southport to Fort Fisher ferry terminal.

Fort Fisher Section

0.1 From the ferry landing on Fort Fisher, turn left onto Fort Fisher Road/U.S. Highway 421 north, which has bike lanes on both sides.

1.3 Turn right onto Loggerhead Road to the Fort Fisher State Recreation Area and beach access and the North Carolina Aquarium.

1.8 Arrive at the North Carolina Aquarium at Fort Fisher. After your visit, turn around and return to Fort Fisher Road.

2.3 Turn right onto Fort Fisher Road.

(continued)

2.7 Arrive at Fort Fisher State Historic Site. After your visit, turn left onto Fort Fisher Road/US 421, heading north, following Bike Routes 3 and 5. *Bail-out:* You have the option of turning right here and heading back to the ferry terminal.

3.7 Enter the town of Kure Beach.

5.7 Enter the town of Carolina Beach.

8.0 Turn left onto Dow Road and then right into Carolina Beach State Park, following the signs.

8.4 Arrive at the visitor center on right. From the visitor center turn right and travel to the marina overlooking the Cape Fear River.

9.5 Arrive at the marina. After your visit, turn around and return to the park entrance.

11.0 Turn left onto Dow Road and then right onto US 421, heading south to return to the Fort Fisher ferry terminal.

19.0 Arrive at Fort Fisher ferry terminal.

conservation of coastal resources; 900 Loggerhead Road, Kure Beach, NC 28449; adults $6.00, seniors $5.00, children six through seventeen $4.00, children under six free; (910) 458–8257, ext. 208; www.ncaquariums.com.

♦ Fort Fisher State Historic Site, one of the largest and most important earthwork fortifications in the South during the Civil War; the visitor center has exhibits and audiovisual presentations; P.O. Box 169, Kure Beach, NC 28449; no charge; (910) 458–5538; www.ah.dcr.state.nc.us/sections/hs/fisher/fisher.htm.

♦ Carolina Beach State Park offers camping, hiking along several different trails, exhibits in the visitor center, and education programs; a concession stand is located at the marina; P.O. Box 475, Carolina Beach, NC 28428; no charge except for camping; office: (910) 458–8206; marina: (910) 458–7770.

RESTAURANTS

♦ Fish Tales Restaurant & Tiki Bar, 606-A West West Street (at Southport marina), Southport, NC 28461; (910) 457–9222. Overlooks Cape Fear River; open daily for seafood, salads, sandwiches; midrange.

♦ Sea Captain Restaurant, 608 West West Street, Southport, NC 28461; (910) 457–0600. Near the marina; open for breakfast and lunch daily, for dinner Tuesday through Saturday; home cooking; midrange.

♦ Concession stand at Carolina Beach State Park, P.O. Box 475, Carolina Beach, NC 28428; (910) 458–7770. Snacks and drinks; low range.

ACCOMMODATIONS

♦ Cape Fear Inn, 308 West Bay Street, Southport, NC 28461; (910) 457–5989. On the waterfront; mid- to upper range, depending on season.
♦ Brunswick Inn, 301 East Bay Street, Southport, NC 28461; (910) 457–5278. Bed-and-breakfast; historic Southport landmark; upper range.

BIKE SHOPS

♦ Two Wheeler Dealer, 4408 Wrightsville Avenue, Wilmington, NC 28403; (910) 799–6444.

REST ROOMS

♦ At the start and finish at the Southport and Fort Fisher ferry terminals.
♦ Mile 1.8 at the North Carolina Aquarium.
♦ Mile 2.7 at the Fort Fisher Historic Site.
♦ At about Miles 8.4 and at 8.6 (Fort Fisher portion) in Carolina Beach State Park.

MAPS

♦ *DeLorme North Carolina Atlas & Gazetteer,* page 87.
♦ North Carolina Department of Transportation's Southport Bicycle Map, 1994.
♦ Carolina Beach State Park map (www.ils.unc.edu/parkproject/visit/cabe/home).

Pamlico Sound Classic

The Pamlico Sound Classic, a century tour, takes you from historic New Bern across two rivers into Pamlico County for a large loop around Gum Tree Swamp and through small coastal communities. The flat terrain makes for easy pedaling through mostly remote areas, except when strong winds prevail. Services are few and far between, so you'll want to stock up when you have the opportunity.

The starting point for this ride is in New Bern, the second oldest town in North Carolina, which was named for the city of Bern in Switzerland by the German and Swiss colonists who settled here in 1710. New Bern was part of the Carolina Charter issued by England's King Charles II, who appointed Royal Governor William Tryon to oversee the colony. Tryon selected New Bern as the site of the first permanent capital of what was to become North Carolina. He erected as his royal residence and capitol building the elegant Tryon Palace, called one of the most beautiful public buildings in America. You'll want to take time to visit the palace either before or after your ride.

From Tryon Palace the route loops through part of the historic district in New Bern, past numerous buildings dating from the eighteenth and nineteenth centuries. A Heritage Tour brochure, available from the visitor center, lists the buildings by address and gives a brief description of each. Of particular note is the interesting architecture of the Fireman's Museum, which you'll see on your right at the intersection with Broad Street as you head north on Hancock Street. Along Johnson Street almost all the buildings on the right side of the street have historic significance, so slow your pace and take a look.

East Front Street, the first post road, curves along the banks of the Neuse River and connects with South Front Street, which parallels the Trent River to Tryon Palace, the route you'll take on your return trip. East Front Street becomes U.S. Highway 70 Business and takes you across the drawbridge over the Trent River. The highway becomes four lanes, divided, but a wide shoulder provides ample room for cyclists. Just remember that bicycles are vehicles and signal your intentions as you take the US 17/NC–55 exit. The ramp circles around and merges into US 70/17 Bypass. You then take the US 17/NC–55 exit to the bridge over the Neuse River. Once you are across the river, you can relax and enjoy pedaling around rural Pamlico County.

Pamlico County is essentially a peninsula surrounded by the Neuse River, Pamlico Sound, the Bay River, and the Pamlico River. Exactly how much shoreline the county has may be subject to debate, but there is no denying that there's a lot of waterfront. Protected by the Outer Banks and surrounding counties of Carteret, Craven, and Beaufort, Pamlico County boasts miles and miles of pristine estuarial waters, the perfect environment for fish, waterfowl, and marshland. During this tour you're seldom more than 5 to 10 miles from the water, and sometimes you'll ride right along the shore.

THE BASICS

Start: The public parking lot for Tryon Palace on Eden Street in downtown New Bern.

Length: 102.0 miles.

Terrain: Mainly level.

Traffic and hazards: You have to cross two rivers to get from New Bern into Pamlico County and must use U.S. Highway 17/North Carolina Highway 55 to cross the bridge over the Neuse River. While US 17/NC–55 is a divided four-lane highway, there is a wide shoulder for bikes. SHARE THE ROAD signs along the highway and on the bridge alert motorists to bicyclists using those facilities.

Getting there: Take US 70 toward New Bern and then follow US 70 Business into New Bern. Turn right onto George Street, which ends directly in front of Tryon Palace. Turn right onto Pollock Street and then left onto Eden Street. The public parking lot will be on the right. See the *DeLorme North Carolina Atlas & Gazetteer,* page 78 A1.

When you exit onto NC–55 (North Carolina Bike Route 3), the road narrows to two lanes with no shoulder, but it's only a short distance to the first turn onto quiet back roads. In places you'll see wide green fields of soybeans against a backdrop of dark green forest. After cycling past forests and farmland, you'll enter Beaufort County and come to the first small town, Aurora. From there the route skirts the perimeter of the Gum Swamp, passes through Goose Creek Game Land (you'll reenter Pamlico County), and follows the Intracoastal Waterway for a short distance before turning south. Canals alongside the roadway are a typical sight here. Signs point the way to wildlife viewing areas.

A long stretch along NC–304 dips and curves around inlets of the Bay River before you reach the small town of Bayboro. You'll find a convenience/grocery store here. As you head east on Highway 55 to Stonewall, keep a look out for the Alligator Control Office, an indication of wildlife in the area you'll want to

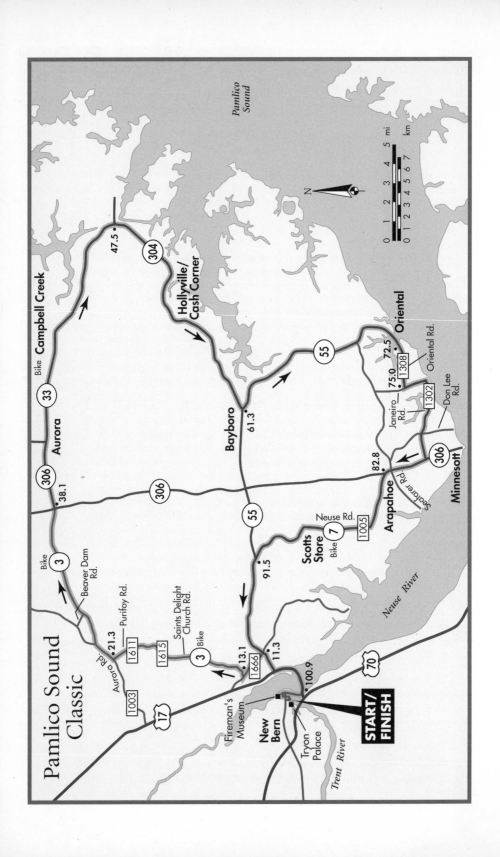

Pamlico Sound Classic

0.0 From the public parking lot for Tryon Palace in New Bern, go right on Eden Street toward the river, which curves around the riverfront side of the palace and becomes Metcalf Street.

0.2 Turn right onto South Front Street.

0.3 Turn left onto Hancock Street. Watch out for the trolley tracks. *Note:* At the intersection with Broad Street, look to your right to see the Fireman's Museum and its interesting architecture.

0.7 Turn right onto Johnson Street. *Note:* Most buildings on your right have historical significance.

1.0 Turn right onto East Front Street.

1.2 At the traffic circle, continue straight on East Front Street and across the drawbridge over the Trent River. Then take the exit for US 17/NC–55 for the bridge across the Neuse River.

5.7 Exit onto NC–55, which is also North Carolina Bike Route 3.

11.3 Turn left onto Broadcreek Road, the name of which changes to Half Moon Road (SR 1666).

13.1 Turn right onto Saints Delight Church Road (SR 1615).

18.8 Bear left onto Purifoy Road (SR 1611).

21.3 Turn right onto Aurora Road (SR 1003) to Cayton.

22.6 Go straight to stay on Aurora Road, then bear right at Beaver Dam Road to stay on Aurora Road. Aurora Road's name changes to Turnstall Swamp Road (SR 1003) when you enter Beaufort County.

31.1 Turn left at the stop sign (no road sign here) and make an immediate right to follow NC–306, which joins NC–33 at this intersection. Take NC–33/306 through the community of Aurora. Bike Route 3 goes to the left just before you enter Aurora.

34.3 Go straight to stay on NC–33 to the community of Campbell Creek.

47.5 Turn right onto NC–304, continuing through Hollyville/Cash Corner.

47.6 Turn left to stay on NC–304 to Bayboro.

61.3 In Bayboro turn left onto NC–55 East to the community of Stonewall and then continue on NC–55 to Oriental. *Note:* Look for the Alligator Control Office!

72.7 North Carolina Highway 55 ends just before you cross the Robert Scott Bridge; the road's name changes to Oriental Road (SR 1308).

75.1 Turn left onto Janeiro Road (SR 1302), which goes straight toward the Neuse River and then curves sharply right.

79.4 Cross Don Lee Road.

80.8 Turn right onto NC–306 North to Arapahoe.

(continued)

82.8 Turn left onto Seafarer Road (SR 1117) and then make an immediate right onto Neuse Road (SR 1005), which is North Carolina Bike Route 7.

87.8 Turn left to stay on Neuse Road (SR 1005) in the community of Scotts Store.

89.6 Turn left to stay on Neuse Road (SR 1005).

91.5 Turn left onto NC–55 West.

100.3 Take NC–55 West toward New Bern, which has signs for Bike Routes 3 and 7.

100.7 Turn right to follow NC–55 and US 70 Business.

100.9 Turn right on NC–55 and US 70 Business West and cross the bridge into New Bern.

101.4 Turn left onto South Front Street.

101.8 Turn left onto Metcalf Street, which curves into Eden Street.

102.0 Turn left into parking lot at Tryon Palace.

avoid. In fact, NC–55 parallels Alligator Creek Road for a short distance then leads you to Oriental, the Sailing Capital of North Carolina because of the large number of sailboats that are docked in the marinas.

Located on the wide shores of the Neuse River, not far from Pamlico Sound, Oriental was originally discovered by one Louis B. Midyette in the 1870s. Legend says that "Uncle Lou," as he was known, anchored his sailboat in the protected waters of Oriental, at the mouth of Smith Creek, to escape a gale. He was sailing from New Bern back to his home in Dare County, where he was a farmer and a fisherman. Storytellers claim that the next morning Lou went ashore and climbed a tree. He was captured by the beautiful landscape and all the waterfront created by the many creeks. He returned home to persuade others to join his family in moving to the area. From Oriental the route winds through the countryside then reconnects with North Carolina Highway 306 to Highway 55 for the trip back to New Bern.

Pamlico County has a rich history. Indian artifacts testify to the county's early inhabitants. Land records date grants from the king of England to colonial farmers, and many residents can trace their family's genealogy to these times. Adding spice to the area's history are the exploits of the infamous Edward Teach— the pirate Blackbeard—who used the numerous coves and inlets in this area as a base for plundering ships. Until more recent times Pamlico County was focused primarily on farming and fishing. Traveling through the county you pass farms and timberland on your way to the many quaint fishing villages nestled among the creeks, forests, and farmland. Here time seems to pass a little slower; you have to accustom yourself to return the wave of friends you haven't met yet.

A tree-lined allée leads to Tryon Palace in New Bern.

♦ New Bern/Craven County Convention & Visitors Bureau, 314 South Front Street, New Bern, NC 28563; (252) 637–9400 or (800) 437–5767; www.visit newbern.com.

♦ Pamlico County Chamber of Commerce, P.O. Box 23, Bayboro, NC 28515 (252) 745–3008; www.pamlico_nc.com/chamber

LOCAL EVENTS/ATTRACTIONS

♦ Tryon Palace, built in 1770 as a residence for Royal Governor William Tryon and the first capitol of North Carolina, has been restored to its eighteenth-century glory with an outstanding collection of antiques and art plus extensive gardens; 610 Pollock Street, New Bern, NC 28562; Governor's Pass (admission to all buildings and gardens) for adults $15.00, children in grades one through twelve $6.00; (252) 514–4900 or (800) 767–1560; www.tryonpalace.org.

♦ Heritage Tour in Historic New Bern, a self-guided tour with information about 142 historic buildings; Craven County Convention & Visitors Bureau, 314 South Front Street, New Bern, NC 28560; no charge; (252) 637–9400 or (800) 437–5767.

♦ Fireman's Museum, a collection of early fire-fighting equipment along with rare photographs and Civil War relics; 408 Hancock Street, New Bern, NC 28560; (252) 636–4087.

♦ Birthplace of Pepsi, the pharmacy where Caleb Bradham invented Pepsi-Cola, which you can taste at the re-created soda fountain; 256 Middle Street, New Bern, NC 28560; no charge; (252) 636–5898.

♦ New Bern Trolley Tours, ninety-minute guided tour covering three centuries of history and architectural beauty; 333 Middle Street, New Bern, NC 28560; adults $12.00, children twelve and under $6.00; (252) 637–7316 or (800) 849–7316; www.newberntours.com.

♦ Oriental Harbor, known as the Sailing Capital of North Carolina, with thousands of sailing vessels of all sizes docked here; Hodges Street, Oriental, NC 28571; no charge; (252) 249–0555.

♦ Circle 10 Art Gallery features original works by local artists: acrylics, oils, watercolors, basketry, fiber art, graphics, jewelry, sculpture, and stained glass; Hodges Street, Oriental, NC 28571; no charge; (252) 249–0298.

♦ Aurora Fossil Museum contains a wide variety of fossils uncovered in the process of mining phosphate, including sharks' teeth and other fossils; Aurora, NC 27806; call for hours; (919) 322–4238.

RESTAURANTS

♦ The Chelsea, a Restaurant and Publick House, 335 Middle Street, New Bern, NC 28560; (252) 637–5469. Casual dining for lunch and dinner Monday through Saturday; mid- to upper range.

♦ Wayside Restaurant, intersection of Highway 306 and Highway 33, Aurora, NC 27806; (252) 322–7299. Breakfast and lunch Monday through Friday; closed weekends; homestyle meals; low range.

♦ Charlie's Country Cooking, Highway 55 West, Bayboro, NC 28515; (252) 745–4551. Monday through Saturday 6:00 A.M.–9:00 P.M.; Sunday 7:00 A.M.– 7:00 P.M.; low range.

♦ Oriental Steam Restaurant & Tavern, Broad Street and Hodges Street, Oriental, NC 28571 (252) 249–3557. Lunch Friday through Sunday; dinner nightly 5:00–9:00 P.M.; retail bakery; midrange.

ACCOMMODATIONS

♦ Comfort Suites Riverfront Park, 218 East Front Street, New Bern, NC 28560; (252) 636–0022.

BIKE SHOPS

♦ Flythe's Bike Shop, 2411 Trent Road, New Bern, NC 28562; (252) 638–1544.

REST ROOMS

♦ At the start and finish at Tryon Palace, when it's open. Also at the visitor center at 314 South Front Street.

♦ At about Mile 31 at the Wayside Restaurant or the Aurora Fossil Museum in Aurora.

♦ At about Mile 61.3 at a convenience/grocery store at the intersection of Highway 304 and Highway 55.

♦ At about Mile 70 at shops and restaurants in Oriental.

MAPS

♦ *DeLorme North Carolina Atlas & Gazetteer,* pages 66–67, 78–79.
♦ New Bern map from Craven County Convention & Visitors Bureau.

Ocracoke to Hatteras Classic

*T*he 67.6-mile Ocracoke to Hatteras Classic covers all of Ocracoke Island and the southern part of Hatteras Island along North Carolina's famed Outer Banks. Much of the route is in the Cape Hatteras National Seashore, which means protected dunes and beaches and no development. Paved shoulders line some of this flat route, but winds can be strong. Also, much of the route travels through remote areas, so plan accordingly for water and food.

The rustic island village of Ocracoke charms visitors with its narrow, curving, sandy streets reminiscent of a bygone era. Known primarily as a center for fishing and bird hunting, Ocracoke more recently has begun to attract tourists, thanks to a large new hotel. Fortunately it retains its rustic charm, and you'll enjoy cycling through the village, built around Silver Lake. The infamous pirate Blackbeard (Edward Teach) met his death in Silver Lake Harbor in 1718. Watching over the village is the Ocracoke Lighthouse, called in one guidebook "a photographer's dream." This lighthouse is the oldest still in service in North Carolina.

Ocracoke has always been an isolated island community because it is accessible only by ferry. Linguists have studied the English spoken by the natives because their isolation helped them retain portions of the Elizabethan accent used by their forebears.

After you leave the village of Ocracoke, you'll enter the Cape Hatteras National Seashore, marked by grass marshes, low scrub trees, and clusters of pines. Just outside the village North Carolina Highway 12 sports modest shoulders for cyclists, which allow motorists to pass more safely. The beaches on this island are among the least populated and most beautiful of the national seashore. You can access the beaches via the public parking areas indicated in the directions. If you want to swim, be wary of the strong tides and currents characteristic of this seashore. There are no lifeguard stations and very few people to help if you run into trouble. Because much of the island is natural—that is, undeveloped—it's important to plan ahead regarding water and other supplies.

A must-see is the Ocracoke Pony Park at Mile 7.5. These ponies, which used to roam wild about the island, are direct descendants of the Spanish mustangs that have long inhabited the island. Concern for the safety and well-being of the ponies led the government to create a fenced pasture for them in the park.

Throughout the national seashore watch for dwarf, misshapen trees, which the strong, salt-laden winds have pruned into unusual shapes. The violent storms that periodically batter the island continually re-create the shoreline, removing sand from one side and redepositing it elsewhere. Historical maps of the Outer Banks illustrate how new inlets are created and others closed as the result of these storms. Such change makes these barrier islands a dynamic part of our natural world.

Myriad birds and ducks populate the island or use its beaches and marshes for their twice-yearly migrations. Birding is popular here in fall and spring during migrating seasons and also in winter. Snow geese, Canada geese, and a variety of ducks are common sights at these times. Besides the plentiful gulls and plovers, it's not uncommon to see white herons and great white egrets in the marsh areas. Sandpipers and rails fascinate with their rapid scurrying on the sand and quick beaks for elusive sea creatures that have washed ashore.

From the northern tip of Ocracoke Island, you take the free ferry to

THE BASICS

Start: Parking lot for Ocracoke Village visitor center, adjacent to the Ocracoke ferry terminal.

Length: 67.6 miles.

Terrain: Flat, but there can be strong winds.

Traffic and hazards: North Carolina Highway 12 is the only main road on the Outer Banks and so carries all the traffic, which can be heavy in the summer months. A paved shoulder from Ocracoke village to the campground and along parts of NC–12 on Hatteras Island helps protect cyclists.

Getting there: To get to Ocracoke from the west or south, you must take either the Cedar Island or Swan Quarter ferries from the mainland, each of which takes more than two hours ($2.00 per bike rider, $10.00 per car). Reservations are a must during the peak summer months. From the north you can take the free ferry from Hatteras Island, which is accessible by car via NC–12 from Nags Head and Manteo. The visitor center parking lot where the ride starts is adjacent to the ferry terminal in Ocracoke village. See the *DeLorme North Carolina Atlas & Gazetteer*, page 68, inset D.

0.0 From the Ocracoke visitor center parking lot, turn left onto the main street, NC–12 going north. Follow NC–12 as it curves through the village. There is a paved shoulder after you leave the village.

2.1 Beach access through the parking lot on the right.

4.1 The pavement narrows when you reach the campground.

7.5 Turn left into Ocracoke Pony Pasture. After your visit, turn left and continue on NC–12 North.

8.3 Beach access through the parking lot.

13.8 Arrive at the ferry terminus for the Hatteras ferry. When you land on Hatteras Island, turn left and continue to follow NC–12.

18.0 Arrive at regional beach access (rest rooms).

22.5 Enter the town of Buxton.

25.9 Turn right into Cape Hatteras Lighthouse National Park.

26.8 Turn right to go to the lighthouse. The old lighthouse site is to the left.

27.2 Arrive at the visitor center.

27.6 Turn left on the entrance road to return to NC–12.

28.5 Turn right onto NC–12 North toward Avon.

35.1 Arrive in Avon. Turn around in Avon and take NC–12 South. *Option:* If you wish you can continue north to the town of Salvo, which is about 30 miles farther north.

54.0 Arrive at the Hatteras ferry landing for ferry to Ocracoke.

60.0 Pass Ocracoke Pony Pasture on the right.

67.6 Arrive at the visitor center parking lot.

Hatteras Island, one of the longest of North Carolina's barrier islands known as the Outer Banks. Thanks to its designation as part of the Cape Hatteras National Seashore, most of the island retains the appearance it must have had when British immigrants first settled here more than 300 years ago.

The natural sights are the biggest attraction for tourists. It's not unusual to see bottlenose dolphins playing in the water near the shore. Because these lands are public property, visitors have free access to the beach, but it's best to use the marked trails in order to preserve the fragile vegetation, which is critical to preventing erosion. The flat terrain makes cycling look really easy, but strong headwinds are common and can be worse than long hills, because there's no letup.

This part of North Carolina has much to recommend it. Historically this stretch of coast has been known as the Graveyard of the Atlantic because the convergence of waters to the south and from the north of the cape make it particularly rough during storms. More than 600 ships have wrecked here—perhaps because of the shallow shoals or storms, and some during war. In World

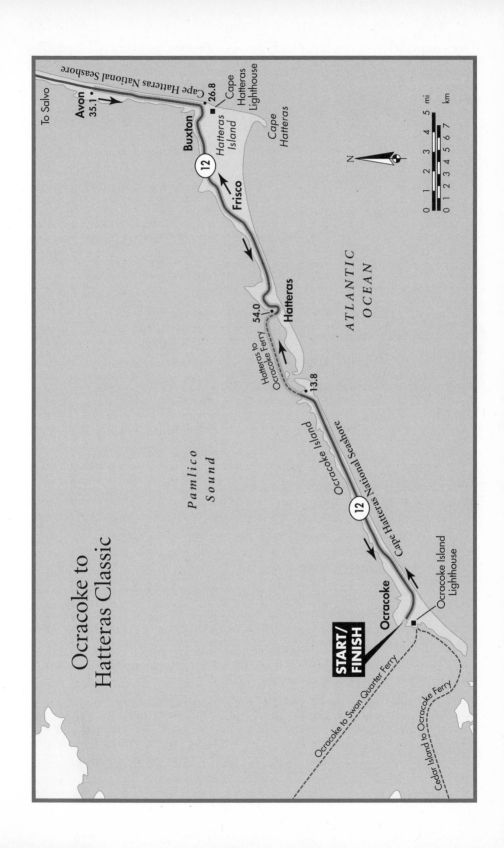

Ocracoke to
Hatteras Classic

Cape Hatteras Lighthouse, now securely guards the coastline after being moved farther inland.

War II German submarines sank so many Allied tankers and cargo ships here that the waters became known as Torpedo Junction.

The Cape Hatteras Lighthouse, like many others, was vital to warning ships of the dangerous Diamond Shoals just offshore and directing them to land. Built in 1870, it stands 208 feet high, the tallest in the United States. Strong storms and beach erosion threatened to tumble the lighthouse into the sea in the late twentieth century. Fortunately sufficient funds were raised to move the lighthouse farther inland in 1999; it now stands 1,600 feet from the ocean, the same distance as when it was first built.

At the lighthouse station are exhibits about the area, including information about the lifesaving endeavors and the large number of ships that have sunk offshore. A park ranger presents talks on different topics during the peak summer tourist season. A self-guiding nature trail begins near the lighthouse and is well marked. This ride takes you to the sea town of Avon, about 6 miles north of the lighthouse. But if the prevailing winds aren't too big a deterrent, you might want to venture farther north to explore the national seashore or even the town of Salvo, about 30 miles away.

LOCAL INFORMATION

♦ Hyde County Chamber of Commerce, P.O. Box 178, Swan Quarter, NC 27885; (888) 493–3826.

♦ Ocracoke Civic & Business Association, P.O. Box 496, Ocracoke, NC 27960; (252) 928–6711.

♦ Dare County Visitors Bureau, 704 South U.S. Highway 64/264, Manteo, NC 27954; (252) 473–2138.

♦ North Carolina Division of Transportation, Ferry Division, 113 Arendell Street, Morehead City, NC 28557; (252) 726–6446 or (800) BY–FERRY; www.ncferry.org.

LOCAL EVENTS/ATTRACTIONS

♦ Ocracoke Preservation Society Museum in the restored David Williams house furnished by the Ocracoke Preservation Society features historical displays, porch talks in summer; located next to the Coast Guard station in Ocracoke; no charge but donations are needed; (252) 928–7375; www.ocracoke-museum.org.

♦ Ocracoke Pony Pens, a herd of wild ponies now protected in a pasture, can be viewed from a wooden platform overlooking the pen; off NC–12 north of Ocracoke village; no charge.

♦ Ocracoke Lighthouse is one of the oldest lighthouses on the East Coast, built in 1823; the grounds are open but the lighthouse is not; Lighthouse Road, Ocracoke Village; no charge; (252) 928–4531.

♦ Cape Hatteras Lighthouse, built in 1870, is the tallest lighthouse in the United States at 208 feet; the visitor center has exhibits and talks; Cape Hatteras; no charge; (252) 995–4474.

RESTAURANTS

♦ Back Porch Restaurant, Back Road, Ocracoke, NC 27960; (252) 928–6401. Casual lunches and upscale dinners; screened porch dining; mid- to upper range.

♦ Dirty Dick's Crab House, Highway 12, Avon, NC 27915; (252) 995–3708; www.dirtydickscrabs.com. Steamed crabs and seafood; midrange.

ACCOMMODATIONS

♦ Berkley Manor, Silver Lake Road, Ocracoke, NC 27960; (800) 832–1223; www.berkley manor.com.

BIKE SHOPS

♦ None.

REST ROOMS

♦ At the start and finish at the Ocracoke village ferry terminal.
♦ At the ferry terminals on each end of the Ocracoke to Hatteras ferry.
♦ On the ferries.
♦ Mile 27.2 at the Cape Hatteras Lighthouse Visitors Center.

MAPS

♦ *DeLorme North Carolina Atlas & Gazetteer,* pages 68–69.

Lake Mattamuskeet Challenge

T he 48.9-mile Lake Mattamuskeet Challenge begins on the south side of the largest natural lake in North Carolina and circles the eastern two-thirds. A short diversion on the eastern end takes you through the small community of Engelhard on the coast of Pamlico Sound. The terrain is flat and most of the roads are straight, allowing you to look for the many varieties of wildlife that seek refuge in this protected area. There are few services available in this fairly remote area, so plan accordingly for water and food.

This tour begins on the south side of Lake Mattamuskeet, the largest natural lake in North Carolina, and crosses the lake on Highway 94, a North Carolina Scenic Byway built on a causeway bisecting the lake. Lake Mattamuskeet is 18 miles long, 7 miles wide, and a swan's neck deep. Wide, grassy areas adjacent to the highway attract fishermen and boaters to the area but also offer spectacular views. The lake itself is the principal attraction in this area, and its survival to this day is testament to the power of Mother Nature, against whom a great battle was waged in the early twentieth century.

At that time Lake Mattamuskeet was purchased, a town called New Holland was established, and canals were built to drain the lake. A pumping station, the world's largest at the time, fueled the drainage. The rich soil at the lakebed could then be farmed. Eventually, however, nature held sway and the lake once again filled with water. In 1934 the lake and surrounding banks became the Lake Mattamuskeet National Wildlife Refuge, which includes about 50,000 acres of marshes, woods, and water. As you enter the refuge proper, about Mile 1.9, you'll shortly see the entrance to the lodge on your right. This lodge is the former pumping station and has exhibits about the history of the area. (You'll also pass the lodge on the Wildlife Drive near the end of the route.)

During fall and spring thousands of migratory birds seek haven here: tundra swans, Canada geese, snow geese, and fifteen kinds of ducks. Other birds common to the area include the bald eagle—our national bird, which has escaped extinction—osprey, great blue heron, common egret, glossy ibis, pileated woodpecker, prothonotary warbler, and indigo bunting. A quiet approach by bike might also allow you to see white-tailed deer (which are plentiful), river otters, muskrats, and perhaps a black bear. It's wise to take extra precautions if you're carrying food on your bike or having a picnic.

In the water's shallower edges, you'll see graceful cypress trees with their "knees" sometimes visible just at the surface. Be prepared to wave to locals you pass on these back roads because they'll frequently throw up a hand in greeting as they pass, whether you're on bike or in a pickup.

THE BASICS

Start: The Mattamuskeet School parking lot on the south side of U.S. Highway 264 near the intersection with SR 1131 and about 0.4 mile west of the intersection with North Carolina Highway 94.

Length: 48.9 miles.

Terrain: Flat.

Traffic and hazards: US 264 is the main road in the area and will have more traffic, although it is usually not heavy. The Wildlife Drive at Mile 37.2 is not paved but is hard-packed with little gravel; it could be muddy after a rain.

Getting there: Take US 264 East to Lake Mattamuskeet in eastern North Carolina and park in the lot for Mattamuskeet School on the south side of US 264 near the intersection with SR 1131 and about 0.4 mile west of the intersection with Highway 94. See the *DeLorme North Carolina Atlas & Gazetteer*, page 68, B1.

Just north of where you turn right onto SR 1311 is the town of Fairfield, which has an interesting historic district, if you're inclined to extend your travels a bit. Continuing on your circumnavigation of the lake will take you past several individual historic properties. For example, the George Israel Watson House is located on Watson Road (SR 1116). Several other historic houses line U.S. Highway 264 along the southeastern shore of the lake. Signs near the road give the home's name and its construction date.

The very flat terrain provides an unusual perspective on wide expanses of corn and other crops, emphasizing the scattered population and the importance of agriculture in this area.

LOCAL INFORMATION

♦ Hyde County Chamber of Commerce, P.O. Box 178, Swan Quarter, NC 27885; (888) 493–3826.

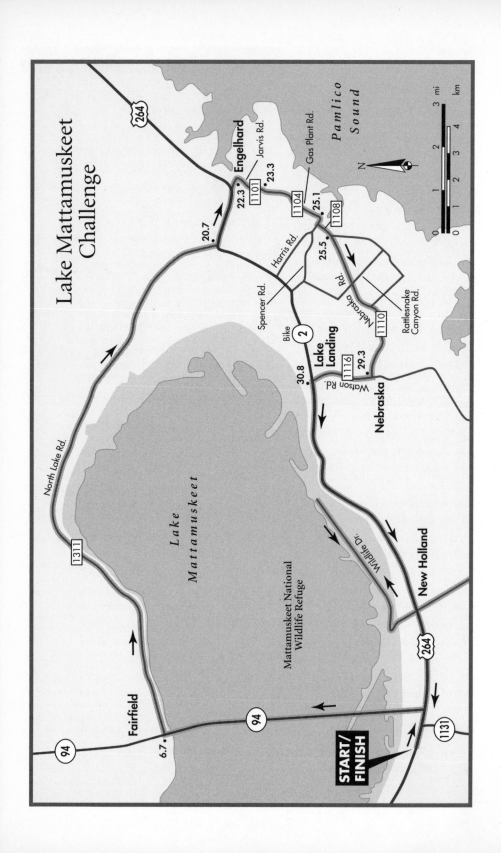

0.0 From the Mattamuskeet School parking lot, turn right onto US 264/NC–94.

0.4 Turn left onto NC–94 and continue across Lake Mattamuskeet.

1.9 Pass the entrance to the Mattamuskeet National Wildlife Refuge.

6.7 Turn right onto North Lake Road (SR 1311). There is no road name sign at the intersection.

20.7 Turn left onto US 264 toward Engelhard. *Note:* A rest area and restaurant are available here.

22.3 Turn right onto Jarvis Road (SR 1101). There is no road name sign at the intersection.

23.3 Turn left onto Gas Plant Road (SR 1104).

25.1 Turn left onto SR 1108 in Middletown (no road name sign at the intersection).

25.5 Turn right onto Nebraska Road (SR 1110) to the community of Nebraska.

29.3 Turn right onto Watson Road (SR 1116).

30.8 Turn left onto US 264 in Lake Landing.

37.2 Turn right onto the road to the wildlife viewing area. You'll pass the wildlife refuge headquarters on the right. Follow the signs for the Wildlife Drive, which has signs for wildlife viewing points along the way. *Bail-out:* If you wish, you can skip this part and continue straight on US 264 to the school.

41.7 Arrive at the end of the Wildlife Drive. Turn around and return to the main road.

46.2 Turn right onto US 264.

48.9 Turn left into the Mattamuskeet School parking lot.

LOCAL EVENTS/ATTRACTIONS

♦ Mattamuskeet National Wildlife Refuge is a protective area for thousands of waterfowl that winter here plus other species including endangered species such as the bald eagle; the lodge has exhibits; 38 Mattamuskeet Road, Swan Quarter, NC 27885; no charge to visit the refuge; (252) 926–4021.

♦ Swan Days Festival, an annual event on the first weekend in December, includes local craft and food vendors, historical displays and presentations, and workshops as well as guided tours of refuge areas not normally accessible by the public; Mattamuskeet National Wildlife Refuge; the tour fee is $7.00 per person with a limited number of spaces available; reservations are required; call (252) 926–4021 November 15–30 only.

RESTAURANTS

♦ Hotel Engelhard, U.S. Highway 264, Engelhard, NC; (252) 925–4400; breakfast and lunch daily; midrange.

Lake Mattamuskeet and hovering clouds are framed by branches on the bank.

ACCOMMODATIONS

♦ Thistle Dew Bed & Breakfast, 443 Water Street, Belhaven, NC 27810; (252) 943–6900 or (888) 822–4409; www.bbonline.com/nc/thistledew; upper range.

BIKE SHOPS

♦ None.

REST ROOMS

♦ At about Mile 21 at the North Carolina Department of Transportation rest area in Engelhard.
♦ At about Mile 21 at the Hotel Engelhard.
♦ At about Mile 37.2 at the wildlife refuge headquarters.

MAPS

♦ *DeLorme North Carolina Atlas & Gazetteer,* page 68.

5

Historic Bath Cruise

The Historic Bath Cruise introduces you to North Carolina's oldest town before directing you through the countryside for a delightful 26.7-mile ride. Except for crossing U.S. Highway 264 and riding along it for a short stretch, you'll see little traffic as you pedal through the countryside. The route takes you past Goose Creek State Park, which has recreational facilities as well as exhibits, before turning back to Bath.

The notorious pirate Blackbeard—real name Edward Teach—was attracted to the North Carolina coast, especially around Bath where he lived for a time, because the numerous inlets and coves offered myriad hiding places. Blackbeard aside, this quaint and attractive town, North Carolina's first, established in 1705, offers much for the inquiring visitor. Whether you choose to tour or simply stroll along the streets, you'll be captivated by this town.

French Protestants from Virginia came here first, followed by English settlers—among them John Lawson, surveyor general of the colony and author of the first history of Carolina in 1709. By 1708 Bath was inhabited by about fifty people living in twelve houses and surviving through the trade of tobacco, naval stores, and furs. The first public library in the colony was established here in 1701 with books sent from England to St. Thomas Parish, which also established a free school for Indians and African-Americans. St. Thomas is the oldest existing church in the state.

The first post road, the road from New England to Charleston over which mail was first regularly carried in North Carolina, passed through Bath. The North Carolina General Assembly met in Bath in 1743, 1744, and 1752, and the town was considered for colonial capital. However, when the Beaufort County government moved up the Pamlico River to the new town of Washington, Bath lost most of its importance and trade.

Start: The Bath visitor center is located on the south side of North Carolina Highway 92.
Length: 26.7 miles.
Terrain: Flat.
Traffic and hazards: Take care crossing U.S. Highway 264 and riding along it for a short stretch.
Getting there: Take US 264 east from Washington, North Carolina, to NC–92, which takes you to Bath. The visitor center is located on the south side of NC–92. See the *DeLorme North Carolina Atlas & Gazetteer,* page 66 B3.

Remaining from those early years are some outstanding examples of architecture: St. Thomas Church (1734); the Palmer-Marsh House (1751), which is noted for the windows in its large double chimney; and the Van Der Veer House (1790). The Palmer-Marsh House, Bath's oldest residence, was the largest residence in the colonial period. These and other historic sites are open to visitors. Fortunately, during the Civil War Bath was spared from Union occupation so that the town remained intact and ready for more recent restoration efforts. The original town limits are the boundaries of a National Register historic district. A park at Bonner Point on Bath Creek offers picnic tables and a good vantage point of the waterfront.

The route from Bath winds through farms and cornfields interspersed with dense forests and small residential communities. Deer frequently graze by the roadside and, unfortunately, sometimes fall victim to motor vehicles at night. The flat terrain and smooth road surfaces allow for plenty of looking around. The dark, rich soil bears testament to the inland sea that used to cover this area and left bounteous nutrients for growing a wide variety of crops.

At Mile 18.9 you'll arrive at Goose Creek State Park, which offers rest rooms, swimming, picnic areas, nature study, and camping. The park is situated at the juncture of Goose Creek and the Pamlico River.

The route then takes you to the small crossroads of Whitepost and across the Pamlico River into Bath along NC–92.

LOCAL INFORMATION

◆ Beaufort County Tourism Office, 409 West Main Street, Suite 107, P.O. Box 1765, Washington, NC 27889; (800) 999–2857; www.washingtonnc tourism.com.

LOCAL EVENTS/ATTRACTIONS

◆ Bath State Historic Site, North Carolina's oldest town with the oldest church and several historic buildings; guided tours available from the visitor center; 207 Carteret Street, Bath, NC 27808; no charge; (252) 923–3971; www.ah.dcr.state.nc.us/sections/hs/bath/bath.htm.

In the historic town of Bath the author cycles past the oldest church in North Carolina. (Photo by R. Bruce Heye)

♦ Goose Creek State Park offers canoeing, swimming, picnicking, hiking, camping, Environmental Education Center with exhibits, outdoor classroom, and boardwalk, regular interpretive programs; 2190 Camp Leach Road, Washington, NC 27889; no charge; (252) 923–2191.

RESTAURANTS

♦ Old Town Country Kitchen, Highway 92, Bath, NC 27808; (252) 923–1840. Country cooking, burgers, salads; three meals served Tuesday through Saturday, closes at 2:00 P.M. Sunday and Monday; low range.
♦ River Forest Manor Restaurant, Water Street, Belhaven, NC 27810; (252) 943–2151; www.riverforestmarina.com.

ACCOMMODATIONS

♦ Thistle Dew Bed & Breakfast, 443 Water Street, Belhaven, NC 27810; (252) 943–6900 or (888) 822–4409; www.bbonline.com/nc/thistledew. Upper range.
♦ River Forest Manor Country Inn, Water Street, Belhaven, NC 27810; (252) 943–2151; www.riverforestmarina.com.

0.0 From the parking lot of the visitor center at the Bath State Historic Site, turn right onto NC–92.

0.1 Turn left onto King Street (SR 1741).

1.6 Turn left onto Post Road (SR 1742).

3.2 Bear left onto South Boyd Road (SR 1528).

4.1 Cross US 264 onto North Boyd Road (SR 1528).

7.7 Turn left onto North White Post Road (SR 1343), which is Bike Route 3.

10.6 Cross US 264 at Everett Crossroads onto South White Post Road (SR 1343).

12.9 Turn right onto NC–92 West, which is part of Bike Route 2.

16.3 Turn left onto US 264.

16.4 Turn left onto Camp Leach Road (SR 1334).

18.9 Turn right into Goose Creek State Park.

19.2 Arrive at the visitor center. After a visit, turn around and return to Camp Leach Road.

19.5 Turn right onto Camp Leach Road (SR 1334).

22.4 Turn left onto Hawkins Beach Road (SR 1334). SR 1336 goes to the right.

24.4 Turn right onto NC–92.

24.5 Turn left onto Delia Wallace Road (SR 1335).

26.0 Turn right onto Creek Road (SR 1339).

26.7 Turn left onto NC–92.

27.6 Turn right into the visitor center parking lot.

BIKE SHOPS

♦ None.

REST ROOMS

♦ At the start and finish at Bath Visitors Center.
♦ Mile 19.2 at Goose Creek Park Visitors Center.

MAPS

♦ *DeLorme North Carolina Atlas & Gazetteer,* page 66.

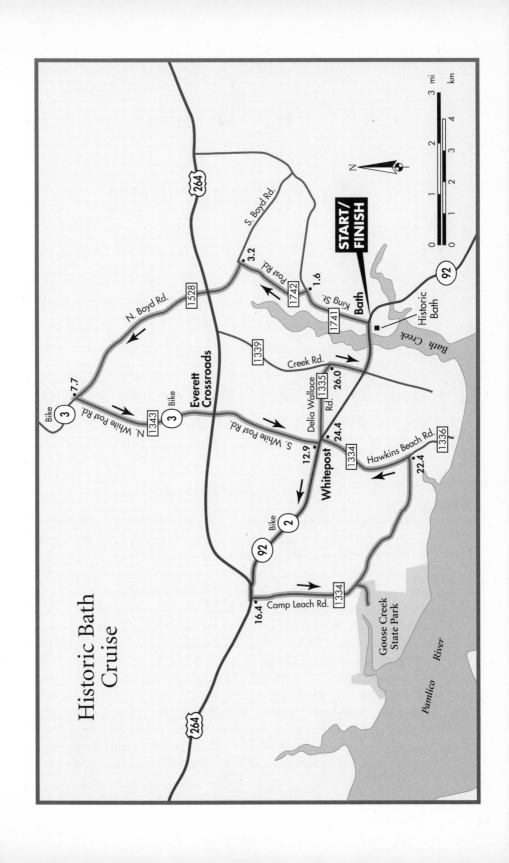

Historic Bath Cruise

START/FINISH

Bath

Historic Bath

Bath Creek

1.6

1741

1742

3.2

S. Boyd Rd.

Post Rd.

King St.

264

1528

N. Boyd Rd.

1339

Creek Rd.

26.0

1335

Delia Wallace Rd.

24.4

Everett Crossroads

7.7

3

Bike

1343

N. White Post Rd.

3

Bike

S. White Post Rd.

12.9

Whitepost

1334

22.4

Hawkins Beach Rd.

1336

92

Bike

2

92

16.4

1334

Camp Leach Rd.

Goose Creek State Park

264

Pamlico River

N

km

3 mi

0 1 2 3 4

0 1 2 3

6

Pottery Country Cruise

As the name implies, the Pottery Country Cruise takes you 35.5 miles along the back roads of Moore County where a community of potters has lived and worked since the 1700s. Beginning at Jugtown Pottery with its weathered wooden buildings and pottery display, the route travels east, parallel to the county line for about 10 miles, before it turns south and then southwest to the town of Robbins. This town, at about the halfway point, offers a few restaurants and a good resting spot. From Robbins the route goes west and then turns north to return to Jugtown Pottery.

The northwestern part of Moore County is noted for the number and variety of potters who live and work in the area. Many are descendants of the English settlers, themselves potters by trade, who were attracted to this area by its abundance of clay. Although pottery was produced here as early as 1750, it gained popularity as a trade only during Reconstruction after the Civil War. At that time the economy had collapsed; farmers could not market their crops, so many began making and selling whiskey jugs. Prohibition greatly reduced demand for such jugs, but renewed interest in pottery as an American craft has seen a resurgence in the industry in the last decade or so.

Jugtown Pottery, where the tour begins, is one of the better-known potteries in the area. A variety of different clay items is on display and for sale in the cozy cabin shop where visitors are welcomed. You can pick up a map of other area potteries if you're interested in more than those along the tour.

You start on Busbee Road (SR 1419) and, just after you cross SR 1003, you'll see Southern Folk Pottery on your right. Howard Mill Road (SR 1456) takes you on rolling hills through fertile farmlands. After you cross the river, you turn right onto George P Road (SR 1461), which presents some challenging hills through the woods and farmland. Chicken and dairy farms line the road, their pastures spotted with small farm ponds. At Mile 11.2, River Road (SR 1606) leads you toward the community of Highfalls. Highway 22 leads you across the river before you turn right on North Moore Road (SR 1470). You'll see a small lake along this road as well as North Moore High School.

Secondary Road 1470 becomes Middleton Street toward Robbins; it becomes Middleton Street (SR 1002) after you cross the intersection with NC–705. Outside town you turn onto Spies Road, which offers a good downhill until you cross Cabin Creek. A rest area is available off the left side of Westside Road (SR 1427) at Mile 32.7 at the intersection with NC–705.

The preponderance of potteries on this tour are located along Busbee Road (after Mile 32.9). Look for the signs for Westmoore Pottery, Millcreek Forge, Hickory Hill Pottery, 7 Springs Farm, O'Quinn Pottery, Yadkin Trail Pottery and Leather, Cady Clay Works, and Owens Pottery. Owens Pottery, which has been in business for more than a century—since 1895—has produced the work of Ben Owens, whose clay designs are well known and exhibited in such places as the Smithsonian. Owens Pottery is renowned for its unique and brilliant glazes, which differ strikingly from many of the traditional glazes still in use.

You'll see a sign for Scott's Pottery as you turn onto Jugtown Road (SR 1420), and more are situated farther down that road past Jugtown Pottery. If you're still in the mood for riding, you would do well to explore more of this area. But be forewarned—you might want to bring panniers or backpacks to haul back the lovely clay pieces that will tempt you.

LOCAL INFORMATION

♦ Sandhills Area Chamber of Commerce, 10677 U.S. Highway 15-501, Southern Pines, NC 28387; (800) 346–5362.

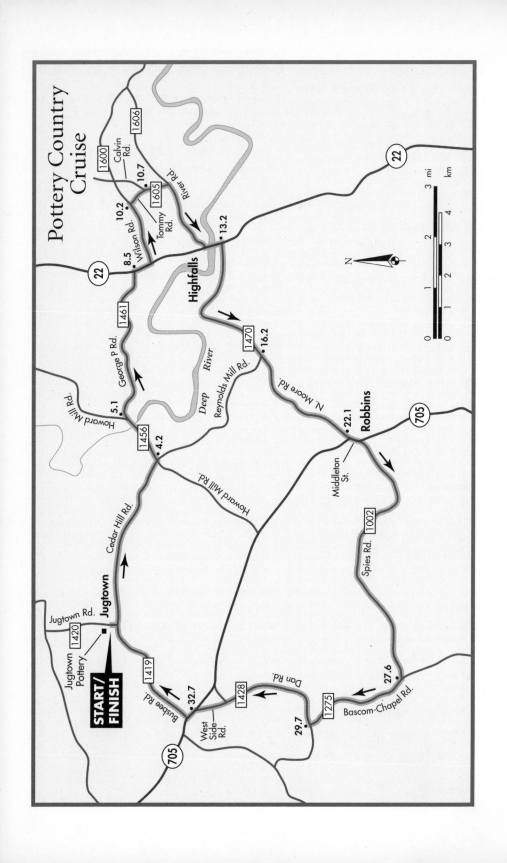

0.0 From Jugtown Pottery on Jugtown Road (SR 1420), turn right onto Jugtown Road (SR 1420).

0.1 Turn left onto Busbee Road (SR 1419).

0.7 Continue straight across SR 1003. Busbee Road's name changes to Cedar Hill Road.

4.2 Turn left onto Howard Mill Road (SR 1456).

5.1 Turn right onto George P Road (SR 1461).

8.5 Turn right onto NC–22.

8.9 Turn left onto Wilson Road (SR 1600).

10.2 Turn right onto Tommy Road (SR 1605).

10.7 Turn right onto Calvin Road (SR 1605). SR 1604 goes to the left.

11.2 Turn right onto River Road (SR 1606).

12.8 Turn left onto NC–22.

13.2 Turn right onto North Moore Road (SR 1470).

16.2 At the intersection with Reynolds Mill Road (SR 1419), continue on North Moore Road (SR 1470).

22.1 In Robbins, North Moore Road becomes Middleton Street but remains SR 1470. After crossing NC–705, SR 1470 becomes SR 1002 but remains Middleton Street.

23.5 Turn right onto Spies Road (SR 1002).

27.6 Turn right onto Bascom-Chapel Road (SR 1275).

29.7 Turn right onto Dan Road (SR 1428).

32.0 Turn left onto West Side Road (SR 1427).

32.7 Turn left onto NC–705.

32.9 Turn right onto Busbee Road (SR 1419).

35.4 Turn left onto Jugtown Road (SR 1420).

35.5 Turn left into Jugtown Pottery.

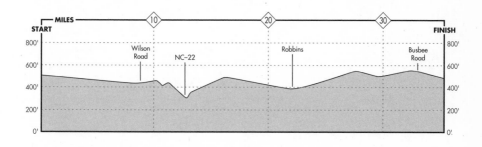

Checking out Hickory Hill Pottery. (Photo by R. Bruce Heye)

LOCAL EVENTS/ATTRACTIONS

♦ Jugtown Pottery, a display of pottery and information about other area potteries; 330 Jugtown Road, Seagrove, NC 27341; no charge for the visit and tour; (910) 464–3266; www.jugtownware.com.

♦ Various other potteries along the route and father down Jugtown Road.

RESTAURANTS

♦ Carolina Fried Chicken, Middleton Street, Robbins, NC 27325; (910) 948–2398. Lunch and dinner; low range.

♦ Little Village Restaurant, 151 Middleton Street, Robbins, NC 27325; (910) 948–2751. Breakfast and lunch; low range.

ACCOMMODATIONS

♦ None.

BIKE SHOPS

♦ None.

REST ROOMS

♦ At the start and finish at Jugtown Pottery.
♦ At restaurants in Robbins.

MAPS

♦ *DeLorme North Carolina Atlas & Gazetteer,* page 60.

Tour de Moore Classic

The Tour de Moore Classic takes its name and its route from the 100-mile bicycle road race around the perimeter of the county every April. This very challenging ride begins at the Campbell House in downtown Southern Pines and makes a clockwise loop around the county. On the way it passes through the Scottish stronghold of Aberdeen, through Jackson Springs and Eagle Springs on the west side of the county, through pottery country in the northwest corner, and along the northern border with Randolph and Chatham Counties. Just north of Glendon it turns due south, skirting Carthage before heading east to Cameron. From there it swoops south to Lobelia then west through horse country as it returns to the starting point in Southern Pines. Most of this route covers very rural areas with minimal services; plan your trip accordingly, and carry sufficient water and snacks.

Moore County in the heart of North Carolina has more than 800 miles of paved roads, and this route covers 113 of them, giving hearty cyclists a wonderful overview of county geography and history. This route incorporates the outer portions of several other popular rides in the county, some of which are included in this book: the Pottery Country Cruise and the Horse Country Ramble (both loops), along with the out-and-back ride to House in the Horseshoe. Because of the Tour de Moore bicycle road race, held in April every year since 1976, motorists and residents in the county are accustomed to cyclists on the road and are usually quite considerate. As you'll soon learn when you ride these roads, Moore County is home to friendly people, charming villages, pleasant countryside, and miles of quiet back roads, making this area ideal for cycling.

Moore County is rich with history dating to the sixth century when Siouan Indians inhabited the area and buffalo migrated annually through the county on the way to coastal marshes. The earliest European settlers—English, German, and Ulster Scots—came in the early 1700s. The mid–eighteenth century brought an influx of Highland Scots who sought to escape the harsh political and economic conditions prevalent in Scotland at that time. These industrious people, finding very poor soil, succeeded by establishing a major industry based on the turpentine and pitch from the indigenous longleaf pine forests.

During the late nineteenth century, a new industry developed here

THE BASICS

Start: Campbell House on Connecticut Avenue in Southern Pines.
Length: 113.3 miles.
Terrain: Rolling to hilly.
Traffic and hazards: Traffic on most roads is light; there's more traffic on North Carolina Highway 211, NC–705, NC–22, NC–24/27, and Glendon-Carthage Road. Watch out for lots of railroad tracks in downtown Aberdeen, and take care when crossing U.S. Highway 1/15-501/NC–211 there.
Getting there: Take US 1 into Southern Pines and follow signs to the downtown area. Campbell House is located on Connecticut Avenue, which intersects with Broad Street, the main street through Southern Pines. Signs point the way to Campbell House, which is east of Broad Street. See the *DeLorme North Carolina Atlas & Gazetteer,* page 60 D3.

around the healthy air and mineral springs, which brought in flocks of people seeking cures and improvement to their health. The spa town of Jackson Springs on this route remains, although its resort hotel is long gone. The tourism spawned by the waters was further augmented with the introduction of golf courses. Very quickly Southern Pines and Pinehurst became popular stopovers for northerners on their seasonal trips to and from Florida. Tourism remains the largest industry of the county today, with the ubiquitous golf courses a major drawing card in the central part of the county. New courses and housing developments are popping up all along North Carolina Highway 211.

The northwestern section of the route winds through pottery country. English potters were attracted to northern Moore County because of plentiful high-quality clay in the region. The number of potters swelled during the 1970s as pottery regained its popularity for its functionality as well as its art. So you may want to allow extra time for visiting some potteries, each of which has distinct styles and designs. The northern area of the county is rural with lots of farms and pastures. The quiet roads, while ideal for cycling, mean that there are no restaurants and few stores, so it's important to carry water and food for this portion of the trip.

The eastern side of the county is crisscrossed with several major highways, so you'll find more options for food and drink. The small town of Cameron, at the confluence of U.S. Highway 1 and NC–24/27, has several restaurants. Be forewarned, though, that many locally owned restaurants are closed on Sunday.

The southeastern portion of the county is covered with large and beautiful horse farms neatly demarcated with the traditional wooden fences. Many of the wealthy tourists who originally just stopped over in Southern Pines took a liking to the area and built large homes and then stables for their horses here. The miles of fenced pastures and neatly tended estates in southeastern Moore County testify to the importance of horse breeding and competitive activities. You may even lure thoroughbreds to the fence to check you out as you whiz past.

Southern Pines, with its relaxed atmosphere and southern charm, will welcome you back and reward your exertion with tasty dishes at the numerous restaurants. Several are located in the downtown area around Broad Street if you want to cycle by. Otherwise, Broad Street and US 1 south of town offer endless restaurant choices.

LOCAL INFORMATION

♦ Convention & Visitors Bureau for Pinehurst & Southern Pines, 10677 U.S. Highway 15-501, Southern Pines, NC 28388; (910) 692–3330.

LOCAL EVENTS/ATTRACTIONS

♦ Campbell House, a cultural visitor center and art gallery; Connecticut Avenue, Southern Pines, NC 28387; no charge; (910) 692–4356.

♦ Weymouth Woods Sandhills Nature Preserve, museum, hiking and nature trails; 1024 Fort Bragg Road, Southern Pines, NC 28387; no charge; (910) 692–2167; www.sandhillsonline.com/attractions/weymouthwoods.

♦ Malcolm Blue House, one of few remaining examples of nineteenth-century Scottish homesteads; Crafts and Skills Festival held there in September; located off Highway 5 in Aberdeen; call for seasonal hours; no charge but donations welcomed; (910) 944–7558.

♦ Union Station in downtown Aberdeen, a 1905 Victorian building on the National Register; open weekdays; no charge; (910) 944–5902.

♦ Jugtown Pottery, a display of pottery and information about other area potteries; 330 Jugtown Road, Seagrove, NC 27341; no charge for the visit and tour; (910) 464–3266; www.jugtownware.com.

Open pastureland is a common site around Moore County.

RESTAURANTS

♦ Sweet Basil, 134 Northwest Broad Street, Southern Pines, NC 28387; (910) 693–1487. Sandwiches and salads (closed Sunday).

♦ Café Mediterraneo, NC-5 Depot, Aberdeen, NC 28315; (910) 944–1717. Lunch Tuesday through Saturday; low range.

♦ The Potter's Café, 201 South Street, Aberdeen, NC 28315; (910) 944–1250. Breakfast and lunch Tuesday through Saturday; low range.

♦ Dewberry Deli; 485 Carthage Street; Cameron, NC 28326; (910) 245–3697. Lunch Tuesday through Saturday; low range.

♦ Pat's Café, U.S. Highway 1, Cameron, NC 28326, (910) 245–3939. Breakfast and lunch Monday through Saturday; low range.

ACCOMMODATIONS

♦ Hampton Inn, 1675 U.S. Highway 1 South, Southern Pines, NC 28387; (910) 692–9266. Midrange.

♦ Knollwood House Bed & Breakfast, 1495 West Connecticut Avenue, Southern Pines, NC 28387; (910) 692–9390; knollwood@pinehurst.net. Upper range.

BIKE SHOPS

♦ Rainbow Cycles, 239 Northeast Broad Street, Southern Pines, NC 28387; (910) 692–4494.

0.0 From Campbell House on Connecticut Avenue in Southern Pines, turn right onto Connecticut Avenue.

2.7 Turn right onto Fort Bragg Road (SR 2074).

6.2 Bear left onto Bethesda Road (NC–5).

11.2 Turn left onto Pee Dee Road in Aberdeen.

11.5 Turn right onto NC–211, then make a right onto East Main Street.

12.4 Turn left onto South Poplar Street.

12.5 Turn right onto South Street. You'll cross railroad tracks, US 1/15-501, and NC–211.

12.6 Turn left onto Pinehurst Street.

13.1 Turn right onto Roseland Road (SR 1112).

20.8 Turn right onto Hoffman Road (SR 1004).

23.3 Turn left onto Jackson Springs Road (SR 1122).

27.7 Turn right onto Hotel Street (SR 1125). Cross NC–73.

28.0 Bear left onto Mill Road (SR 1126).

29.6 Turn right onto Flowers Road (SR 1137).

33.9 Turn left onto NC–211.

34.4 Turn right onto NC–705 in Eagle Springs.

38.4 Turn left onto Bensalem Road (SR 1270).

41.5 Turn right onto Big Oak Church Road (SR 1275).

44.0 Cross NC–24/27.

47.0 Cross SR 1002. Big Oak Church Road's name changes to Bascom-Chapel Road (SR 1275).

49.2 Turn right onto Dan Road (SR 1428).

51.5 Turn left onto West Side Road (SR 1427).

52.2 Turn left onto NC–705, which is a North Carolina Scenic Byway.

52.3 Turn right onto Busbee Road (SR 1419).

54.9 Turn left onto Jugtown Road (SR 1420) to Jugtown Pottery and Museum. After the tour go back to Busbee Road and turn left. The road's name changes to Cedar Hill Road (SR 1419) after you cross Needham Grove Road (SR 1003).

58.4 Turn left onto North Howard Mill Road (SR 1456).

(continued)

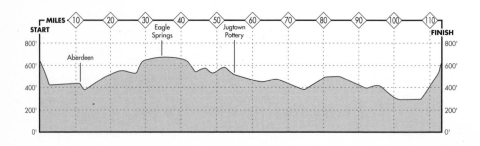

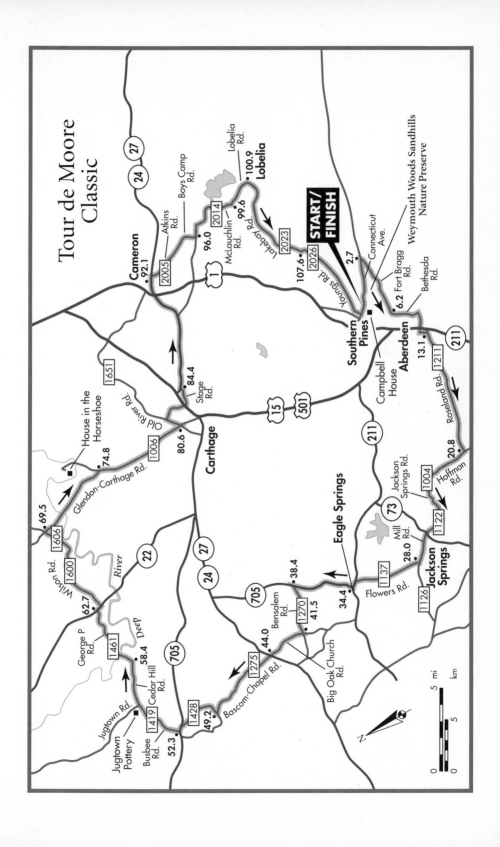

59.4 Turn right onto George P Road (SR 1461).

62.7 Turn right onto NC–22.

63.1 Turn left onto Wilson Road (SR 1600).

67.0 Turn left onto River Road (SR 1606).

69.5 Turn right onto Glendon-Carthage Road (SR 1006).

74.8 Turn right onto Glendon-Carthage Road (SR 1006) where it intersects with South Carbottom Road (SR 1621).

80.6 Turn left onto Old River Road (SR 1651).

81.5 Turn right onto Priest Hill Road (SR 1653).

83.4 Turn left onto Union Church Road (SR 1805).

83.7 Turn left onto Stage Road (SR 1804).

84.4 Turn right onto NC–24/27.

92.1 Turn right onto Atkins Road (SR 2005).

94.1 Continue straight on Boys Camp Road (SR 2007).

96.0 Turn left onto Cranes Church Road (SR 1825).

96.7 Turn right onto McLauchlin Road (SR 2014).

99.6 Turn left onto Lobelia Road (SR 1001).

100.9 Turn right onto Lakebay Road (SR 2023).

107.6 Turn left onto Youngs Road (SR 2026).

112.8 Turn left onto Ridge Street in Southern Pines.

113.3 Turn left onto Connecticut Avenue and return to Campbell House.

REST ROOMS

♦ At the start and finish at the Campbell House.

♦ At about Mile 3.7 at the Weymouth Woods Sandhills Nature Preserve.

♦ Mile 12.4 at restaurants in downtown Aberdeen.

♦ Mile 20.8 at a convenience store on Hoffman Road.

♦ At Mile 51.5 there's a rest area on West Side Road at its intersection with NC–705.

♦ Mile 55.1 at Jugtown Pottery and Museum.

♦ Mile 84.4 on NC–24/27 at a convenience store in Cameron just after the railroad tracks.

♦ After Mile 99.6 there's a convenience store on Lobelia Road.

MAPS

♦ *DeLorme North Carolina Atlas & Gazetteer,* page 60.

♦ Moore County Map, produced by the Convention & Visitors Bureau.

House in the Horseshoe Ramble

The House in the Horseshoe Ramble, a relatively easy 20.5-mile ride, starts at Courthouse Square in the charming small town of Carthage. With just a few turns, the route travels along rural roads with pastures and forests directly to the Revolutionary War site at the Alston House, also known as the House in the Horseshoe. The ride is an out-and-back, part of which follows the Tour de Moore bike route.

This fairly easy ride offers a firsthand look at longleaf pine forests in Moore County in the Sandhills Region of North Carolina. This area is recognized as one of the last remaining strongholds of longleaf pine in the entire southeastern United States. This pine, which was once the dominant tree throughout the Southeast from Virginia to Texas covering approximately 92 million acres, is recognizable by its long needles—up to 15 inches in length—and its long narrow cones, which range from 6 to 10 inches.

The region takes its name from the rolling hills topped with deep coarse sands that dominate the landscape and clearly differ from the red clay of the Piedmont area of the state. It is now believed that sediment-filled rivers millions of years ago formed a delta in this area where the rivers flowed into the sea. Over 40 to 50 million years, erosion from sandy winds and streams carved the hilly terrain.

Despite a harsh, desertlike environment, an amazing variety of plant and animal life flourishes here. And fire has played an important role in the life cycles of certain animal and plant species. It is thought that summer lightning or Native American fire practices caused fire to sweep across vast areas about every two to seven years. Some plants, such as the longleaf pine and the abundant wire grass, depend on the periodic fires for their reproduction.

Look for wildlife such as deer and fox squirrels as you ride along the

Relaxing on the steps in front of the House in the Horseshoe.

Glendon-Carthage Road. Besides the forests, the smooth surface will take you past farmlands and open, rolling pastures broken only by small stands of trees and clumps of low-growing shrubs. This part of the route takes you up and down the rolling countryside.

At Mile 7.5 you'll bear right onto South Carbottom Road (SR 1621), even though one of the Moore County bike routes follows SR 1006 to the left. About 2.5 miles later you'll see a sign for the Alston House, which is also known as the House in the Horseshoe. The elegant house itself, about half a mile down this road, was so named because it is situated on a hilltop in the horseshoe bend of the Deep River. Built in 1772, it was home to Philip Alston, the wealthiest man in newly formed Moore County, who became a colonel in the revolutionary army.

During the American Revolution, the backcountry of North Carolina was the site of periodic battles between groups of citizen-soldiers who were either revolutionaries (Whigs) or loyalists (Tories). On the morning of August 5, 1781, Alston and his revolutionary comrades were camped at his house when they were attacked by a larger unit of Tories. The numerous bullet holes in both the front and back of the house still bear witness to the battle. Fortunately Mrs.

Alston and her children were sheltered in one of the large fireplaces in the house to protect themselves from the bullets.

During the battle, the Tories tried to set fire to the house by rolling a cart filled with burning straw against its wall. Seeing himself outnumbered and wanting to prevent the destruction of his lovely home, Alston surrendered. He survived the Revolution and became clerk of court and then a state senator. However, he became embroiled in a very bitter local political feud, during which time he was twice accused of murder, jailed as an accessory to murder, and relieved of his position as clerk of court. In 1790 he sold the house and plantation and left the state.

The house and 2,500-acre plantation were bought in 1798 by Governor Benjamin Williams, who called the estate his "Retreat." He had served as governor of North Carolina, as a captain under George Washington, as a member of the first board of trustees of the University of North Carolina, and as a member of the National Congress in Philadelphia.

THE BASICS

Start: Courthouse Square on Monroe Street in Carthage.
Length: 20.5 miles.
Terrain: Rolling with a couple of long gradual climbs and a rather steep climb back to Carthage.
Traffic and hazards: There is some traffic along Glendon-Carthage Road, but otherwise traffic is light. The parking lot at House in the Horseshoe is gravel, but the distance is short.
Getting there: Take North Carolina Highway 22 north from Southern Pines to Courthouse Square in Carthage. There is on-street parking around the courthouse (two-hour limit) and in the municipal parking lots south of the square behind the government buildings. Start the ride at the intersection of Courthouse Square and Monroe Street. See the *DeLorme North Carolina Atlas & Gazetteer,* page 60 C3.

LOCAL INFORMATION

♦ Sandhills Area Chamber of Commerce, 10677 U.S. Highway 15-501, Southern Pines, NC 28387; (800) 346–5362.

LOCAL EVENTS/ATTRACTIONS

♦ House in the Horseshoe Historic Site offers guided tours of the house and farm buildings; closed Monday; 324 Alston Road, Sanford, NC 27330; no charge but donations welcomed; (910) 947–2051.

RESTAURANTS

♦ Pep's Whitehorse Restaurant, 138 Union Church Road, Carthage, NC 28327; (910) 947–9697. Casual dining.

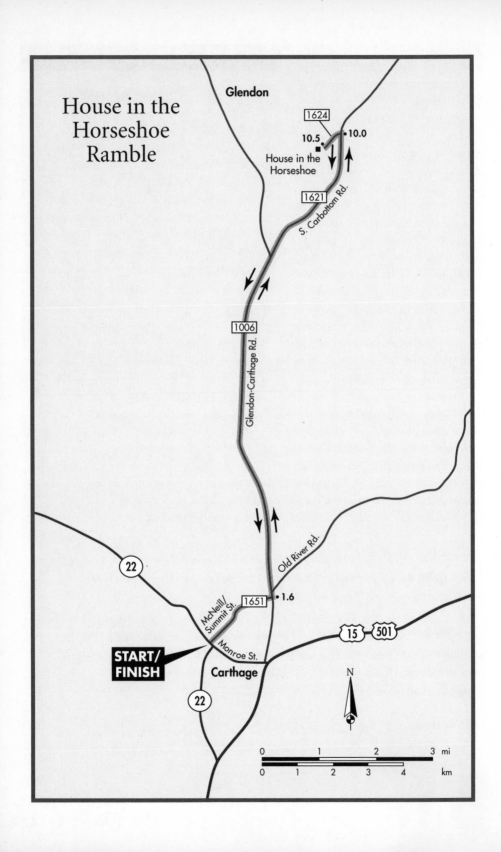

House in the
Horseshoe
Ramble

Glendon

1624

10.5 ◾   • 10.0

House in the
Horseshoe

1621

S. Carbottom Rd.

1006

Glendon-Carthage Rd.

22

Old River Rd.

McNeill/
Summit St.   1651   • 1.6

15   501

Monroe St.

**START/
FINISH**

Carthage

22

N

| 0 | | 1 | | 2 | | 3 | mi |

| 0 | 1 | 2 | 3 | 4 | km |

0.0 From Courthouse Square at Monroe Street in Carthage, turn right onto Monroe Street.

0.1 Turn left onto McNeill Street, which becomes Summit Street and then Old River Road (SR 1651).

1.6 Turn left onto Glendon-Carthage Road (SR 1006).

7.5 Go straight on South Carbottom Road (SR 1621). Glendon-Carthage Road (SR 1006) goes to the left.

10.0 Turn left onto SR 1624 to the Alston House—the House in the Horseshoe.

10.5 Arrive at the house. After your visit, exit by turning right onto SR 1624.

11.0 Turn right onto South Carbottom Road (SR 1621).

13.5 Turn left onto Glendon-Carthage Road (SR 1006).

19.4 Turn right onto Old River Road (SR 1651), which becomes Summit Street and then McNeill Street.

20.9 Turn right onto Monroe Street to Courthouse Square.

♦ Peking Wok, 1005 Monroe Street, Carthage, NC 28327; (910) 947–7770. Chinese food.

ACCOMMODATIONS

♦ The Old Buggy Inn Bed & Breakfast, 301 McReynolds Street, Carthage, NC 28327; (910) 947–1901 or (800) 553–5247; www.oldbuggyinn.com. Mid- to upper range.

BIKE SHOPS

♦ None.

REST ROOMS

♦ At the start and finish at the public library in Carthage.

♦ Convenience stores on McNeill Street and one on Monroe Street at start and finish.

♦ Mile 10.5 at House in the Horseshoe.

MAPS

♦ *DeLorme North Carolina Atlas & Gazetteer,* page 60.

Pinehurst Ramble

The Pinehurst Ramble at 16.8 miles is a fairly easy ride from downtown Southern Pines to Pinehurst, through the village, then back again. Much of the route is tree-lined, and traffic speeds are low, except along Midland Road where the speed limit is 45 mph. However, the four lanes on Midland Road offer additional space for cyclists in the right lane. Maneuvering around the traffic circle between the two towns requires that cyclists behave like vehicle operators, yielding to traffic already in the circle but staying on the right side of the lane for easy exit on Midland Road. The effort is worth it as you tour the quaint village of Pinehurst before returning along the same route to Southern Pines.

As you leave Southern Pines, you'll take Northwest Broad Street to Vermont Avenue, cross the railroad tracks, and then go right on Northeast Broad, where the street becomes two-way again. At Delaware Street the road divides into four lanes with trees in the middle; Northwest Broad Street becomes Midland Road. If you had no idea you were in the middle of golf country, you might figure it out on this tour, which takes you past some of the most prestigious golf resorts in the Southeast.

At Mile 1.7 you'll pass Mid-Pines Plantation, a well-known golf resort and conference center. Then you'll pass several golf resorts on your right surrounded by attractive residential areas. Longleaf pines line the roadsides and the medians, reinforcing the identity of the Sandhills and providing welcome shade for cyclists.

Golf was first introduced in the Sandhills area around the turn of the twentieth century. This region already had several noted resorts where people came from the North to take the waters and improve their health. The introduction of golf fairly well cinched the area's draw as a resort location and has helped the area become known as the Golf Capital of the World. More than thirty-five championship golf courses are located in the vicinity of Pinehurst.

At Mile 5.1 you'll come to a large traffic circle—or roundabout, as the British say—where you want Midland Road. Follow the signs to Pinehurst Village District, which has been carefully and intentionally preserved to show off the New England–style parks and roadways, laid out by Frederick Law Olmsted, who designed New York's Central Park and Asheville's Biltmore Gardens. The town's streets are lined with handsome Georgian Colonial homes and estates.

According to local lore, since Pinehurst was founded after Southern Pines—and Southern Pines was laid out in a strict grid system—the designers of Pinehurst were instructed to do anything except a grid. The resulting curving maze of streets can be a challenge, even with a good map. But the route I've selected will show you a good cross section of the town without leaving you stranded.

One of the central showpieces of the town is the historic Pinehurst Hotel. As you cycle up the circular drive, you'll revel in the broad porches with awnings from another era stocked with plenty of old-fashioned rockers and ceiling fans, all overlooking beautiful gardens. You can see why people have been drawn to this resort for more than a hundred years. The most recent addition to the resort is the Pinehurst Spa, an elegant building offering luxurious spa services to guests waiting to be pampered.

Be sure to allow some time to stroll the neat sidewalks in the village area before heading back to Southern Pines via Midland Road.

0.0 From the intersection of Broad Street and New Hampshire Avenue, turn left onto Broad Street.

0.2 Turn left onto Vermont Avenue, cross the railroad tracks, then turn right onto Northeast Broad Street, which becomes two-way at this point. The road's name changes to Midland Road as you leave Southern Pines.

1.2 Cross under US 1 on Midland Road.

5.1 At the large traffic circle, take Midland Road (NC–2), following the signs to Pinehurst Village District.

6.3 Turn right onto Fields Road, then left onto Cherokee Avenue.

6.7 Turn right onto Chinquapin Road and follow it through the village shopping area.

7.1 Turn left onto Graham Road, then right onto McLean Road.

7.3 Cross Beulah Hill Road (NC–5) onto Linden Road.

7.7 Turn left onto McKenzie Road.

8.1 Turn left onto Ritter Road. Cross Beulah Hill Road (NC–5).

8.3 Turn left into Pinehurst's Carolina Hotel, circle through the hotel drive and entrance, then continue straight on Carolina Vista Road.

8.7 Turn left onto Azalea Road, then make a ninety-degree left onto Midland-Palmetto Road (NC–2) and continue to the traffic circle.

10.0 At the traffic circle, take Midland Road (NC–2) back toward Southern Pines. As you enter Southern Pines, Midland Road becomes Northeast Broad Street.

16.8 Turn right onto New Hampshire Avenue and return to the parking lot.

LOCAL INFORMATION

♦ Convention & Visitors Bureau for Pinehurst & Southern Pines, 10677 U.S. Highway 15-501, Southern Pines, NC 28388; (910) 692–3330.

LOCAL EVENTS/ATTRACTIONS

♦ Shops and buildings in historic Pinehurst.
♦ Pinehurst Resort (Carolina Hotel, Pinehurst Spa, Holly Inn).

RESTAURANTS

♦ Villager Deli, Pinehurst Square, Pinehurst, NC 28374; (910) 295–1005. Breakfast and lunch Monday through Saturday; low range.
♦ Theo's Taverna, 140 Chinquapin Road, Pinehurst, NC 28374; (910) 295–0780. Greek dishes; lunch and dinner Monday through Saturday; midrange.

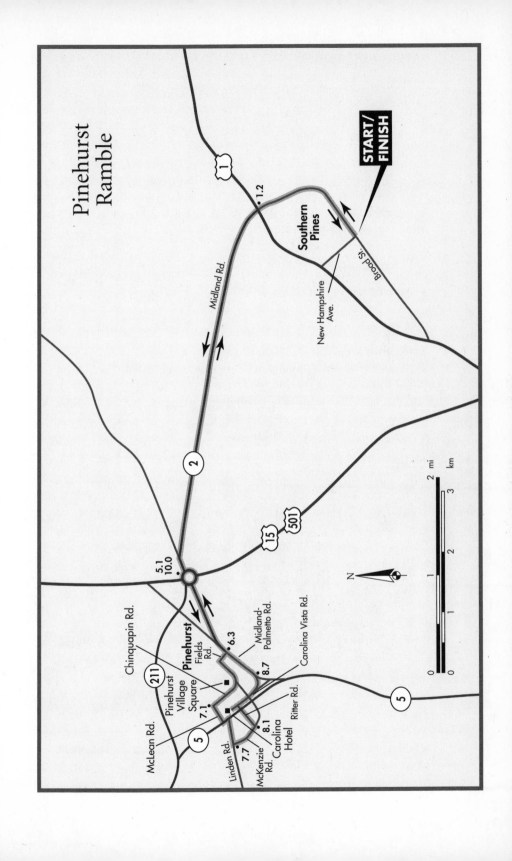

Pinehurst Ramble

♦ Hampton Inn, 1675 U.S. Highway 1 South, Southern Pines, NC 28387; (910) 692–9266. Midrange.

♦ Knollwood House Bed & Breakfast, 1495 West Connecticut Avenue, Southern Pines, NC 28387; (910) 692–9390; knollwood@pinehurst.net. Upper range.

BIKE SHOPS

♦ Rainbow Cycles, 239 Northeast Broad Street, Southern Pines, NC; 28387 (910) 692–4494.

REST ROOMS

♦ At restaurants in Pinehurst.

MAPS

♦ *DeLorme North Carolina Atlas & Gazetteer,* page 60.
♦ Moore County Map, produced by the Convention & Visitors Bureau.

The Spa at Pinehurst offers massages and other services for tired cyclists.

Southern Pines Ramble

The Southern Pines Ramble is a short, easy ride that will fully acquaint you with some of the history and the distinctive character of this charming town. The main street, with its graceful magnolia trees and central railroad tracks, retains the ease and spirit of a bygone era. The ride starts at one of the major estates in the town, which is now a cultural center, then winds through some of the beautiful streets with large seasonal homes before heading toward the Weymouth Woods Nature Preserve. After this brief foray into the more rural parts of town, the ride returns to town via Indiana Avenue and circles through some downtown streets before returning to the Campbell House.

Southern Pines has a very interesting history. It began as a health resort developed by John Patrick in 1883. He named the streets for the New England states to tempt northerners to move south. Since Southern Pines is situated halfway between New York and Florida along the major north–south rail line, it was the ideal location for stopovers for northerners traveling to Florida for the winter or vice versa. As a result, five or six large resort hotels were built in the town, and people started building their own English-style cottages around the hotels. They would spend November through January in Southern Pines, holding foxhunts and big parties until they moved on to Florida or New York. The mild climate and sandy terrain with no rocks made the area ideal for horses (good footing) and for golf (no puddles on the courses). These two sports continue to be popular today.

The ride starts at the Campbell House, but the story of the family who built it actually starts on the other side of Connecticut Avenue at what is now the

Start: The Campbell House on Connecticut Avenue.
Length: 9.5 miles.
Terrain: Rolling with a few gradual climbs.
Traffic and hazards: Traffic is light on most of these roads. Be aware that the traffic patterns in downtown Southern Pines are somewhat unusual because the train tracks run through the middle of the main street. Fortunately the streets cross the tracks at right angles. However, along Broad Street traffic crossing the tracks has the right-of-way, while traffic approaching from the side streets must stop.
Getting there: Take U.S. Highway 1 into Southern Pines and follow signs to the downtown area. Campbell House is located on Connecticut Avenue, which intersects with Broad Street, the main street through Southern Pines. Signs point the way to Campbell House, which is east of Broad Street. See the *DeLorme North Carolina Atlas & Gazetteer,* page 60 D3.

Weymouth Center for the Arts and Humanities. James Boyd, grandson of the original owner, and his wife Katharine had the remaining portion of the original home redesigned about 1920 and used "Weymouth" for extensive entertaining for their literary and artistic friends. In honor of the Boyds, the estate now houses the Center for the Arts and Humanities, including the North Carolina Literary Hall of Fame. Save some time to visit the center before or after the tour.

The Campbell House is the other portion of James Boyd's original house, which his grandson Jack moved across Connecticut Avenue and later sold to the Campbells. It is now home to a gallery for local artists and to the Moore County Arts Council. To the right of the main house is the Train House, where Boyd's model trains are kept.

As you travel out of town on Connecticut, you'll see several English Tudor houses that were originally built around the Highland Hotel. On your left is the beginning of Moore County's horse country. The area along Highland Road is considered by some to be the prettiest block in Southern Pines. Some of these big houses are occupied only from October through May; the owners spend the rest of the year in Boston or other northern cities. As you turn right onto Connecticut again, you'll pass Duncraig Manor, which belongs to members of the Quaker Oats family. All the roads to the left are dirt for the benefit of the horses. Throughout this part of the county, horse-riding trails interlace the area.

At Mile 3.4 you turn right onto Fort Bragg Road—so named because it skirts the perimeter of the military installation. Turn into Weymouth Woods Sandhills Nature Preserve at Mile 5.3 and check out the visitor center, which has exhibits about how the pine forests were used to produce turpentine and other naval stores. The preserve, which was the first natural area brought into the North Carolina state parks system, contains the largest longleaf pine tree in the state. The museum, interpretive programs, and nature trails at Weymouth

Woods allow visitors to observe and better understand the natural history of the region.

As you come back into Southern Pines on Southeast Broad Street, you'll pass the Princess Movie Theater on the right—now an antiques store—which was the first talking-movie house in North Carolina. Enjoy the remaining gorgeous magnolia trees that line the railroad tracks through the middle of town. You can see how the railroad was literally the lifeblood of this town for so many years and still carries passengers from the Amtrak station on Broad Street, in the heart of the town.

Near the train station in the area around Vermont Avenue, you'll see some of the early Southern Pines houses, which were small boardinghouses. Some were also tourist homes for people of less affluent means who were traveling through the area. As you return to the Campbell House, you'll cross North Ridge Street, which was the outer boundary on the original Southern Pines grid laid out by John Patrick.

LOCAL INFORMATION

♦ Convention & Visitors Bureau for Pinehurst & Southern Pines, 10677 U.S. Highway 15-501, Southern Pines, NC 28388; (910) 692–3330.

The Weymouth Center is home to the North Carolina Literary Hall of Fame.

0.0 From the Campbell House, turn right onto Connecticut Avenue.

0.2 Turn right onto North Valley Road.

0.6 Turn left onto Massachusetts Avenue.

0.7 Turn left onto Highland Road.

1.1 Turn right onto Connecticut Avenue.

3.5 Turn right onto Fort Bragg Road.

5.3 Turn right into the Weymouth Woods Sandhills Nature Preserve. After your visit turn around and return to Fort Bragg Road.

5.7 Turn right onto Fort Bragg Road.

6.2 Turn right onto Indiana Avenue.

8.1 Turn right onto Southeast Broad Street.

8.2 Turn left onto Massachusetts Avenue.

8.3 Turn right onto Bennett Street.

8.9 Turn right onto West Maine Avenue.

9.0 Turn right onto Northwest Broad Street.

9.1 Turn left onto Connecticut Avenue.

9.5 Turn right into the Campbell House parking lot.

LOCAL EVENTS/ATTRACTIONS

♦ Weymouth Center for the Arts and Humanities houses the North Carolina Literary Hall of Fame and offers lectures and concerts in addition to other special events; 555 East Connecticut Avenue, Southern Pines, NC 28388; admission fees vary according to the event; (910) 692–6261; weymouthcenter@pinehurst.com.

♦ Weymouth Woods Sandhills Nature Preserve offers a museum, plus hiking and nature trails; 1024 Fort Bragg Road, Southern Pines, NC 28387; no charge; (910) 692–2167; weymouth@pinehurst.net; www.sandhillsonline.com/attractions/weymouthwoods.

RESTAURANTS

♦ The Ice Cream Parlor, 176 Northwest Broad Street, Southern Pines, NC 28387; (910) 692–7273. Sandwiches and ice cream.

♦ Sweet Basil, 134 Northwest Broad Street, Southern Pines, NC 28387; (910) 693–1487. Sandwiches and salads (closed Sunday).

ACCOMMODATIONS

♦ Hampton Inn, 1675 U.S. Highway 1 South, Southern Pines, NC 28387; (910) 692–9266. Midrange.

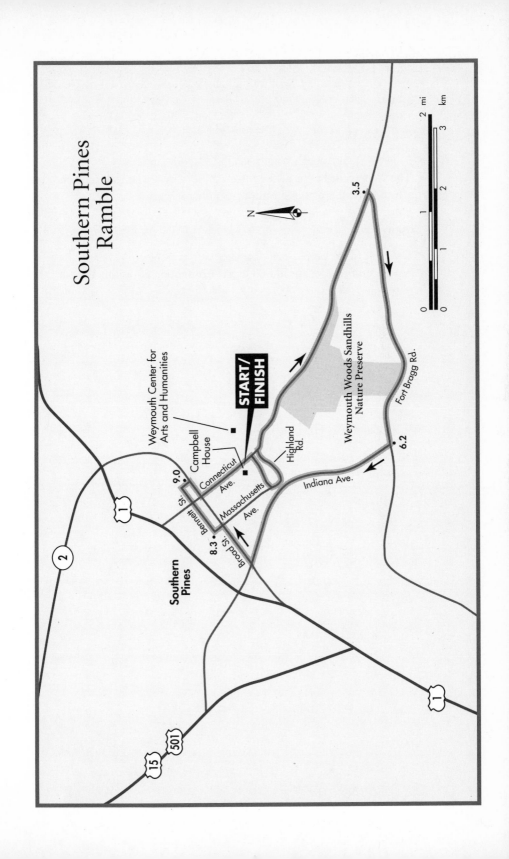

Southern Pines Ramble

Weymouth Center for Arts and Humanities

START/FINISH

Campbell House

Weymouth Woods Sandhills Nature Preserve

Connecticut Ave.

Highland Rd.

Massachusetts Ave.

Indiana Ave.

Fort Bragg Rd.

Bennett St.

Broad St.

Southern Pines

3.5

6.2

8.3

9.0

N

2 mi

km

0   1   2   3

0   1   2

1

2

1

15

501

1

BIKE SHOPS

♦ Rainbow Cycles, 239 Northeast Broad Street, Southern Pines, NC 28387; (910) 692–4494.

REST ROOMS

♦ Mile 5.3 at Weymouth Woods Sandhills Nature Preserve.
♦ The Ice Cream Parlor at the intersection of New Hampshire Avenue and Northwest Broad Street in downtown Southern Pines.

MAPS

♦ *DeLorme North Carolina Atlas & Gazetteer,* page 60.
♦ Moore County Map, produced by the Convention & Visitors Bureau.

Horse Country Ramble

A delightful 22.3-mile ride, the Horse Country Ramble loops through the southeastern part of Moore County, home to myriad horse farms and stables. The route begins at the Campbell House in Southern Pines then heads east toward the crossroads of Hog Island. At Mile 12.4 the route turns north toward Lakeview then meanders through the countryside before turning south toward the small town of Niagara. From there the route returns in a fairly straight shot to Southern Pines and the Campbell House.

It won't take you long to see why this tour is called Horse Country Ramble—and why it's one of my favorites. Thoroughbreds will lazily glance at you as you pass their lush pastures and luxurious accommodations. There are also caution signs warning of horseback riders and of horses and carriages all along the route. In fact, this part of Moore County is so engrossed in horses that deeds for the farms in this area are specially drawn up to allow horseback riders to cross the property of others.

The horse people in the area can be divided into three interest groups: the hunter-jumpers, the foxhunters, and the carriage drivers. The hunter-jumpers participate in three-day events for dressage, cross-country, and stadium. Carriage drivers have four special horse shows in fall and four more in spring. Some old photographs of Southern Pines show the foxhunters coming right through the center of town on Broad Street. Horses are so important to these people that many build their own living quarters over the stables that house their horses. Watch for these along the route—many are situated away from the road, so you have to really look.

Pappy and Ginny Moss were original horse lovers in the area who

THE BASICS

Start: The Campbell House on Connecticut Avenue in Southern Pines.
Length: 22.3 miles.
Terrain: Rolling with a few good hills.
Traffic and hazards: Traffic on most of the route is light, although it will be heavier along Niagara-Carthage Road. Exercise caution when crossing U.S. Highway 1, as it is a very busy highway.
Getting there: Take US 1 to Southern Pines and follow signs to the Campbell House on Connecticut Avenue, which intersects with Broad Street, the main street through Southern Pines. See the *DeLorme North Carolina Atlas & Gazetteer,* page 60 D3.

established the Moss Foundation to preserve open land for horseback riding. In many places you'll see sandy dirt roads crossing the paved ones to allow gentler surfaces for the horses' hooves.

As you head right on Youngs Road (SR 2026), you'll pass through a residential area with lots of longleaf pines. But soon you'll see the miles of horse fences and farms with names like Economy Farm, Greedy Mother Farm, Land's End, and Sweet and Sourwood Farm. A tobacco field here and there keeps the horse pastures from totally dominating the region.

The rolling hills along Lakebay Road (SR 2023) frame even more horse farms. Look along here for houses with the stables underneath. After you cross US 1 and the railroad tracks in Lakeview (there's a convenience store at the intersection), you'll see Crystal Lake on the left. After you turn right onto Airport Road (SR 1843), there's a sharp turn after the next 0.1 mile. Niagara-Carthage Road at Mile 19.1 is wider with slight paved shoulders. More horse farms are situated along the left side of this road.

On Valley View Road (SR 1857) after Mile 19.2, you'll pass the Equine Hospital and Equine Center with lots of practice fields for riding and jumping. This road merges into North May Street (SR 2080) after a mile.

When you return to the Campbell House, take some time to visit. Originally a private home, Campbell House was given to the town of Southern Pines by Major and Mrs. W. D. Campbell in 1966 to serve "the cultural and social enrichment of the inhabitants of the community." The house's large room—called the Board Room or Permanent Gallery—was part of the Boyd home built in 1903 on the site of the present Weymouth Center. In the 1920s grandsons of the original Boyd moved this part of the house to its current site on Connecticut Avenue, where it became Jack Boyd's home.

The house grew with new additions. Then in 1946 Major Campbell bought the property and made extensive changes. The original frame house was faced with valuable old ballast brick from Charleston, South Carolina. The house now serves as an exhibition center for local artists and a meeting place for about twenty-five organizations.

A sporty cyclist sails past a horse farm in southern Moore County.

LOCAL INFORMATION

♦ Convention & Visitors Bureau for Pinehurst & Southern Pines, 10677 U.S. Highway 15-501, Southern Pines, NC 28388; (910) 692–3330.

LOCAL EVENTS/ATTRACTIONS

♦ Campbell House is a cultural visitor center and art gallery; Connecticut Avenue, Southern Pines, NC; no charge.

♦ Weymouth Center for the Arts and Humanities houses the North Carolina Literary Hall of Fame and offers lectures and concerts in addition to other special events; 555 East Connecticut Avenue, Southern Pines, NC 28388; admission fees vary according to the event; (910) 692–6261; weymouthcenter@pinehurst.com.

RESTAURANTS

♦ The Ice Cream Parlor, 176 Northwest Broad Street, Southern Pines, NC 28387; (910) 692–7273. Sandwiches and ice cream.

♦ Sweet Basil, 134 Northwest Broad Street, Southern Pines, NC 28387; (910) 693–1487. Sandwiches and salads (closed Sunday).

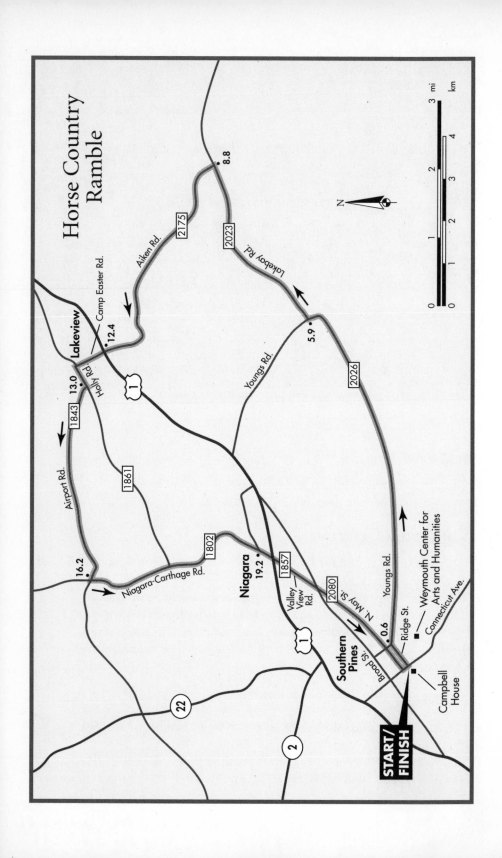

Horse Country Ramble

0.0 From the Campbell House on Connecticut Avenue in Southern Pines, turn left onto Connecticut Avenue.

0.2 Turn right onto Ridge Street.

0.6 Turn right onto Youngs Road (SR 2026). Delaware Avenue goes off to the right at a sharp angle.

5.9 Turn right onto Lakebay Road (SR 2023).

8.8 Turn left onto Aiken Road (SR 2175) to Lakeview.

12.4 Cross US 1. The road's name changes to Camp Easter Road (SR 1853).

12.8 Turn left onto Holly Road (SR 1861).

13.0 Bear right on Airport Road (SR 1843).

16.2 Turn left onto Niagara-Carthage Road (SR 1802) and follow it into Niagara.

19.1 Arrive at Niagara; continue on Niagara-Carthage Road (SR 1802).

19.2 Turn right onto Valley View Road (SR 1857).

20.2 Turn right onto North May Street (SR 2080).

22.0 Turn left onto Connecticut Avenue.

22.3 Turn right into the Campbell House.

ACCOMMODATIONS

♦ Hampton Inn, 1675 U.S. Highway 1 South, Southern Pines, NC 28387; (910) 692–9266. Midrange.

BIKE SHOPS

♦ Rainbow Cycles, 239 Northeast Broad Street, Southern Pines, NC 28387; (910) 692–4494.

REST ROOMS

♦ At the start and finish at the Campbell House.
♦ The Ice Cream Parlor at the intersection of New Hampshire Avenue and Northwest Broad Street in downtown Southern Pines.

MAPS

♦ *DeLorme North Carolina Atlas & Gazetteer,* pages 60–61.
♦ Moore County map, produced by the Convention & Visitors Bureau.

Scotland County Ramble

The Scotland County Ramble, 19.1 miles in length, begins on the campus of St. Andrews Presbyterian College in the small town of Laurinburg, then winds through the countryside to the small community of Laurel Hill and on to the Richmond Hill community before heading back toward Laurinburg. The return route takes you through downtown Laurinburg on tree-lined streets, then busy Main Street on the way back to the campus.

This tour begins on the lovely campus of St. Andrews Presbyterian College in Laurinburg. With a relatively young campus built in the late 1950s, St. Andrews presents a contemporary and well-thought-out campus with a unified architectural style. The new college opened its doors in 1961, consolidating the programs of Flora McDonald College (a woman's college) and Presbyterian Junior College (for men). Take some time to walk around the campus and cross the large lake, the college's centerpiece.

As you can imagine, Scotland County takes its name from the homeland of many of the settlers in this area, who had names like McNair and McLaurin. Since many of these folks were brought up in the Calvinist tradition, there are many Presbyterian churches in the area. These congregations, along with business leaders in the community, banded together to raise enough money to have the new college built here. In subsequent years new manufacturing plants and other businesses have found Scotland County an attractive place to locate.

As you leave the campus, you'll head toward Scotia Village, a large retirement community affiliated with the college. After crossing the busy McColl Road (U.S. Highway 15-401), you'll head out into the country on Blues Farm Road (SR 1117) past pine forests and pleasant residential areas. The Lakeview development is built around a typical lake for the area with stands of cypress trees, populated with ducks and swans. X-way Road leads to the community of Crossway, the site of the old X-way Mill.

Calhoun Road bisects large fields of soybeans and corn, then forests on either side. You pass through Livingston Quarters before arriving in the pleasant community of Laurel Hill. St. Johns Church Road (SR 1148) changes both name and number to Morgan Street (SR 1001) after you cross U.S. Highway 74. At Mile 10.8 bear right onto Old Wire Road (SR 1319) and watch for an old, but active mill wheel on the left at 11.5 miles. Tobacco fields, too, are around, but not as plentiful as in other parts of the state.

Richmond Mill with its requisite millpond was the site of a cannon factory during the Civil War. Contemporary textile industries are situated along Fieldcrest Road (SR 1303). U.S. Highway 74 Business has only light to moderate traffic because most through traffic takes the bypass. As you enter Laurinburg, Andrew Jackson Highway turns into West Church Street, edged with stately homes and two large churches, one of which is Presbyterian.

THE BASICS

Start: The intersection of Magnolia Street and Dogwood Mile on the St. Andrews Presbyterian College campus.

Length: 19.1 miles.

Terrain: Fairly level with a few ups and downs.

Traffic and hazards: Traffic is light on the back roads; take care crossing busy U.S. Highway 15-401 on Hasty Road, and US 74 in Laurel Hill. Traffic will be heavy on Main Street as you return to the college. Be prepared to move across lanes so you can turn left at the second light.

Getting there: Take US 74 to Laurinburg, exiting at Business US 15-401, which is Main Street. After Business US 15-401 merges with the US 15-401 Bypass, turn left onto Elm Avenue through the main entrance of St. Andrews Presbyterian College. Go three-quarters of the way around the traffic circle to Dogwood Mile (toward the residential side of campus). Take the next right onto Magnolia Street and park in any of the parking lots. See the *DeLorme North Carolina Atlas & Gazetteer*, page 72 C3.

Atkinson Street, which parallels tree-lined Main Street, has magnificent trees of its own and less traffic. Atkinson ends at a more southern point on Main Street where you face 0.6 mile of fairly heavy traffic because so many fast-food restaurants are along this part of the highway. Numerous traffic lights slow the traffic and allow cyclists to negotiate their way into the left-turn lane to return to the St. Andrews campus via the second entrance on the residential side of the lake.

LOCAL INFORMATION

♦ Chamber of Commerce, 606 South Atkinson Street, Laurinburg, NC 28352; (910) 276–2200.

0.0 From the intersection of Magnolia Street and Dogwood Mile on the campus of St. Andrews Presbyterian College, turn left onto Dogwood Mile.

0.7 At the traffic circle, travel three-quarters of the way around.

1.0 Turn right onto Elm Avenue, which is the first road, toward Scotia Village.

1.3 Turn right onto Sycamore Lane (SR 1632), then turn left onto Oakwood Drive (SR 1608).

1.7 Turn right onto Hasty Road (SR 1615).

1.9 Cross US 15–401.

2.3 Turn left onto Blues Farm Road (SR 1117).

3.9 Turn right onto Crossway Road (SR 1008). The sign says X-WAY ROAD.

4.0 Turn left onto Blue Woods Road (SR 1116).

4.8 Turn left onto Calhoun Road (SR 1119).

6.6 Turn left onto Gibson Road (North Carolina Highway 79) at Springfield Mills.

7.1 Turn right onto Old Rockingham Road (SR 1126).

8.8 Turn right onto St. Johns Church Road (SR 1148).

10.2 When you cross US 74, St. Johns Church Road's name changes to Morgan Street (SR 1001) in Laurel Hill.

10.8 Bear right onto Old Wire Road (SR 1319).

11.9 Turn right onto Fieldcrest Road.

15.1 Turn left onto Andrew Jackson Highway/US 74 Business, which becomes West Church Street in Laurinburg.

17.2 Turn right onto Atkinson Street.

18.4 Turn right onto Main Street. (After you cross under US 74 Bypass, prepare to turn left at the second light.)

18.9 Turn left onto Lauchwood Drive, then make an immediate right onto Dogwood Mile on the St. Andrews campus.

19.1 Turn left onto Magnolia Street to the parking lots.

LOCAL EVENTS/ATTRACTIONS

♦ Campus of St. Andrews Presbyterian College, a coed liberal arts college with award-winning campus architecture; 1700 Dogwood Mile, Laurinburg, NC 28352; no charge; (910) 277–5000.

RESTAURANTS

♦ Wooly McDuff's Neighborhood Grill (next to the Comfort Inn), 1709 U.S. Highway 401 Bypass South, Laurinburg, NC 28352. American food; midrange.

♦ Champ's Fine Food & Spirits, 1500 U.S. Highway 401 Bypass South, Laurinburg, NC 28352. American food; midrange.

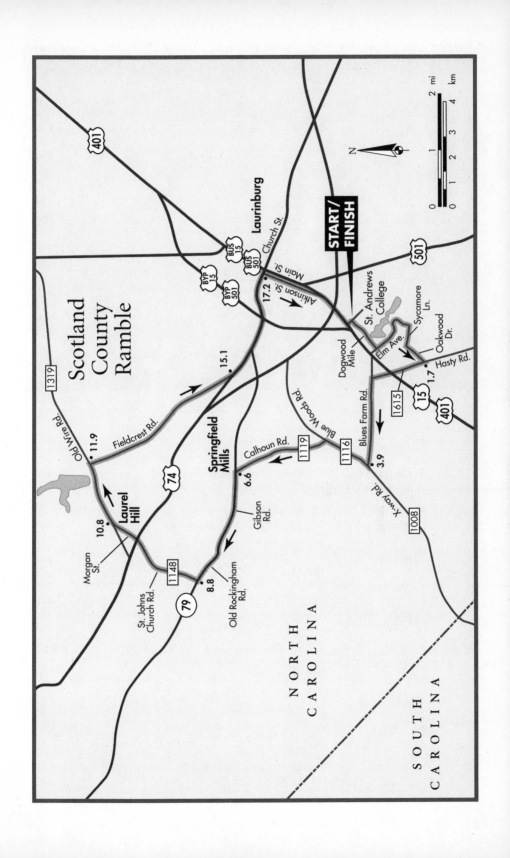

Cypress trees and cattails fill one end of the lake on the St. Andrews campus.

ACCOMMODATIONS

♦ Comfort Inn, 1705 U.S. Highway 401 Bypass South, Laurinburg, NC 28352; (910) 277–7788. Midrange.
♦ Hampton Inn, 115 Hampton Circle (off U.S. Highway 401 Bypass South), Laurinburg, NC 28352; (910) 277–1516. Midrange.

BIKE SHOPS

♦ None.

REST ROOMS

♦ At the start and finish in the Belk Student Union Center at the St. Andrews Presbyterian College campus on Magnolia Street.

MAPS

♦ *DeLorme North Carolina Atlas & Gazetteer,* page 72.

Richmond County Cruise

The *Richmond County Cruise links three charming and historic small towns in Richmond County—Ellerbe, Rockingham, and Hamlet—on a 33.7-mile ride. The tour begins at the Rankin Museum in Ellerbe at the edge of peach country, then travels cross-country to the county seat of Rockingham, where the main street circles the county courthouse in the downtown. From Rockingham it's a short distance to Hamlet, which served as a major hub for the Seaboard Atlantic Railroad at its picturesque and historic depot. The return route passes Ledbetter Lake then retraces the initial part of the route beginning at the intersection at Greenleaf Church.*

The Rankin Museum of American Heritage, the starting point for this route, includes a diverse collection of cultural artifacts and natural history items from South America to the Arctic and from Africa to Alaska. Here you can see an Arctic polar bear, a Central American jaguar, fossils from the Paleozoic era, and an eclectic collection of rocks, minerals, and gems—many from Richmond County. Artifacts of North Carolina pottery, nineteenth-century tools, and beadwork from the Plains Indians of North America are some of the other interesting exhibits in this most varied collection. Try to spend some time here, although museum hours are somewhat limited—Monday through Friday, 10:00 A.M.– 4:00 P.M., and Saturday and Sunday 2:00–5:00 P.M.

From Ellerbe with its antiques-shop-lined Main Street, we head across country on smooth pavement to enjoy the forests and rolling terrain. Pine forests, so typical of the Sandhills Region, abound but are interspersed by lush pastures where horses lazily graze.

Start: The Rankin Museum of American Heritage on Church Street in downtown Ellerbe.

Length: 33.7 miles.

Terrain: Rolling with a few short, moderate hills.

Traffic and hazards: Traffic is light except in the towns. Be careful crossing the numerous railroad tracks in Hamlet.

Getting there: Take U.S. Highway 220 into the town of Ellerbe, where U.S. Highway 220 becomes Main Street. Turn west onto Church Street (there's a large Citgo station on the corner—street signs are not highly visible, but there are signs for the Rankin Museum). The Rankin Museum of American Heritage is on the left in the second block. Parking is available in front of the museum. See the *Delorme North Carolina Atlas & Gazetteer,* page 71 A7.

At Mile 4.3, where you turn right onto Bear Branch Road, you'll see the pretty white building of Greenleaf Church, an example of the historic churches in the county. The churches or meetinghouses served as a stabilizing force for law and order in the early wilderness and had a profound influence on the lives of these hardy early settlers. After passing through scrub forests, you reach the small community of Roberdel with its cluster of frame houses. After a sharp bend in the road and a short climb, the road's name changes to Roberdel Road.

As you enter Rockingham, Fayetteville Road takes you past the historic district with its many restored homes from the late nineteenth and early twentieth centuries. In the downtown area you'll circle the Richmond County Courthouse (built in 1922) and the U.S. Federal Building (1935), both of which are on the National Register of Historic Places. Rockingham serves as the seat of Richmond County.

As you pedal toward Hamlet on County Home Road (SR 1624), you'll see a wide variety of homes. Note the sandy soil of the area. The sand remains from a large dune system that in prehistoric times was the edge of the sea, which came this far inland. Wire Grass Road, named for the popular roadside plant in this area, has ups and downs as it leads into Hamlet. The large stately homes along Main Street point to the historic district, which lies off to the right. Be careful of the road edges in Hamlet because, even where there are curbs, the repaving has left a 2- to 3-inch drop-off in many places.

Hamlet is home to the National Railroad Museum, housed in the old Seaboard Railroad Station off Lackey Street. The distinctive architecture of this building alone makes it worth a stop. As you leave the station, you'll go right onto Lackey Street, the name of which changes to Raleigh Street after you cross the railroad tracks. At the intersection of Raleigh Street and Hamlet Road, be especially careful because this one block covers a busy section of U.S. Highway

74 through Hamlet. Stay in the left lane so you're in the proper position to turn left onto Spring Street at the next light.

Right after you turn left onto Ledbetter Road (SR 1442), look to your right for the dam and waterfall on Ledbetter Lake. This road takes you back to Ellerbe, the center point for many fruit and vegetable farms in the area. In summer many produce stands operate in the vicinity, especially when local peaches are ripe. A juicy ripe peach makes a wonderful reward for your physical efforts during this delightful ride.

Antique shops line Main Street in Ellerbe.

LOCAL INFORMATION

♦ Richmond County Chamber of Commerce & Tourist Bureau, 505 Rockingham Road, Rockingham, NC 28379; (910) 895–9058.

LOCAL EVENTS/ATTRACTIONS

♦ The Rankin Museum of American Heritage offers diverse collections of natural and cultural history from several continents; 131 West Church Street, Ellerbe, NC 28338; adults $3.00, students $1.00; (910) 652–6378; www.rankin museum.com.

♦ The National Railroad Museum and Hall of Fame, Inc. is housed in the Victorian depot built in 1900; the museum's exhibits demonstrate the major role of railroads in this country's development; 23 Hamlet Avenue, Hamlet, NC 28345; open Saturday and Sunday; no charge.

♦ The Seaboard Festival, held the last Saturday of October each year; 201 Main Street, Hamlet, NC 28345; (910) 582–2651; www.hamletnc.org.

RESTAURANTS

♦ Ellerbe Springs Inn and Restaurant, 2537 North U.S. Highway 220, Ellerbe, NC 28338; (910) 652–5600 or (800) 248–6467; www.ellerbesprings.com. Traditional southern dishes; breakfast, lunch, dinner; midrange.

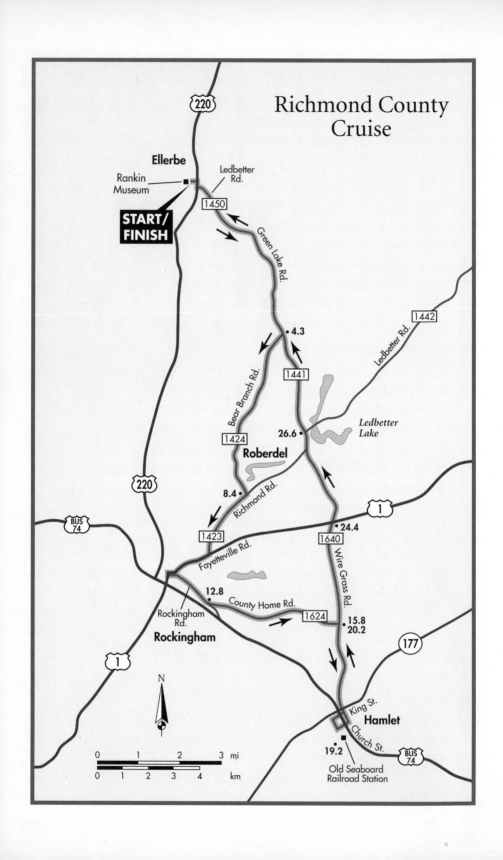

Richmond County Cruise

220

Ellerbe

Rankin Museum

Ledbetter Rd.

START/FINISH

1450

Green Lake Rd.

• 4.3

1441

1442

Ledbetter Rd.

Ledbetter Lake

Bear Branch Rd.

1424

26.6 •

Roberdel

8.4 •

Richmond Rd.

1

220

BUS 74

1423

24.4 •

1640

Fayetteville Rd.

Wire Grass Rd.

12.8 •

County Home Rd.

1624

15.8
20.2 •

Rockingham Rd.

Rockingham

1

177

N

King St.

Hamlet

Church St.

BUS 74

19.2 •

Old Seaboard Railroad Station

0   1   2   3 mi

0 1 2 3 4 km

0.0 From the intersection of Church and Second Streets, adjacent to the Rankin Museum in Ellerbe, turn right onto Church Street.

0.1 Turn right onto Main Street.

0.3 Turn left onto Ledbetter Road (SR 1450), which is also North Carolina Bike Route 23. Ledbetter Road's name changes to Green Lake Road, but it remains SR 1450.

4.3 Turn right onto Bear Branch Road (SR 1424), the name of which changes to Roberdel Road after you pass the Roberdel community.

8.4 Turn right onto Richmond Road (SR 1423).

10.1 Turn right onto Fayetteville Road (US 1) toward Rockingham.

10.9 Bear right on US 1 but stay in the left lane on the one-way street.

11.2 Turn left onto Hancock Street (US 1).

11.3 Turn left onto Franklin Street (US 1 North).

11.5 Bear right onto Rockingham Road (SR 1648).

12.8 Turn left onto South Long Street at the light (a hospital is on the left), then immediately right onto County Home Road (SR 1624).

15.8 Turn right onto Wire Grass Road (SR 1640) going into Hamlet.

17.7 Turn left onto Spring Street.

17.8 Turn right onto King Street (NC–177 South) and cross US 74 Business.

18.4 Turn left onto Hylan Avenue.

18.5 Turn left onto Main Street in Hamlet.

19.1 Turn left onto Lackey Street.

19.2 Turn right into the Old Seaboard Railroad Station. When you exit after your tour, turn right onto Lackey Street. Lackey Street's name changes to Raleigh Street after you cross the railroad tracks.

19.5 Turn left onto Spring Street (a one-way street).

20.2 Turn right onto Wire Grass Road (SR 1640). Continue straight past the intersection with County Home Road (SR 1624).

24.4 Cross US 1.

24.7 Bear left onto Ledbetter Road (SR 1442).

26.6 Turn left onto the Green Lake Road (SR 1441).

29.1 At the intersection by Greenleaf Church, the road number changes from SR 1441 to SR 1450. Green Lake Road's name changes back to Ledbetter Road in Ellerbe.

33.4 Turn right onto Main Street in Ellerbe.

33.7 Turn left onto Church Street to return to the Rankin Museum.

ACCOMMODATIONS

◆ Ellerbe Springs Inn and Restaurant, 2537 North U.S. Highway 220, Ellerbe, NC 28338; (910) 652–5600 or (800) 248–6467; www.ellerbesprings.com. Mid-range.

BIKE SHOPS

◆ None.

REST ROOMS

◆ At the start and finish at the Rankin Museum.
◆ Mile 8.4 at a convenience store at the intersection of Roberdel and Richmond Roads.
◆ Mile 17.8 at a convenience store at the intersection of King Street and U.S. Highway 74.
◆ Mile 24.4 at a convenience store at the intersection of U.S. Highway 1 and Wire Grass Road.

MAPS

◆ *DeLorme North Carolina Atlas & Gazetteer,* pages 71–72.

Capital City Ramble

The Capital City Ramble offers a relatively easy 12.2-mile tour of Raleigh. It starts at the main entrance to an established girls' school then heads toward the State Capitol and downtown Raleigh. After a few blocks on streets in the center city, it takes you east through historic Oakwood and past St. Augustine's College. Winding back on itself, the route then passes the Governor's Mansion and two museums before it turns north to meander through different old-time Raleigh neighborhoods. The route returns to Hillsborough Street through neighborhoods surrounding North Carolina State University.

Named for Sir Walter Raleigh, this state capital is relatively friendly to cyclists. This route circles through some of the most interesting sights in the center city and traverses a historic district before wandering through some of Raleigh's older, tree-lined neighborhoods. Raleigh retains much of its longtime southern charm, which belies the rapid growth of Raleigh and Wake County outside the beltline.

St. Mary's, at our starting point, is an Episcopal school for girls that was established in 1842 by the Reverend Albert Smedes on the site of an earlier school for boys. At the edge of St. Mary's campus is the site of the Joel Lane House, which was built before 1770 and was the meeting place where it was decided to locate the town of Raleigh on Lane's land in 1792.

Hillsborough Street leads directly to the State Capitol Building, which stands majestically on Capitol Square and has been restored to its neoclassical splendor. Built in 1833–40, the building is open for tours and now houses the governor's office and other executive functions.

This Victorian mansion serves as the residence for North Carolina's governor.

On Martin Street, after you cross Blount Street at Mile 1.1, you'll see Moore Square Park on your left with its huge acorn sculpture paying tribute to the mighty oak trees that surround it. Across the street is the rejuvenated City Market with lots of interesting shops and restaurants. The City Cemetery on East Street (Mile 1.5) was established in 1798.

You enter the historic district of Oakwood after you turn right onto Jones Street (Mile 1.8). This elegant turn-of-the-twentieth-century community was declining rapidly when visionary Raleigh residents formed a preservation group to encourage families to move in and restore these charming homes. This street is also part of Raleigh Bike Route 9.

St. Augustine's College, on Oakwood Avenue at Mile 2.9, is one of the earliest African-American colleges in the South, and it continued to produce educated and talented alumni, even during the dark days of the Jim Crow era. Among its most famous alumni were the Delany sisters, one an educator and the other a dentist, both of whom lived to be more than one hundred years old. They told their lively and interesting story in the best-seller *Having Our Say.*

As you go west on Oakwood Avenue, you pass the Oakwood Cemetery and reenter the Oakwood Historic District. Blount Street takes you past the elegant Victorian house on the left that serves as the Governor's Mansion. Then you'll pass the North Carolina Museum of History and the Museum of Natural Sciences on your right as you head west on Edenton Street at Mile 4.4.

From there the route winds its way through neighborhoods from different eras in the city's development. Although a great number of Raleigh's famed trees were decimated by a major hurricane in the late 1990s, many remain to grace these neighborhoods "inside the beltline" and proffer welcomed shade for cyclists.

At Mile 8.8 the route turns back toward Hillsborough Street via a 2-mile stretch on the neighborly Brooks Avenue, which leads to the North Carolina State University campus. When you come to a stop at Hillsborough Street, the university campus will be directly across the street; you'll likely see many students and university personnel along this part of the route.

THE BASICS

Start: The main entrance to St. Mary's School on Hillsborough Street.

Length: 12.2 miles.

Terrain: Rolling terrain with a few good hills.

Traffic and hazards: Traffic can be heavy in the downtown area during the week, although the travel speeds are low. Hillsborough Street around the university is busy.

Getting there: Take the Hillsborough Street exit off I–440 on the west side of Raleigh. Go east on Hillsborough Street toward downtown. St. Mary's School is on your left about 2.5 miles toward downtown. There is usually ample on-street parking in this area. See the *DeLorme North Carolina Atlas & Gazetteer,* page 40 C2.

0.0 From the main entrance to St. Mary's School on Hillsborough Street, turn left onto Hillsborough Street and head east toward downtown Raleigh.

0.8 Turn right onto Salisbury Street.

1.0 Turn left onto Martin Street.

1.4 Turn left onto East Street.

1.8 Turn right onto Jones Street.

2.6 Turn left onto Hill Street.

2.8 Turn left onto Oakwood Avenue.

3.6 Turn right onto East Street.

3.7 Turn left onto Polk Street.

4.0 Turn left onto Blount Street (one-way south).

4.3 Turn right onto Edenton Street (one-way west).

4.8 Turn right onto Harrington Street.

5.1 Turn left onto West North Street.

5.3 Turn right onto Boylan Avenue.

5.4 Turn left onto West Johnson Street.

5.5 Turn right onto St. Mary's Street.

6.3 Turn right onto Williamson Drive.

6.6 Turn left onto Carr Street.

6.8 Turn right onto Harvey Street.

6.9 Turn left onto Cowper Drive.

7.6 Turn left onto Fairview Road.

8.4 Turn right onto Cambridge Road.

8.8 Turn left onto Lake Boone Trail.

9.0 Turn left onto Brooks Avenue.

11.0 Turn left onto Hillsborough Street.

12.1 Bear left to stay on Hillsborough Street.

12.2 Arrive at the main entrance to St. Mary's School.

At Mile 12.1 the main street bears to the right to join Morgan Street, which is one-way east. You will need to turn left to remain on Hillsborough Street and return to the main entrance of St. Mary's School.

LOCAL INFORMATION

◆ Greater Raleigh Convention and Visitors Bureau, 421 Fayetteville Street Mall, Suite 1505, Raleigh, NC 27602; (919) 834–5900 or (800) 849–8499; www.raleighcvb.org.

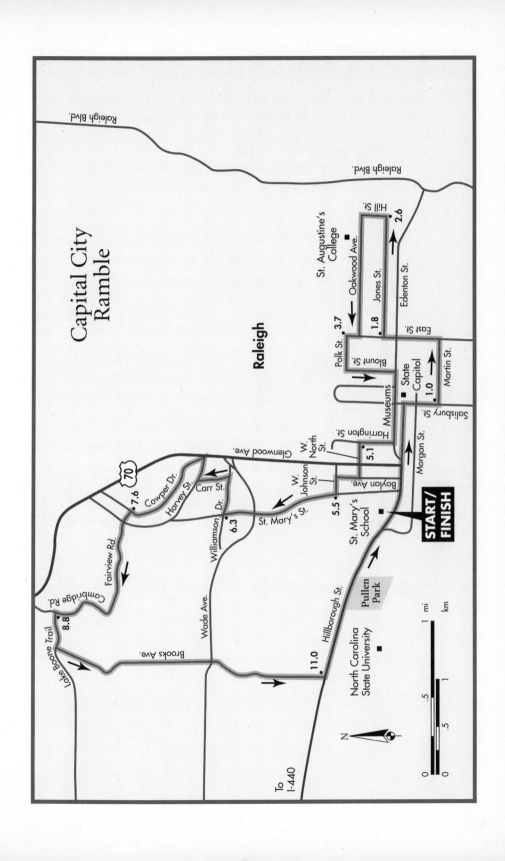

Capital City
Ramble

Raleigh

LOCAL EVENTS/ATTRACTIONS

♦ North Carolina Museum of History, an enlarged museum, has a variety of exhibits; 5 East Edenton Street, Raleigh, NC, 27601; no charge, but donations are welcomed; (919) 715–0200; ncmuseumofhistory.org.

♦ North Carolina Museum of Natural Sciences offers a wide variety of science exhibits and free programs, often featuring live animals; 11 West Jones Street (at the corner of Jones and Salisbury Streets), Raleigh, NC 27601; no charge, but donations are welcomed; (919) 733–7450 or (877) 4–NATSCI.

RESTAURANTS

♦ Irregardless Café, 901 West Morgan Street (where Hillsborough joins Morgan at Mile 12.1), Raleigh, NC 27603; (919) 833–8898. Lunch and dinner daily plus Sunday brunch; varied menu with vegetarian specials.

♦ The Charter Room (in the Velvet Cloak Inn), 1505 Hillsborough Street, Raleigh, NC 27605; (919) 828–0333; www.velvetcloakinn.com. Casual American dining; voted Best Seafood Restaurant in the Triangle.

ACCOMMODATIONS

♦ The Velvet Cloak Inn, 1505 Hillsborough Street, Raleigh, NC 27605; (919) 828–0333; www.velvetcloakinn.com. Mid- to upper range.

♦ The Brownstone (a Holiday Inn hotel), 1707 Hillsborough Street, Raleigh, NC 27605; (919) 828–0811 or (800) HOLIDAY; www.brownstonehotel.com. Midrange.

BIKE SHOPS

♦ All-Star Bike Shops, 3530 Wade Avenue, Raleigh, NC 27607; (919) 833–5070; www. allstarbikeshop.com

♦ Cycle Logic, 1211 Hillsborough Street, Raleigh, NC 27603; (919) 833–4588.

REST ROOMS

♦ Mile 4.3 at the Museum of History or Museum of Natural Sciences.

MAPS

♦ Raleigh Bike Map, produced by the North Carolina Department of Transportation and the Raleigh City Transportation Department, reprinted in 1997.

Duke-Durham Cruise

T he 26.1-mile Duke-Durham Cruise takes you on a delightful sight-seeing tour of Durham, home of Duke University. The ride begins in front of the famous Duke Chapel, winding through the West and then the East Campus before skirting the downtown area. It next heads north past the Museum of Life and Science, past numerous parks, and through different neighborhoods as it heads west. The route then curves through University Estates to historic Bennett Place. The longest single stretch follows North Carolina Highway 751 through Duke Forest on a North Carolina Scenic Byway that ends at Duke University's West Campus. You can end the route here or do the extra loop through south Durham, returning via downtown and Ninth Street to the starting point.

This sight-seeing tour will give you a good feel overall for Durham as well as introducing you to the many parks and attractions in this lovely city. The ride begins at one of the city's most famous attractions, Duke Chapel on the West Campus of Duke University, known for its impressive Gothic architecture. The chapel, the central and dominant structure on campus, houses a fifty-bell carillon and a Flentrop organ with five keyboards. You'll want to walk around inside the chapel before or after your tour.

The first part of the route winds along shaded Campus Drive through the West Campus and then connects to the East Campus after passing under two overpasses for the Durham Freeway and Main Street. The Duke University Museum of Art, which merits a visit, is located on the East Campus, which is noted for its striking Georgian architecture. You'll take Buchanan Boulevard,

Start: From the parking lot in front of Duke Chapel on the Duke University West Campus.

Length: 26.1 miles.

Terrain: Rolling with some hills.

Traffic and hazards: The route follows neighborhood streets as much as possible, but there are some sections with heavier traffic. Roxboro Street is also U.S. Highway 15-501 Business, though it's one-way. Watch for sleeping policemen (speed humps) on many neighborhood streets. Poor visibility is a problem where you turn left onto Murray Avenue and again at Broad Street. Hillsborough Road is a busy major road. Also, take care in crossing Hillsborough Road.

Getting there: From I-85 in Durham, take North Carolina Highway 751 to Duke University Road. Turn left onto Duke University Road and then left onto Wannamaker Drive. At the traffic circle, take Chapel Drive to the parking area in front of Duke Chapel on the Duke University campus where the ride starts. See the *DeLorme North Carolina Atlas & Gazetteer*, page 39 A7.

which skirts the eastern edge of campus, before turning onto Trinity Avenue with its lovely early-twentieth-century houses. Duke University was founded as Trinity College, from whence came the street's name. You'll pass the Historic Durham Athletic Park on Washington Street. Durham's baseball team gained national prominence with the release of the film *Bull Durham*, which was shot in the city.

The route soon turns north, passing Duke Park and Northgate Park before arriving at the Museum of Life and Science, an interesting hands-on museum that appeals to adults as well as children. Across the street from the museum sits an old Piedmont Airlines plane, a shock to see next to a city street. Along Club Boulevard you'll pass the North Carolina School of Science and Math, a residential high school for juniors and seniors who excel in those subjects. At the end of Club Boulevard, you'll be facing the large lake that serves as the city's reservoir. Hillandale Golf Course lines both sides of Sprunt Road before you turn south onto LaSalle Street.

Morreene Road and American Drive curve through quiet residential areas, but watch out for the numerous speed humps that slow down both bikes and motor vehicles. The next sight is Bennett Place, which marks the location of the surrender that ended the Civil War on April 26, 1865, for Florida, Georgia, and the Carolinas, seventeen days after Lee's surrender at Appomattox, Virginia. Here General Joseph E. Johnston surrendered most of the Confederate army remaining in the field. The triumphant Union general was William T. Sherman, who had just completed his March to the Sea. Each April a reenactment ceremony retells this historic event.

The original home burned in 1921, and a replica was built in 1961. The site now includes the restored homestead and a visitor center where you can see exhibits on North Carolina's role in the Civil War along with photographs, flags, guns, and uniforms. An audiovisual presentation is available on request, as are guided tours. The shady grounds offer picnic facilities.

From there Hillsborough Road leads you to NC–751, a North Carolina Scenic Byway through refreshing Duke Forest to the West Campus of Duke University. You have the option of turning left onto Duke University Road here or continuing the ride by bearing right onto Academy Road. The next section of the route follows quiet streets through southern Durham neighborhoods before turning north toward downtown. On Enterprise Drive you have the option of following part of the American Tobacco Trail, a paved greenway route that will bring you back to the route on Blackwell Street. You'll pass the current Durham Bulls Athletic Park just before you reach the main part of downtown. You'll see a bit of downtown then head west on Morgan Street, where the Durham Civic Center and restored Carolina Theater are located.

On Morgan Street at the intersection with Gregson Street, you have the option of detouring one block to your left to Brightleaf Square, a complex of shops and restaurants in renovated tobacco buildings. After a short stint on Main Street, a right turn onto Ninth Street takes you through a charming neighborhood of eclectic shops, restaurants, and an ice cream parlor, which might prove irresistible at this point in the ride. From Club Boulevard you'll take short Oval Drive around aptly named Oval Park to Oakland. Watch for the busy intersection and short jog on Hillsborough Road to Fifteenth Street, which becomes Anderson Street after you cross Main. You'll see the entrance to the Sarah P. Duke Gardens on your right just before you turn right onto Campus Drive and return to Duke Chapel.

LOCAL INFORMATION

◆ Durham Convention & Visitors Bureau, 101 East Morgan Street, Durham, NC 27701; (919) 680–8302 or (800) 446–8604; www.Durham-NC.com.

LOCAL EVENTS/ATTRACTIONS

◆ Duke University Chapel, a magnificent Gothic structure that houses a fifty-bell carillon with bells ranging in size from 10 to 11,200 pounds and a five-keyboard Flentrop organ; Chapel Drive on the Duke University West Campus; open daily 8:00 A.M.–5:00 P.M.; no charge; (919) 684–2572 or (919) 681–1704; www.chapel.duke.edu.

◆ Museum of Life and Science, packed with hands-on science, technology, and nature exhibits; 433 Murray Avenue, Durham, NC 27704; open Monday through Saturday 10:00 A.M.– 5:00 P.M., Sunday noon–5:00 P.M. (until 6:00 P.M. on weekends in summer); adults $8.50, seniors sixty-five-plus $7.00, children three through twelve $5.50, under three free; (919) 220–5429; www.ncmls.org.

◆ Bennett Place State Historic Site, the restored Bennett House and site where General Joseph Johnston surrendered most of the Confederate armies at the

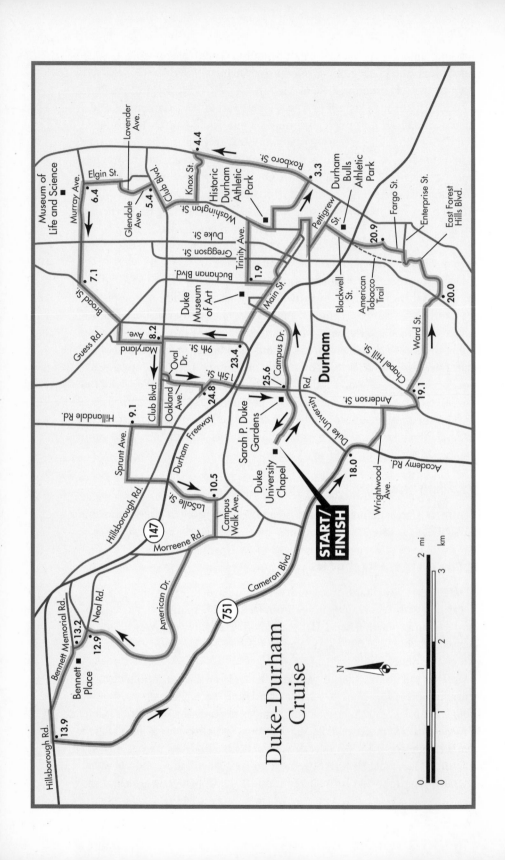

Duke-Durham Cruise

0.0 Start from the parking lot in front of Duke Chapel on the Duke University West Campus. Take Chapel Drive away from the chapel.

0.3 Go around the traffic circle and turn right onto Campus Drive, which connects the West and East Campuses of the university. The road will go under two streets and then curve back to the left to Main Street.

1.6 Turn right onto Main Street.

1.7 Turn left onto Buchanan Boulevard.

1.9 Turn right onto Trinity Avenue. You'll cross Gregson and Duke Streets.

2.4 Turn right onto Washington Street.

2.6 Turn left onto Corporation Street. Historic Durham Athletic Park is on the left.

2.8 Turn right onto Rigsbee Avenue.

3.0 Turn left onto East Seminary Avenue. Downtown is straight ahead.

3.3 Turn left onto Roxboro Street, which is one-way north. Stay in the right lane to go straight at the intersection with Markham Avenue.

4.4 Turn left onto Knox Street. Duke Park is on the right.

4.9 Turn right onto Washington Street.

5.2 Turn right onto Club Boulevard.

5.4 Turn left onto Glendale Avenue.

5.6 Turn right onto Lavender Avenue. Northgate Park is on the left.

5.8 Turn left onto Elgin Street.

6.1 Turn left onto Murray Avenue

6.3 The entrance to the Museum of Life and Science is on the right. A Piedmont Airlines plane is on the left.

7.1 Turn left onto Broad Street. Take care because of poor visibility.

7.6 Turn right onto Sunset Avenue. Don't take the sharp right, which is Guess Road.

7.8 Turn left onto Maryland Avenue. *Note:* North Carolina School of Science and Math is on the left.

8.2 Turn right onto Club Boulevard, which is wide with parking on both sides.

8.9 Turn right onto Hillandale Road. Straight ahead is the lake for the Durham Water Works.

9.1 Turn left onto Sprunt Avenue.

9.6 Turn left onto LaSalle Street.

9.8 Cross Hillsborough Road. Watch out for rough railroad tracks.

10.5 Turn right onto Campus Walk Avenue.

10.8 Turn right onto Morreene Road, which is wide with three lanes.

11.1 Turn left onto American Drive.

12.9 Turn left onto Neal Road.

13.2 Turn left onto Bennett Memorial Road. *Note:* Entrance to Bennett Place is on your left.

(continued)

13.7 Turn left onto Hillsborough Road.

13.9 Turn left onto NC–751/Cameron Boulevard.

18.0 Bear right. The road's name changes to Academy Road. *Bail-out:* You can turn left onto Duke University Road to return to the starting point at the chapel.

18.2 Turn left onto Wrightwood Avenue.

18.6 Turn right onto Anderson Street.

18.9 Turn left onto Chapel Hill Street.

19.1 Turn right onto Ward Street.

19.8 At the intersection with West Forest Hills Boulevard, go straight onto West Forest Hills Boulevard. This boulevard also goes to the left.

20.0 Cross University Drive and go straight onto East Forest Hills Boulevard. Ignore the sign for a turn on the bike route.

20.5 Turn right onto Overhill Terrace.

20.6 Turn right onto Enterprise Street. The American Tobacco Trail crosses Enterprise Street. *Option:* You can turn left here onto the American Tobacco Trail and take it to Blackwell Street near the Durham Bulls Athletic Park, where you will rejoin the route.

20.7 Turn left onto Fargo Street. *Note:* Great view of the Durham skyline.

20.9 Turn left onto South Street. At the traffic signal, the road's name changes to Blackwell Street. You'll pass under the Durham Freeway.

21.3 Pass the Durham Bulls Athletic Park on the right.

21.5 Turn left onto Pettigrew Street.

21.8 Turn right onto Chapel Hill Street.

21.9 Turn right at the second stop sign.

22.0 Turn left onto Foster Street.

22.1 Turn left onto Morgan Street.

22.3 Turn right to stay on Morgan Street.

22.7 Turn right—not the sharp right—onto Main Street.

23.4 Turn right onto Ninth Street.

24.1 Turn left onto Club Boulevard.

24.4 Turn left onto Oval Drive.

24.5 Turn left onto Oakland Avenue. Go straight at the small traffic circle.

24.8 Turn left onto Hillsborough Road.

24.9 Turn right onto Fifteenth Street. The road's name changes to Anderson Street after you cross Main Street. Watch out for the rough railroad tracks.

25.6 Turn right onto Campus Drive.

25.8 Go around the traffic circle and then turn right onto Chapel Drive.

26.1 Arrive at parking lot in front of Duke Chapel.

end of the Civil War; 4409 Bennett Memorial Road, Durham, NC 27705; guided thirty-minute tours plus a slide show every thirty minutes; call ahead for hours; no charge; (919) 383–4345.

♦ Historic Durham Athletic Park, the film location for the movie *Bull Durham* (which starred Kevin Costner, Susan Sarandon, and Tim Robbins), is now home to the Durham Americans after fifty years as the original home of the Durham Bulls; 500 West Corporation Street, Durham, NC 27701; (919) 956–9555.

♦ Durham Bulls Athletic Park, the stadium where the Durham Bulls baseball team plays; ticket prices vary; for ticket information tickets@durhambulls.com or (919) 956–BULL; for general information (919) 687–6500.

♦ American Tobacco Trail, a 30-mile rails-to-trails project located in the Triangle Region of North Carolina that crosses through the city of Durham and through Durham, Chatham, and Wake Counties; no charge; (919) 680–8302 or (800) 446–8604; www.Durham-NC.com.

♦ Sarah P. Duke Gardens, fifty-five acres of native plants and a 300-bush rose garden; on Anderson Street, Durham, NC 27705; open daily 8:00 A.M.–dusk; no charge; (919) 684–3698.

♦ Duke University Museum of Art, changing exhibits plus permanent displays of Greek and Roman antiquities, Chinese jade, American and European paintings, drawings, and sculptures; on the Duke University East Campus just off East Main Street, Durham, NC 27701; open Tuesday through Friday, 10:00

Duke Chapel, the starting point for the ride, stands as the centerpiece of Duke University's three campuses in Durham. (Photo courtesy of Durham Convention and Visitor's Bureau)

A.M.–5:00 P.M., Saturday 11:00 A.M.–2:00 P.M., Sunday 2:00 P.M.–5:00 P.M.; no charge; (919) 684–5135.

RESTAURANTS

♦ Caterpillar Café, Museum of Life and Science, 433 Murray Avenue, Durham, NC 27704; (919) 220–5429. Pizza, hot and cold sandwiches, snacks, and ice cream; midrange.

♦ Blue Corn Café, 716-B Ninth Street, Ninth Street District, Durham, NC 27705; (919) 286–9600. Latin American cuisine; open Monday through Saturday 11:30 A.M.–9:30 P.M.; closed Sunday; midrange.

♦ Bahn's Cuisine, 750 Ninth Street, Ninth Street District, Durham, NC 27705; (919) 286–5073. Open Monday through Saturday 11:00 A.M.–8:00 P.M.

ACCOMMODATIONS

♦ Old North Durham Inn, Debbie and Jim Vickery , 922 North Mangum Street, Durham, NC 27701; (919) 683–1885; dvick1885@aol.com; www.bbonline. com/nc/oldnorth. Close to downtown; complimentary tickets to all Durham Bulls games; upper range.

♦ Duke Tower Residential Suites, 807 West Trinity Avenue, Durham, NC 27701; (919) 687–4444. Close to Duke University; midrange.

BIKE SHOPS

♦ Cycle Center, 639 Broad Street, Durham, NC 27705; (888) 286–2453 or (919) 286–BIKE.

REST ROOMS

♦ At the start and finish in the Duke Student Union, which is on the left as you approach the circle in front of Duke Chapel.

♦ At about Mile 6.1 at Edison Johnson Center in Rock Quarry Park at 600 Murray Avenue.

♦ At about Mile 8.2 at fast-food restaurants on Club Boulevard at Buchanan Street (just as it turns into Guess Road).

♦ At about Mile 10.8 at Morreene Road Center at 11 Morreene Road.

♦ At about Mile 22.1 at the Durham Convention & Visitors Bureau at 101 East Morgan Street.

♦ Mile 22.3 at Brightleaf Square, one block to the left on Gregson Street where you cross it on Morgan Street.

MAPS

♦ City Map of Durham by Riley Marketing, Inc., 2001.
♦ Maps by the City of Durham Planning Department.

Orange County Ramble

The Orange County Ramble will let you relax and enjoy your ride with few turns. The ride begins in the small town of Carrboro with its mainly residential streets. Major improvements along Greensboro Street provide ample room for cyclists even at the busiest times. You'll quickly leave the town behind. Then the long, peaceful stretches of road wind through dairy country—hence the name Dairyland Road for one of the longest segments. This route is popular with local cyclists, especially on weekends, so be prepared for some friendly waves.

This ride starts at Carr Mill Mall, a combination historic site and shopping center situated at the convergence of Main, Weaver, and Greensboro Streets. Distinctive shops and restaurants can be found in this area. The mill, listed on the National Register of Historic Places, was originally the Durham Hosiery Mills in the early twentieth century. The mill's owner, Julian S. Carr, agreed to provide electricity for the town's 1,000 residents and, in his honor, the town of Venable renamed itself Carrboro. The mills closed during the Great Depression, making the University of North Carolina the largest employer in the area.

Mainly a residential community, Carrboro grew up around the railroad when a spur from the Durham-Greensboro Southern Railway was extended to connect university students to the outside world. The town has one of the most extensive bikeway systems in the state and, in 2001, earned its seventeenth consecutive Tree City U.S.A. Award from the National Arbor Day Foundation for its effort to plant and maintain trees.

As you leave Carrboro on Hillsborough Road, you'll find the houses

Start: Carr Mill Mall on Weaver Street in Carrboro.
Length: 24.3 miles.
Terrain: Rolling with a few good climbs but also some level stretches.
Traffic and hazards: Weaver and Greensboro Streets and Hillsborough Road can be very busy at peak times, but Greensboro Street is wide with marked bike lanes. Borland Road is curvy with poor visibility.
Getting there: Take North Carolina Highway 86 south from I-40 toward Chapel Hill. As you enter Chapel Hill, North Carolina Highway 86 is called Airport Road and merges with Columbia Street. Turn right when you reach Rosemary Street, which becomes Main Street when you enter Carrboro in just a few blocks. Turn right onto Weaver Street and you'll see Carr Mill Mall and the parking lot on your right. See the *DeLorme North Carolina Atlas & Gazetteer,* page 39 B6.

becoming farther apart, separated by golden fields of grain with a few new housing developments. One of these new developments, called Arcadia, to the north of town provides an innovative housing model concentrating on sustainable, energy-efficient construction using active and passive solar features in its buildings.

In the crossroads community of Calvander (Mile 3.4), you'll take Dairyland Road, which takes its name from the many dairy farms that grace this part of the county. Pristine white fences, expansive fields of corn, rolling hills, and grazing cattle characterize this part of the ride. Borland Road (Mile 13.8) offers lots of curves, so be sure to ride far enough into the lane that cars approaching the curve can see you in time.

You'll want to save some time—at either the beginning or end of your ride—to visit the sights in Chapel Hill. Franklin Street is the main street in this lovely historic town. Lots of interesting shops and restaurants line its streets, which are busy year-round with university students and staff. The Morehead Planetarium on East Franklin just east of Columbia Street is part of the University of North Carolina and contains a walk-in model of the solar system. Planetarium shows are presented evenings and for weekend matinees.

The Ackland Art Museum, just south of Franklin Street on Columbia, offers displays of paintings, drawings, sculptures, and other artworks representing Oriental, classical, twentieth-century, and North Carolina folk art.

The University of North Carolina, chartered in 1789, is one of the oldest state-chartered universities in the country and was the first to accept and graduate students. The Old Well, a symbol of the university, can be found by walking through the campus behind the Morehead Planetarium. Parking is limited on campus, so biking and walking are the preferred modes of transportation here.

Three cyclists enjoy a flat stretch along Dairyland Road.

Both Carrboro and adjacent Chapel Hill are part of the Research Triangle area of North Carolina, which also includes Durham and Raleigh. The area was so named because of the three major universities in the area, one of which is the University of North Carolina at Chapel Hill, the oldest school in the UNC system.

LOCAL INFORMATION

♦ Chapel Hill/Orange County Visitors Bureau, 501 West Franklin Street, Suite 104, Chapel Hill, NC 27516; (888) 968–2060; www.chocvb.org.

LOCAL EVENTS/ATTRACTIONS

♦ The University of North Carolina campus, including the Morehead Planetarium, 250 East Franklin Street, Chapel Hill, NC 27514; (919) 962–0522; call for show times; $4.50 for adults, $3.50 for students, children, and senior citizens.
♦ Ackland Art Museum houses 14,000 objects broadly covering the history of European painting and sculpture, South Columbia Street off East Franklin

0.0 Turn right onto Weaver Street as you exit the Carr Mill Mall parking lot.

0.1 Turn right onto Greensboro Street, which has bike lanes.

1.4 Bear right on Hillsborough Road when Greensboro Street ends.

3.4 Turn left onto Dairyland Road (SR 1104) in Calvander. Chapel Hill Road goes off to the right.

10.2 Turn right onto Orange Grove Road (SR 1006).

13.4 Turn right onto Dodsons Crossroads Road (SR 1102).

13.8 Turn left onto Borland Road (SR 1107). This road is curvy.

16.5 Turn right onto Arthur Minnis Road (SR 1113).

17.1 Turn left onto Union Grove Church Road (SR 1179).

20.5 Turn left onto Dairyland Road (SR 1104).

21.1 Turn right onto Hillsborough Road in Calvander.

21.8 Bear left on Hillsborough Road.

23.1 Bear left on Greensboro Street.

24.3 Turn left onto Weaver Street then left into the parking lot at Carr Mill.

Street in Chapel Hill; free but with a suggested donation of $3.00; (919) 966–5736.

♦ Interesting shops along Franklin Street in Chapel Hill and on Main Street in Carrboro.

♦ Serene rural settings.

RESTAURANTS

♦ Spotted Dog Restaurant & Bar, 111 East Main Street, Carrboro, NC 27510; (919) 933–1117. Imaginative casual fare, including vegetarian and healthy options.

♦ Crazie Mae's, Carr Mill Mall, Weaver Street, Carrboro, NC 27510; (919) 933–1117. Lighter fare and homemade desserts.

ACCOMMODATIONS

♦ The Carolina Inn, 211 Pittsboro Street, Chapel Hill, NC 27516; (800) 962–8519. Listed on National Register of Historic Places; a AAA four-diamond hotel.

♦ Days Inn, 1312 Fordham Boulevard (U.S. Highway 15-501), Chapel Hill, NC 27514; (919) 929–3090. Moderate rates.

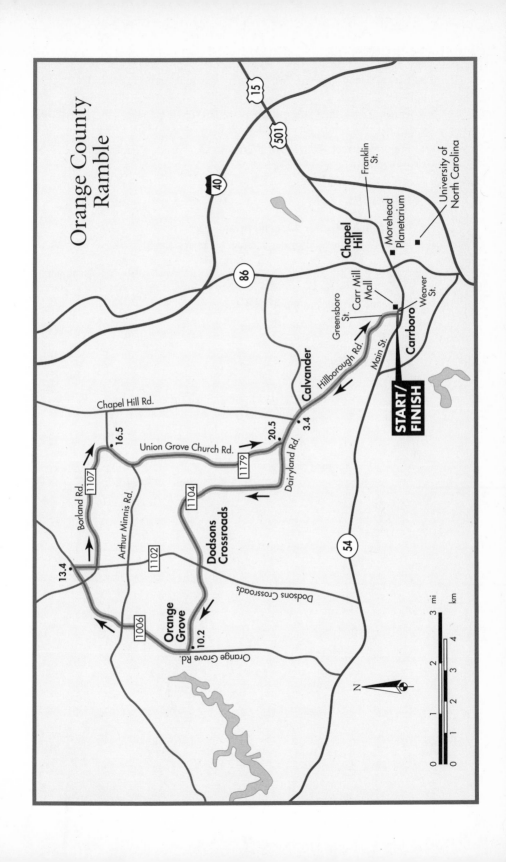

Orange County Ramble

BIKE SHOPS

♦ Clean Machine, 104 West Main Street, Carrboro, NC 27510; (919) 967–5104.

♦ Performance Bike Shop, 404 East Main Street, Carrboro, NC 27510; (919) 933–1491.

♦ Franklin Street Cycles, 210 West Franklin Street, Chapel Hill, NC 27516; (919) 929–0213.

REST ROOMS

♦ Carr Mill Mall at the start and finish.
♦ Talbert's Grill in Calvander at Mile 3.4 and Mile 20.5.

MAPS

♦ *DeLorme North Carolina Atlas & Gazetteer,* page 39.

Historic Alamance County Cruise

T he Historic Alamance County Cruise rambles through the quiet countryside in this section of North Carolina's Piedmont. The gently rolling landscape provides the exhilaration of coasting downhill with the challenge of gradual climbs. This cruise explores three historic sites from the eighteenth and nineteenth centuries. Alamance Battleground commemorates the last battle of the War of Regulation, a precursor to the American Revolution. The Alamance Historical Society includes a restored nineteenth-century manor and outbuildings with recently restored gardens. Historic Snow Camp with its outdoor dramas provides a glimpse of life for the Quakers who settled here in the mid-eighteenth century. The route also crosses Cedar Rock Park, offering a verdant respite from the rigors of cycling.

Our starting point for this tour is the Alamance Battleground, "Where the Regulators and Militia Met to End the War of Regulation" in the early 1770s. This battlefield, memorialized with an 1880 granite monument, commemorates the struggle of North Carolina Regulators against the abuses and excesses of the royal government of this British colony under Royal Governor William Tryon. Tryon's army of fewer than 1,000 men rested on the banks of Alamance Creek before confronting the 2,000 Regulators who had assembled 5 miles away.

The two-hour battle resulted in nine fatalities for each side, although the better-equipped and trained militia also took fifteen prisoners and executed six of them. While the Regulators' efforts at effecting reform were unsuccessful, they demonstrated the high level of discontent among the colonists and fore-

A cannon looks out over the Alamance Battleground.

told the boldness of the colonists and their eventual success during the War of Independence a decade or so later.

The visitor center at the battleground offers an audiovisual presentation of the historical event; a map near the field illustrates the battle and gives a brief history. Also located at the battleground is the Allen House. This log house typifies those used extensively by frontier settlers in the western part of the colony. According to family sources, the house was probably constructed around 1780 by John Allen and was moved from nearby Snow Camp, then restored and refurbished with its original furnishings. John's sister Amy was married to Hermon Husband, a Quaker and pamphleteer active in the Regulator movement.

Just a short distance from the battleground (Mile 1.9) is the Alamance County Historical Museum, whose grounds include the Holt family cemetery. The next sight to see along the route comes at Cedar Rock Park, which the route crosses. The road passes through lovely rural areas with scattered houses and farmland broken by clusters of woods. The terrain is rolling so uphill climbs are rewarded with nice downhill runs.

At Mile 18.4 the route takes you into Saxapahaw. The town is built into a hillside overlooking the Haw River and offers an optional side trip for those who are interested in more miles than the route provides. First settled by the Sissipahaw Indians, the town was the site of a pioneer cotton mill built by Quaker John Newlin in 1844 and revived in 1927. Senator B. Everett Jordan from North Carolina had his home here. At Saxapahaw, we turn around and head to Snow Camp.

Snow Camp at Mile 27.6 was founded by the Quakers in 1749. During the American Revolution, General Cornwallis camped in this area after the Battle of Guilford Courthouse, using the home of Simon Dixon as his headquarters. An outdoor drama, *The Sword of Peace,* recounts the history of the area and the convictions and activities of the Quakers who lived here. On Drama Road—a North Carolina Scenic Byway—you can see the log cabins that remain from the Quaker settlement. Ye Old Country Kitchen Restaurant serves dinner and offers a welcome break.

The return loop weaves through the rural countryside and returns you to Alamance Battleground along quiet country roads.

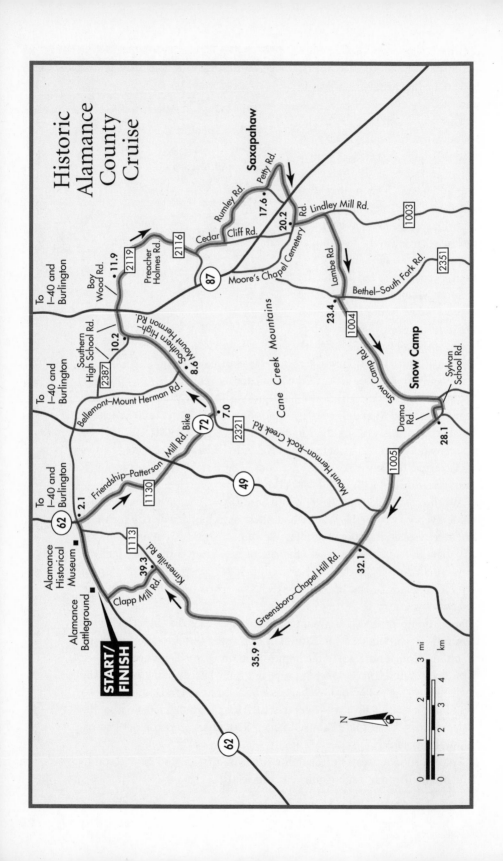

Historic Alamance County Cruise

0.0 From the parking lot at Alamance Battleground, turn left onto NC–62.

1.9 Alamance Historical Museum is on your left.

2.1 Turn right onto North Carolina Bike Route 72, Friendship–Patterson Mill Road (SR 1130).

5.3 At the stop sign at NC–49, continue straight. Signs for Bike Route 72 and Cedar Rock Park are across the highway.

5.6 Cross Cedar Rock Park.

7.0 At the stop sign turn left onto Mt. Hermon–Rock Creek Road, (SR 2321), Bike Route 72.

8.6 At the stop sign bear right on Bellemont–Mt. Hermon Road (SR 2321).

8.9 Turn left onto SR 2321, Southern High–Mt. Hermon Road (Bike Route 72 sign).

10.2 At the stop sign turn right onto Southern High School Road (SR 2387). Follow Bike Route 72. Diagonally across the road is Southern High School.

11.0 At a stoplight at the intersection with NC–87, go straight following Bike Route 72. Boy Wood Road—SR 2119 (also shown on some signs as Boy Woods)—is the road's name on the other side of NC–87.

11.9 Turn right onto Preacher Holmes Road (SR 2116).

14.7 Turn left onto Cedar Cliff Road (SR 2176).

15.5 Turn left onto Rumley Road (SR 2178).

17.6 Turn left onto Petty Road (SR 2173).

18.3 Turn left onto Moore's Chapel Cemetery Road, following Bike Route 72 signs into Saxapahaw.

18.4 Intersection with Church Road. The town of Saxapahaw is to the left. Turn back onto Moore's Chapel Cemetery Road. (SR 2172). Begin Bike Route 72. Stay to the left instead of turning right onto Petty Road.

19.4 At the stop sign continue straight across NC–87.

20.2 At the stop sign turn left onto Lindley Mill Road (SR 1003).

21.0 Turn right onto Lambe Road (SR 2335).

23.3 Turn right onto Bethel-South Fork Road (SR 2351).

23.4 At the stop sign turn left onto Snow Camp Road (SR 1004).

26.6 Go straight across Greensboro–Chapel Hill Road at the flashing red light and head toward Snow Camp.

(continued)

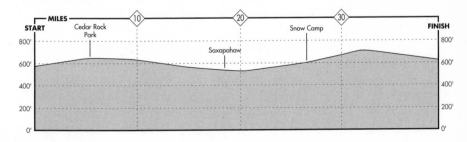

27.4 Turn right onto Sylvan School Road (SR 2360) at the sign about the outdoor drama *The Sword of Peace*.

27.6 Turn right on Drama Road.

28.1 Turn right onto Sylvan School Road (SR 2360).

28.5 Continue straight onto Greensboro–Chapel Hill Road (SR 1005; Bike Route 2).

32.1 At an intersection with NC–49, continue straight across, staying on Greensboro–Chapel Hill Road (SR 1005). Follow Bike Route 2 signs.

35.9 At the stop sign turn right onto Kimesville Road (SR 1113), beginning Bike Route 74. *Note:* SR 1005 and Bike Route 2 both go to the left here.

39.3 Turn left onto Clapp Mill Road (SR 1129).

41.0 Turn right onto NC–62. (The bike route goes to the left here.)

41.1 Turn left into Alamance Battleground Park.

LOCAL INFORMATION

♦ Burlington and Alamance County Convention & Visitors Bureau, 610 South Lexington Avenue, P.O. Drawer 519, Burlington, NC 27216; (336) 570–1444 or (800) 637–3804; www.burlington-area-nc.org.

LOCAL EVENTS/ATTRACTIONS

♦ Alamance Battleground displays information and monuments about the battlefield where the War of the Regulation came to an end; no charge; call for hours; 5803 North Carolina Highway 62 South, Burlington, NC 27215; (336) 227–4785; www.ah.dcr.state.nc.us/alamance/alamanc.htm.

♦ Alamance County Historical Museum is housed in a nineteenth-century home, restored both inside and outside to display period rooms, outbuildings, and gardens; tours are available at no charge; call for hours; 4777 North Carolina Highway 62 South, Burlington, NC 27215; (336) 226–8254.

♦ *The Sword of Peace* Historical Outdoor Drama reenacts the struggles the peaceful Quakers had to face during the Revolutionary War; two other theatrical offerings alternate during the summer months: *Pathway to Freedom,* an exciting account of the Underground Railroad, and *Cane Creek Calamities,* a musical comedy based on North Carolina legend and folklore; adults $12.00, children under twelve $5.00; seniors (sixty and older) $10.00; Drama Road, Snow Camp, NC 27349; (336) 376–6948 or (800) 726–5115; www.snowcamp drama.com

RESTAURANTS

♦ Azalea's, 5371 North Carolina Highway 62 South, Burlington, NC 27215; (336) 227–6131. Buffet and salad bar; limited hours, so call first.
♦ Ye Old Country Kitchen, 327 Drama Road, Snow Camp, NC 27349; (336) 376–6991. Country-style buffet; limited hours but open on evenings before the dramas.
♦ Yesterday's Grill, 716 West Greensboro–Chapel Hill Road, Snow Camp, NC 27349; (336) 376–1833. Daily specials and casual dining.

ACCOMMODATIONS

♦ Ramada Inn, 2703 Ramada Road (near exit 143 on I–40), Burlington, NC 27215; (336) 227–5541). Midrange.

BIKE SHOPS

♦ Shannon's Cycle Center, 721 Chapel Hill Road, Burlington, NC 27215; (336) 228–7130.

REST ROOMS

♦ Alamance Battleground, at the start and end.
♦ Mile 11 at a convenience store at the intersection of NC–87 and Southern High School Road.
♦ Mile 26.6 at a convenience store at the intersection of Snow Camp Road and Greensboro–Chapel Hill Road.
♦ Mile 27.6 at historic Snow Camp.

MAP

♦ *DeLorme North Carolina Atlas & Gazetteer*, page 38.

Randolph County Classic

T he Randolph County Classic offers 82.4 miles of beautiful scenery, interesting attractions, and challenging hills. Starting in downtown Asheboro, the seat of Randolph County, the route heads east to the town of Staley on the border of Chatham County. Taking a southwestern direction from Staley, the route cuts a diagonal line toward the southernmost point of Seagrove, stopping for a visit at the North Carolina Zoological Park. From there it heads west into the Uwharrie National Forest, where you can see one of the last remaining wooden covered bridges in North Carolina and the North Carolina Aviation Museum with vintage World War II aircraft. The route then curves north, then east, past Lake Lucas to return to downtown Asheboro via less traveled streets. The remnants of an ancient mountain range make the county very hilly. The southern part of the county is less populated and therefore has fewer services, so you need to take plenty of snacks and water with you.

This 82.4-mile route, which could be called the route of lakes and parks, covers the southern half of Randolph County, starting in Asheboro and passing through many small Randolph towns before returning to Asheboro from the west. Curvy and undulating, the route passes widely spaced houses and forests interspersed with pastoral settings along fairly smooth roads.

The town of Franklinville's Riverside Park on Main Street offers picnic tables and a playground on the banks of the Deep River. Between Franklinville and Ramseur, you'll pass Ramseur Lake and the Pell Recreation Facility, which has rest rooms. Rural scenes provide a diversion as the route heads east to the town of Staley. From Staley, the route turns southwest toward Seagrove.

In the community of Grantville, outfitters offer canoe rentals on the historic Deep River, which joins with the Haw River to form the Cape Fear. Over the years the river has been used by Indians, steamboats, and colonists to move goods and passengers. The landscape is dotted here and there with picturesque structures such as an old wooden schoolhouse and an unusual wooden barn, reminders of bygone eras.

A short distance off the main route via Old Cox Road is the North Carolina Zoological Park. You can enter the park through the African Exhibits at a less busy entrance. With its 500 acres of natural habitat, the zoo is definitely worth seeing. The county's premier tourist attraction, it draws about 800,000 visitors each year. The North American side of the facility is home to seals and polar bears, bison, and elk, as well as the indoor Streamside and Sonora

THE BASICS

Start: Intersection of Salisbury Street and North Cox Street in downtown Asheboro, North Carolina, near the municipal parking lot behind the Randolph County Courthouse.
Length: 82.4 miles.
Terrain: Very hilly for most of the route, with a few sections that are more rolling.
Traffic and hazards: While most of the route follows less traveled secondary roads, there are a few places where the route uses main roads; extra care is advised on North Carolina Highways 22, 49, and 42. Also use caution when crossing major highways such as U.S. Highway 64. Old Cox Road at the North Carolina Zoological Park can be very busy during the summer and on weekends.
Getting there: Take US 220 to Asheboro. Exit at US 64 East toward Asheboro. Go north on US 220 Business, which is also Fayetteville Street, the main north–south street in Asheboro. Turn right onto Salisbury Street; the municipal parking lot will be on your right, behind the Randolph County Courthouse. See the *DeLorme North Carolina Atlas & Gazetteer,* page 37 D7.

Desert Pavilions. The zoo's African habitats feature nine large outdoor exhibits for zebras, ostriches, baboons, elephants, gorillas, giraffes, and rhinoceros. The luxuriant vegetation of the Forest Aviary offers ample perches for the brilliantly colored tropical birds that call this home.

The southernmost point of the route is the town of Seagrove, headquarters for North Carolina's pottery industry. You'll see numerous potteries along the way into Seagrove, the location for the North Carolina Pottery Center, a combination museum and art gallery. You should plan to spend a little time here viewing the exhibits and the displays of the many varied styles of pottery produced in the area.

The southwestern part of the route takes you to the old Pisgah Covered Bridge, one of only two remaining in North Carolina, and the North Carolina

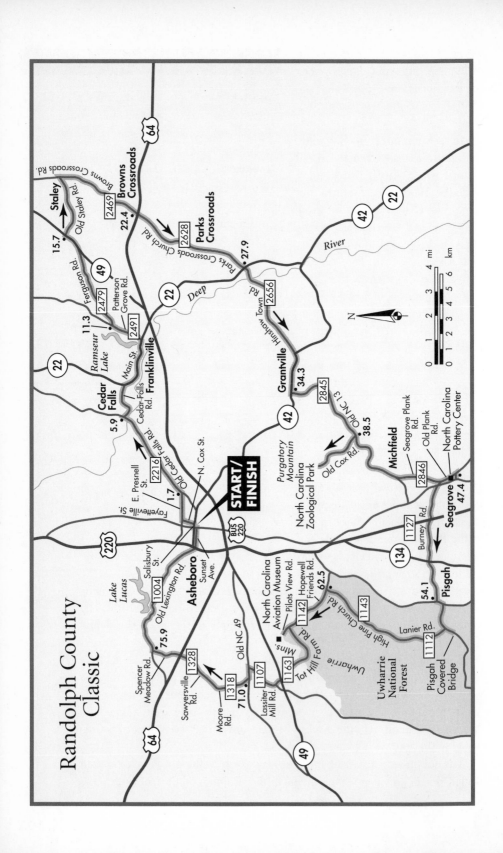

Randolph County Classic

0.0 From the municipal parking lot behind the Randolph County Courthouse, turn right onto Salisbury Street and then left onto North Cox Street.

0.5 Turn right onto East Presnell Street, which has a paved shoulder.

1.7 Turn left onto Old Cedar Falls Road (SR 2216).

5.7 Turn left to stay on Old Cedar Falls Road (SR 2216).

5.9 Turn right onto Cedar Falls Road (SR 2226).

7.5 North Carolina Highway 22 comes in from the left. The road name changes to Main Street as you enter Franklinville.

8.4 Turn left onto NC–22/Main Street in Franklinville.

9.4 The entrance to Kermit Pell Recreation Facility at Ramseur Lake.

9.8 Turn left onto Patterson Grove Road (SR 2491).

11.3 Turn right onto Ferguson Road (SR 2479).

12.5 At a stop sign cross Ramseur-Julian Road (SR 2442) and continue on Ferguson Road.

13.4 At a stop sign cross Low Bridge Road (SR 2481) and continue on Ferguson Road.

15.0 Turn left onto NC–49.

15.7 Turn right onto Old Staley Road (SR 2470). The road's name becomes Columbia Street in Staley.

18.4 Turn right onto South Main Street in Staley. The road's name change to Browns Crossroads (SR 2469) after you leave Staley.

22.4 Cross US 64. Browns Crossroads' name changes to Parks Crossroads Church Road (SR 2628).

27.9 Cross NC–22. Parks Crossroads Church Road's name changes to Hinshaw Town Road (SR 2656).

32.6 Turn right onto NC–42.

34.3 Turn left onto Old North Carolina Highway 13 (SR 2845) through Grantville.

38.5 Turn right onto Old Cox Road (SR 2834) to the North Carolina Zoological Park.

(continued)

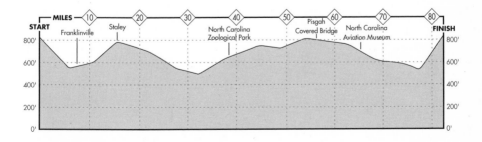

40.0 Arrive at the entrance to the zoo through the African Exhibits. After the visit, turn around and turn left onto Old Cox Road.

41.5 Turn right onto NC–13.

44.8 Turn left onto Seagrove Plank Road (SR 2846), which becomes Old Plank Road as you enter Seagrove.

47.4 Turn right onto Main Street, which is also NC–705, in Seagrove.

47.7 The visitor information center is on the left near the intersection with US 220 Business. The North Carolina Pottery Center is on the right. After the visit, turn around and retrace your steps on Main Street.

48.0 Turn left onto Old Plank Road.

48.8 Turn left onto Seagrove Plank Road Extension (SR 2850).

49.0 Turn right onto US 220 and then make an immediate left onto Burney Road (SR 1127).

51.7 At a stop sign cross New Hope Church Road (SR 1121) and continue on Burney Road.

52.3 At a stop sign cross NC–134 and continue on Burney Road.

54.1 Turn left onto Pisgah Covered Bridge Road (SR 1114).

54.4 Turn right to stay on Pisgah Covered Bridge Road as you enter the Uwharrie National Forest.

56.0 Arrive at Pisgah Covered Bridge. After your visit, exit the park and go right on Pisgah Covered Bridge Road (SR 1114).

56.4 Turn left onto Lanier Road (SR 1112), which is a North Carolina Scenic Byway.

58.3 Turn right onto High Pine Church Road (SR 1143).

62.5 Turn left onto Hopewell Friends Road (SR 1142).

64.9 Go straight onto Pilots View Road at the intersection of Hopewell Friends, Pilots View, and Tot Hill Farm Roads.

65.3 Arrive at the North Carolina Aviation Museum. After your visit, turn around and return to the intersection of Pilots View Road, Hopewell Friends Road, and Tot Hill Farm Road.

65.6 Turn right onto Tot Hill Farm Road (SR 1163).

68.8 Cross Highway 49. Tot Hill Farm Road's name changes to Science Hill Road (SR 1163).

69.1 Turn right onto Lassiter Mill Road (SR 1107).

70.5 Turn left onto Old Highway 49 (SR 1193).

71.0 Turn right onto Moore Road (SR 1318).

72.9 Turn right onto Sawyersville Road (SR 1328).

74.6 Cross US 64. Sawyersville Road's name changes to Spencer Meadow Road (SR 1418).

75.9 Turn right onto Old Lexington Road (SR 1416).

(continued)

77.7 The entrance to Lake Lucas. Continue on Old Lexington Road, whose name changes to Lexington Road; the state road number changes to SR 1004.

81.4 Cross the bridge over US 220. Lexington Road's name changes to Sunset Avenue.

82.3 Turn left onto North Fayetteville Street in downtown Asheboro.

82.4 Turn right onto Salisbury Street to the parking lot.

Aviation Museum with its unique collection of vintage warplanes, most of which are still airworthy. The route passes through the lovely forested areas of the Uwharrie National Forest on a Scenic Byway and then winds its way through the pastoral waysides. The area's topography means lots of hills and curves, but the vistas and points of interest make it well worthwhile. The southern part of the county is remote with few services, so plan to take water and snacks with you. Just a few miles off the route is the Birkhead Mountain Wilderness in the national forest where hiking trails beckon cyclists for a change of pace.

After winding through the countryside, the route passes Lake Lucas before entering Asheboro on less traveled streets.

LOCAL INFORMATION

♦ Randolph County Tourism, P.O. Box 4774, Asheboro, NC 27204; (336) 626–0364 or (800) 626–2672; www.VisitRandolph.org.

♦ Asheboro-Randolph Chamber of Commerce, 317 East Dixie Drive, Asheboro, NC 27203; (336) 626–2626; chamber.asheboro.com.

LOCAL EVENTS/ATTRACTIONS

♦ Ramseur Lake/Kermit Pell Recreation Facility has rest rooms, picnic facilities, and boat rentals; 549 Ramseur Lake Road (just off Highway 22), Ramseur, NC 27316; no charge; (336) 824–4646.

♦ North Carolina Zoological Park, acknowledged as one of the nation's finest all-natural habitat zoos, spreads over 500 acres; 4401 Zoo Parkway (the entrance is also off Old Cox Road), Asheboro, NC 27205; admission is $8.00 for adults, $5.00 for children two through twelve and seniors sixty-two and over; (800) 488–0444; www.nczoo.org.

♦ North Carolina Pottery Center offers permanent exhibits that trace the history and development of North Carolina pottery plus changing exhibits of work by the state's potters; just off Main Street, Seagrove, NC 27341; adults

The Pisgah Covered Bridge is one of the few remaining covered bridges in North Carolina.

$3.00, students kindergarten through twelfth grade $1.00; (336) 873–8430; www.ncpotterycenter.com.

♦ Pisgah Covered Bridge, one of the last remaining wooden covered bridges in North Carolina, is located in a small park with picnic tables and a short trail; Pisgah Covered Bridge Road; no charge.

♦ North Carolina Aviation Museum features examples of airworthy American warplanes from World War II through Vietnam, plus an extensive collection of authentic military uniforms and memorabilia; P.O. Box 1814, Asheboro, NC 27204; admission is $5.00 for adults, free for children under ten; (336) 625–0170.

♦ Warbird Airshow, an annual event on the first full weekend in June, is held at the Asheboro Airport; (336) 625–0170.

♦ Uwharrie National Forest, a large recreation area in southwestern Randolph County, encompasses much of the Uwharrie Mountains, remnants of an ancient chain of island volcanoes that were active some 600 million years ago; no charge; information is available from the USDA Forest Service at (910) 576–6391.

♦ Birkhead Mountain Wilderness, 13 miles of interconnected trails in the Uwharrie National Forest; trailheads are located on Lassiter Mill Road; no charge; information is available from the Forest Service at (910) 576–6391.

RESTAURANTS

♦ Baileys Coffee & News, 23 South Fayetteville Street, Asheboro, NC 27203; (336) 625–8451. Sandwiches; breakfast, lunch, and dinner Monday through Saturday but hours vary; midrange.
♦ Franklinville Restaurant, 159 West Main Street, NC–22, Franklinville, NC 27248; (336) 824–2117. Breakfast and lunch, Monday through Saturday; sandwiches; midrange.
♦ Captain Tom's Seafood, Browns Crossroads Road, Franklinville, NC 27248; (336) 824–2371. Family dining; dinner Tuesday through Saturday, lunch and dinner Sunday; closed Monday (long lines on weekends).
♦ Main Street Grill, 126 Main Street, Staley, NC 27355; (336) 622–1306. Sandwiches, hamburgers; breakfast & lunch Monday through Saturday.
♦ Seagrove Grocery, Main Street near its intersection with U.S. Highway 220, Seagrove, NC 27341 Snacks and beverages.

ACCOMMODATIONS

♦ Comfort Inn, 825 West Dixie Drive (U.S. Highway 64), Asheboro, NC; 27205 (336) 626–4414 or (800) 752–2518. AAA rated; continental breakfast; midrange.
♦ Holiday Inn Express, 1113 East Dixie Drive, Asheboro, NC 27203; (336) 636–5222 or (800) 465–4329; www.hiexprss.com. AAA rated; continental breakfast; midrange.

BIKE SHOPS

♦ None.

REST ROOMS

♦ At the start and finish at the Randolph County Courthouse during working hours.
♦ Mile 9.4 at Kermit Pell Recreation Facility in Ramseur.
♦ Mile 34.3 at Clark's General Store at the intersection of Old North Carolina Highway 13 and NC–42.
♦ Mile 40.0 at the North Carolina Zoological Park.
♦ Mile 47.7 at Seagrove visitor center or the North Carolina Pottery Center.
♦ Mile 65.3 at the North Carolina Aviation Museum.
♦ Mile 77.7 at Lake Lucas Park in Asheboro.

MAPS

♦ *DeLorme North Carolina Atlas & Gazetteer,* pages 37, 38, 59, and 60.
♦ Map of Asheboro from the North Carolina Department of Transportation.

High Point Cruise

The High Point Cruise takes you on a 35.9-mile tour of south-western Guilford and northeastern Davidson Counties, also slicing off a small tip of Randolph County. Because it links the towns of High Point and Thomasville, the route passes through a lot of residential areas as it skirts downtown High Point and passes through the heart of Jamestown and Thomasville. The terrain can be quite hilly in places, and some of the roads have quite a bit of traffic, so this route is recommended for more experienced cyclists.

This route links the two Piedmont towns of High Point and Thomasville and offers a variety of scenery and neighborhoods in between. The ride starts in the heart of furniture country in High Point, which got its name by being the "high point" on the original survey for the old North Carolina Railroad. Called the Furniture Capital of the World, it is known around the world as host twice a year for the International Home Furnishings Market (mid-October and mid-April), which swells the area's population by tens of thousands. Of the 125 furniture plants in the area, fifteen are among the world's largest. In fact, 60 percent of all furniture made in the United States is made within a 200-mile radius of High Point.

The campus of High Point University is our jumping-off point. This main campus, which attracts primarily traditional students, is complemented by a second location in Winston-Salem geared primarily to evening students who are working adults. Take a stroll around the campus with its lovely Georgian Revival buildings either before or after your ride.

The first part of the route meanders through an older residential section of town, with stately homes and established trees, passing the High Point Museum and Historical Park at Mile 0.9, where you turn onto East Lexington Avenue. The route uses sections of four High Point bike routes with some unsigned connections linking them. After you turn onto Hickswood Drive, the houses become more spaced out as you head north and away from the city.

The turn onto Penny Road changes the direction to south along this somewhat busy road. To avoid some of the traffic and add some natural scenery to the ride, the route uses part of the High Point Greenway connecting Penny Road to East Fork Road. There are some steep inclines along the trail that must be negotiated by wood stairs. Fortunately, there's a track so you can roll your bike smoothly along as you walk the stairs. There's also another point where you have to dismount to go through a stile. Otherwise the greenway is paved and pleasant for riding.

THE BASICS

Start: From the main entrance of High Point University on Montlieu Avenue.
Length: 35.9 miles.
Terrain: Mainly rolling, but with some short but steep climbs.
Traffic and hazards: These roads can be quite busy, especially during peak morning and evening hours: East Lexington Avenue, Penny Road, East Fork Road, Main Street in Jamestown, National Highway (four-lane).
Getting there: Take U.S. Highway 311 (which becomes Main Street) into High Point. Turn left onto Montlieu Avenue (to the east) off Main Street, north of the downtown area. High Point University is about 1.1 mile on the left on Montlieu Avenue. Turn left into the main entrance at the university. There is visitor parking around the circle as well as plenty of on-street parking in the area. See the *DeLorme North Carolina Atlas & Gazetteer*, page 37 B5.

At Mile 8.0 you'll enter the historic district in Jamestown and pass the town hall briefly before you turn left onto Oakdale Road. You'll pedal past another furniture landmark on Harvey Road, the huge Furnitureland South Distribution Center. The route then alternates between residential and rural until you get to Archdale-Trinity. What is now Duke University in Durham was founded in Trinity in 1838 as Brown's School House.

The longest single stretch on this route is Turnpike Road, the name of which changes to Trinity Street when you enter Davidson County and the town of Thomasville, known as the chair city. You'll want to pause in awe at the Big Chair, the largest chair in the world, at the intersection of Main and Salem Streets in downtown Thomasville. Although it appears to be built of wood, the 30-foot chair actually has a steel skeleton covered with wire mesh coated with a mixture of cement and granite dust to a thickness of about half an inch. The chair was then painted to look like wood with a striped, upholstered seat. The Big Chair has hosted governors, university presidents, mayors, beauty queens, and even an evangelist.

From the downtown you'll wind your way past Cushwa Stadium and the

Thomasville schools on your way back to High Point. You may want to slow down to enjoy the section on Ferndale Boulevard, a wide street with a grassy median and trees. High Point Central High School with its beautiful classic architecture will be on your right. Brookside Drive at Mile 34.6 is another lovely street with a park down the middle. After weaving your way along some charming residential streets, you'll soon find yourself back at High Point University.

LOCAL INFORMATION

♦ High Point Convention & Visitors Bureau, 300 South Main Street, P.O. Box 2273, High Point, NC 27261; (336) 884–5255 or (800) 720–5255; www.high point.org.
♦ Thomasville Tourism Commission; (800) 611–9907.

LOCAL EVENTS/ATTRACTIONS

♦ High Point University, a campus of Georgian Revival buildings from the 1920s for educating 3,000 students; Montlieu Avenue, High Point, no charge; www.highpoint.edu.
♦ Furniture Discovery Center, the museum of furniture manufacturing offering self-guided tours; 101 West Green Drive (behind the visitor center), High Point, NC 27260; hours vary with the season; adults $5.00, seniors and students over fifteen $4.00, children six through fifteen $2.00, children under six free with adult; (336) 887–3876; www.furniturediscovery.org.
♦ Angela Peterson Doll & Miniature Museum showcases more than 1,600 dolls and miniatures from all over the world; 101 West Green Drive (in the same building with the Furniture Discovery Center), High Point, NC 27260; Monday through Friday 10:00 A.M.–4:30 P.M., Saturday 9:00 A.M.–4:30 P.M., Sunday 1:00–4:30 P.M.; adults $4.50, seniors and children over fifteen $3.50, children six through fifteen $2.50, children three through five $1.00, children under three free; (336) 885–DOLL.
♦ High Point Museum and Historical Park offers exhibits portraying the history of High Point including eighteenth-century buildings as well as exhibits on local industry; 1859 East Lexington Avenue, High Point, NC 27260; the museum is open Tuesday through Saturday 10:00 A.M.–4:30 P.M.; the historical park is open dawn to dusk daily; voluntary donations requested; (336) 885–1859; www.highpointmuseum.org.
♦ Piedmont Environmental Center, a nature preserve with a solar-heated environmental education building, offers workshops and outings; 1220 Penny Road, High Point, NC 27265; the building is open Monday through Saturday 9:00 A.M.–5:00 P.M., Sunday 1:00–5:00 P.M.; trails are open daily dawn to dusk; fees vary for activities; (336) 883–8531; www.piedmontenvironmental.com.
♦ Big Chair in Thomasville, a 30-foot replica of a Duncan Phyfe chair, is the

The Big Chair in Thomasville is the city's most famous landmark.

0.0 From the visitor parking area near the main entrance to High Point University, go out the main gate and turn left onto Montlieu Avenue.

0.1 Turn left onto College Drive.

0.4 Turn right onto McGuinn Drive.

0.9 Turn right onto East Lexington Avenue. *Note:* The High Point Museum and Historic Park are just across Lexington Avenue.

1.2 Turn left onto Carolina Street. *Note:* Look for the North Carolina Bike Route 3 sign.

1.3 Turn right onto Woodruff Avenue.

1.8 Turn left onto Deep River Road.

3.1 Cross the Deep River and turn right onto Hickswood Drive. *Note:* University Park is on the right.

4.2 Turn right onto Willard Road.

4.5 Turn right onto Penny Road. Bike Route 3 goes to the left. *FYI:* Exercise caution when making the next left turn because of traffic in this area.

5.2 Turn left into the main entrance for the Piedmont Environmental Center, then make an immediate left onto the paved greenway. Watch out for boardwalk sections that include stairs! *FYI:* This trail is part of the High Point Greenway.

6.7 From the greenway, turn right onto East Fork Road.

7.3 Turn right onto Guilford Road.

8.0 At Perry Drive turn right onto Main Street in Jamestown. *FYI:* Position yourself defensively on the roadway so you can make the next left turn.

8.1 Turn left onto Oakdale Road.

9.3 Turn right onto Harvey Road.

11.0 Turn right onto Kivett Drive. Bike Route 2 goes to the left.

11.5 Turn left onto Triangle Lake Road.

12.3 Turn left onto Baker Road.

13.3 Turn left onto Cox Avenue.

14.0 Turn right onto Jackson Lake Road.

15.2 Turn right onto East Fairfield Road, which is North Carolina Highway 610.

15.7 Turn left onto Ranch Drive, then bear right to stay on Ranch Drive.

15.9 Turn left onto Greenoak Drive (SR 1168). There is no road name sign at the intersection.

16.2 Turn right onto Liberty Road.

16.7 Cross Main Street/US 311. Liberty Road's name changes to Trindale Road, which is NC–62. *Note:* The Archdale Historical Museum will be on the right.

16.9 Cross Archdale Road.

18.4 Turn right onto Mendenhall Road SR 1599).

19.0 Turn left onto Surrett Drive (SR 1595).

(continued)

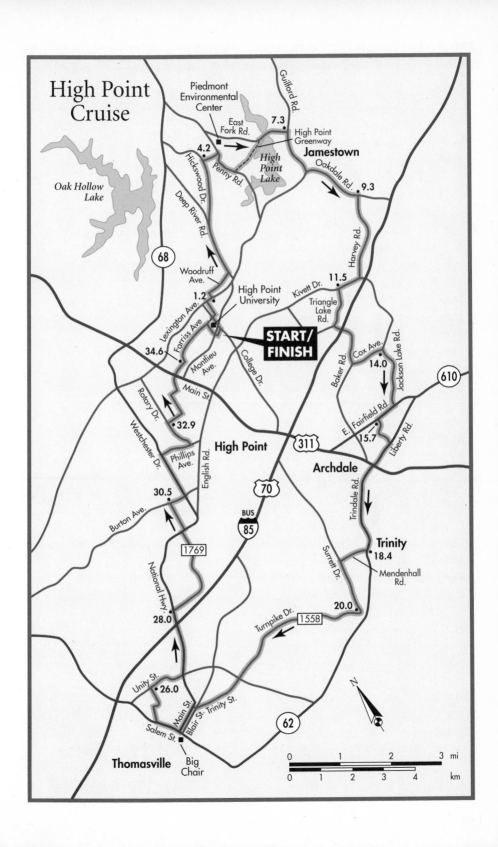

High Point Cruise

Oak Hollow Lake

Piedmont Environmental Center

East Fork Rd.

Guilford Rd.

7.3

High Point Greenway

Jamestown

4.2

Penny Rd.

Hickswood Dr.

Deep River Rd.

High Point Lake

Oakdale Rd.

9.3

Harvey Rd.

⑥⑧

Woodruff Ave.

High Point University

1.2

Lexington Ave.

Farriss Ave.

34.6

Monlieu Ave.

College Dr.

Kivett Dr.

11.5

Triangle Lake Rd.

Baker Rd.

Cox Ave.

Jackson Lake Rd.

14.0

⑥¹⁰

Main St.

Rotary Dr.

32.9

High Point

E. Fairfield Rd.

15.7

Liberty Rd.

Westchester Dr.

Phillips Ave.

English Rd.

③¹¹

Archdale

Trindale Rd.

30.5

Burton Ave.

⑦⓪

BUS
⑧⑤

Surrett Dr.

Trinity
18.4

Mendenhall Rd.

1769

National Hwy.

28.0

20.0

Turnpike Dr. 1558

N

Unity St.

26.0

Main St.

Blair St.

Trinity St.

⑥²

Salem St.

Thomasville

Big Chair

START/ FINISH

0	1	2	3 mi

| 0 | 1 | 2 | 3 | 4 km |

20.0 Turn right onto Turnpike Road (SR 1558). Turnpike Road's name changes to Trinity Street (SR 1558) when you cross into Davidson County and enter Thomasville.

24.1 Turn left onto Blair Street.

24.2 Turn right onto Julian Avenue then left onto East Main Street in Thomasville. *FYI:* Don't be confused—there are two parts to East Main Street, one on either side of the railroad tracks that run through downtown. You want to turn left onto the north part of East Main Street.

24.7 Turn right onto Salem Street. *Note:* The Big Chair for which Thomasville is known is diagonally across Main Street. Pose for a photo.

25.2 Turn right onto Stadium Drive. *Note:* Memorial Park will be on the left.

25.5 Turn right onto Lodge Drive past Cushwa Stadium.

25.6 Turn right onto Culbreth Avenue.

25.7 Turn left onto Memorial Park Drive.

26.0 Turn right onto Unity Street.

26.6 Turn left onto National Highway.

27.7 Cross Business I–85.

28.0 Turn right onto Pleasant Grove Church Road (SR 1769). This road changes names to South Road once it passes into Randolph and Guilford Counties.

29.9 Cross English Road.

30.5 Turn right onto Burton Avenue.

30.8 Turn left onto Westchester Drive/NC–68.

31.7 Turn right onto Phillips Avenue. *Note:* West End Park will be on the right.

32.3 Turn left onto Rotary Drive and cross Chestnut Street.

32.9 Turn right onto Ferndale Boulevard *Note:* High Point Central High School has interesting, classic architecture.

33.2 Turn left onto Council Street.

33.6 Turn right onto West Ray Avenue.

33.8 Turn left onto North Lindsay Street, which curves into Parkway Avenue.

34.1 Cross Main Street, staying in the right lane, then bear right onto North Hamilton Street.

34.3 Turn left onto Woodrow Avenue.

34.6 Turn left onto Brookside Drive.

34.8 Turn left onto Forrest Street then right onto East Farriss Avenue. Cross Centennial Street.

35.3 Turn right onto West College Drive.

35.7 Turn left onto Montlieu Avenue toward the entrance to the university.

35.9 Turn left into the main entrance at High Point University.

symbol of Thomasville, the Chair City; next to the railroad tracks at the intersection of Main and Salem Streets in downtown Thomasville; no charge.

RESTAURANTS

♦ Jed's Barbecue, National Highway, Thomasville, 27360; (336) 475–5806. Monday through Saturday 10:30 A.M.–9:00 P.M.; barbecue, steaks, seafood; low range.
♦ Great China Chinese Restaurant, 110 East Fairfield Road, #114, High Point, NC 27263; (336) 434–8688. Monday through Sunday; Chinese; low range.
♦ Fast-food restaurants along National Highway.

ACCOMMODATIONS

♦ High Point Inn, 400 South Main Street, High Point, NC 27260; (336) 882–4103. AAA-approved; midrange.
♦ Radisson Hotel City Center, 135 South Main Street, High Point, NC 27260; (336) 889–8888. Mid- to upper range.

BIKE SHOPS

♦ Spinz Bike Shop, 3029 South Main Street, High Point, NC 27263; (336) 861–6480.
♦ Bicycle Toy & Hobby Sales, 2000 North Main Street, High Point, NC 27262; (336) 889–2453.

REST ROOMS

♦ At the start and finish in the administration building at High Point University.
♦ Mile 0.9 at the High Point Historical Park.
♦ Mile 5.2 at the Piedmont Environmental Center.
♦ At about Mile 16.7 at a convenience store at the intersection of Liberty Road and Main Street.
♦ Mile 25.2 at Memorial Park on Stadium Drive in Thomasville.
♦ Mile 30.8 at McDonald's or a convenience store on Westchester Drive.
♦ Mile 31.7 at a portable toilet in West End Park.

MAPS

♦ *DeLorme North Carolina Atlas & Gazetteer,* page 37.
♦ North Carolina Department of Transportation's High Point Area Bicycle Map, 1998.

Guilford Courthouse Cruise

The 30.4-mile Guilford Courthouse Cruise begins with a 2-mile tour of the Guilford Courthouse National Military Park before heading out of town on Lake Brandt Road. The historic exhibits in the military park give way to residential areas, and then to rolling farmland. Traffic will subside along Air Harbor Road but can pick up again on Church Street for a mile before you turn onto Archergate Road. The next 16 miles take you through lovely farmland and past scattered houses before bringing you back toward Greensboro on Lake Brandt Road.

The principal attraction along this route is the Guilford Courthouse National Military Park at the starting point. Covering about 220 acres, the park memorializes the Revolutionary War battle fought here in March 1781 between General Nathanael Greene's mixed Continental and militia army and the British forces of Lord Cornwallis. Although Cornwallis won the battle, he suffered severe losses and failed to destroy the revolutionary force. Despite his defeat, Greene helped force Cornwallis to Virginia, where he finally surrendered at Yorktown in October 1781.

The park includes wayside exhibits and markers along a 2.5-mile route. The monuments include those for John Penn and William Hooper, signers of the Declaration of Independence. In the middle of a large grassy area stands the statue of General Greene astride his horse. The Cavalry Monument recognizes the contributions of the American cavalry, among them "The Goliath of the Revolution," as Peter Francisco of Virginia was known. He is alleged to have wielded a 5-foot sword to protect his massive 260-pound, 6-foot-6 body during the battle. The sword was said to have been a gift from General George Washington.

The park itself is a lovely retreat with large expanses of grass and winding trails. It's a popular spot with both cyclists and joggers, especially at the end of the workday and on weekends. The city of Greensboro has built numerous greenways, both paved and unpaved, that connect to the park, if you're interested in exploring beyond the route described here.

As you turn right onto Old Battleground Road after you've finished the tour in the park, you'll see a wide, paved path adjacent to the road that you may prefer to take if traffic is heavy on Old Battleground Road, as it usually is at rush hour. The bike path ends at Lake Brandt Road, where you turn right. Lake Brandt is wide with a middle turn lane, so although it's busy, there's ample room for motorists to pass safely. Air Harbor Road, which was named for the small private airport that was next to the road, is quieter and leads into the countryside of Guilford County.

The route passes residential developments, which thin out as the route moves farther into the coun-

THE BASICS

Start: The visitor center for Guilford Courthouse National Military Park during the hours the park is open (8:00 A.M.–5:00 P.M.). Otherwise, use the parking lot to the north of the intersection of New Garden Road and Old Battleground Road.

Length: 30.4 miles.

Terrain: Mainly level to rolling with a few hills.

Traffic and hazards: Parts of the route are very busy at peak hours; try to avoid riding at those times. Otherwise, take extra care along Old Battleground Road, Church Street, and North Carolina Highway 150. Lake Brandt Road in the city is wide with a center turn lane that allows extra room for cars to pass. New Garden Road can be busy also.

Getting there: From I-40 in Greensboro, take the Guilford College exit and turn north onto Guilford College Road toward Greensboro. You'll cross over Market Street after 1.1 miles and then Friendly Avenue after another 1.0 mile. After you cross Friendly Avenue, the road's name changes to New Garden Road. Go 0.7 mile and turn right to stay on New Garden Road. After 3.6 miles, you'll cross Battleground Avenue. The entrance to the Guilford Courthouse National Military Park visitor center will be 0.3 mile on your right.

tryside. The two large lakes on the route—Lake Brandt and Lake Townsend—are the principal water supplies for the city of Greensboro. The route dips briefly into Rockingham County before turning south again toward Greensboro.

Tannenbaum Historic Park and Greensboro Country Park, two of Greensboro's city parks adjacent to the military park, also include markers related to the Battle of Guilford Courthouse. Both parks have picnic areas. A bicycle/foot trail leads to Greensboro Country Park from the tour drive through the military park. Tannenbaum Historic Park preserves a portion of Joseph Hoskins's farmstead, where General Cornwallis's troops formed for battle. Ironically, Hoskins had left for Pennsylvania after his farm suffered damages during the Philadelphia campaign. Exhibits in the Colonial Heritage Center and historic buildings depict life before, during, and after the Battle of Guilford Courthouse.

Greensboro's Natural Science Center is located within Greensboro Country Park. The Natural Science Center houses a hands-on museum, zoo, planetarium, Dinosaur Gallery, and Jaycee Herpetarium. The varied exhibits include traveling displays as well as permanent exhibits.

LOCAL INFORMATION

♦ Greensboro Visitor Information Center, 317 South Greene Street, Greensboro, NC 27401; (336) 274–2282 or (800) 344–2282; www.greensboronc.org.

LOCAL EVENTS/ATTRACTIONS

♦ Guilford Courthouse National Military Park, more than 200 acres and twenty-eight monuments honoring combatants in the March 15, 1781, battle of the American Revolution; the visitor center houses exhibits and

A lone cannon represents the fierce battle of the American Revolution fought at Guilford Courthouse.

shows films; 2332 New Garden Road, Greensboro, NC 27410; no charge; (336) 288–1776; www.nps.gov/guco or (friends' group) www.guilford battlegroundcompany. org.

♦ Tannenbaum Historic Park, portrays the story of everyday life in eighteenth-century North Carolina; 2200 New Garden Road, Greensboro, NC 27410; no charge; (336) 545–5315; www. ci.greensboro.nc.us/leisure/ tannenbaum.

♦ Anniversary Commemoration of the Battle of Guilford Courthouse; held annually on the weekend closest to March 15; partnership of Guilford Courthouse National Military Park, Greensboro Country Park, and Tannenbaum Historic Park; no charge; (336) 288–1776; www.nps. gov/guco or (friends' group) www.guilfordbattleground company.org.

♦ Guilford College, the first coeducational institution in the South, founded by the

This statue honors General Nathanael Greene, who led the revolutionary forces at Guilford Courthouse.

Quakers in 1837 in the New Garden Community; 5800 West Friendly Avenue (at its intersection with New Garden Road), Greensboro, NC 27410; no charge; (336) 316–2000; www.guilford.edu.

♦ Eastern Music Festival, an annual five-week feast of recitals, chamber music, and symphony concerts from late June to early August; ticket prices vary; (336) 333–7450 or (877) 833–6753; www.easternmusicfestival.com.

♦ Natural Science Center, a hands-on museum, zoo, and planetarium; 4301 Lawndale Drive in Greensboro Country Park, Greensboro, NC 27455; admission is $6.00 for adults, $5.00 for children under thirteen and seniors over sixty-five; (336) 288–3769; www.naturalsciencecenter.org.

0.0 From the visitor center at Guilford Courthouse National Military Park, turn left to begin the tour route through the park. The road through the park is one-way with a wide bicycle lane on the left side.

0.5 Cross Old Battleground Road.

2.2 Turn right onto Old Battleground Road. As an option, a paved bikeway parallels Old Battleground Road to the intersection with Lake Brandt Road.

2.7 Turn right onto Lake Brandt Road.

3.8 Turn left to stay on Lake Brandt Road. Lawndale Drive goes off to the right.

4.2 Turn right onto Air Harbor Road.

6.8 Turn left onto Church Street.

7.8 Turn right onto Archergate Road (SR 2516).

8.7 Turn left onto Yanceyville Road (SR 2523).

9.4 Turn left to stay on Yanceyville Road (SR 2523).

12.3 Turn left onto NC–150.

13.9 Turn right onto Church Street (SR 1001A), which crosses into Rockingham County.

17.8 Turn left onto Scalesville Road (SR 1002).

22.2 Turn left onto Witty Road (SR 2305).

23.7 Turn left onto Lake Brandt Road (SR 2347).

29.3 Turn left onto Old Battleground Road.

29.8 Turn right onto New Garden Road.

30.4 Turn left into the visitor center at Guilford Courthouse National Military Park.

RESTAURANTS

♦ Talk of the Town Café, 2130-B New Garden Road, Greensboro, NC 27410; (336) 286–6481. Breakfast and lunch Sunday through Tuesday; brunch, lunch, and dinner Wednesday through Saturday. American cuisine; midrange.

♦ Stuzzico Antica Pizzeria, 2109-E New Garden Road, Greensboro, NC 27410; (336) 282–9660. Lunch and dinner daily; pizza, Italian dishes, sandwiches; midrange.

♦ Danny's Restaurant, 2109-A New Garden Road, Greensboro, NC 27410; (336) 545–0055. Breakfast and lunch Monday through Friday; breakfast Saturday; southern food; low range.

ACCOMMODATIONS

♦ Battleground Inn, 1517 Westover Terrace (just off Battleground Avenue), Greensboro, NC 27408; (336) 272–4737. Midrange.

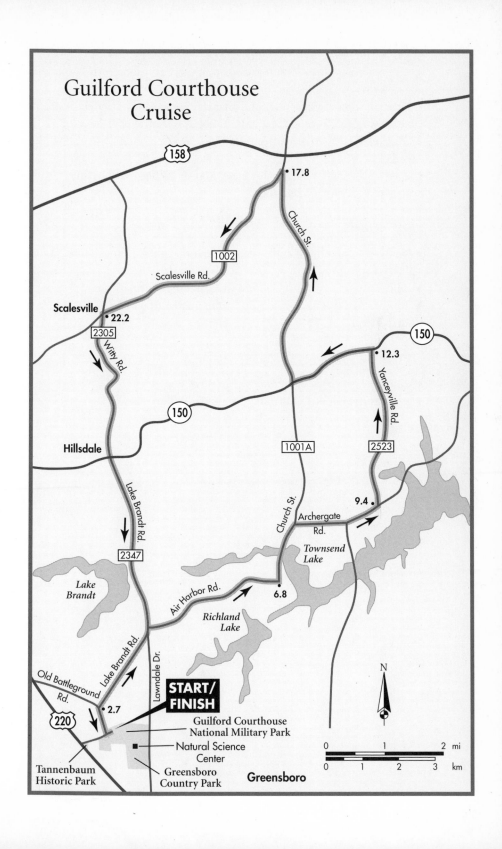

Guilford Courthouse Cruise

158

• 17.8

Church St.

1002

Scalesville Rd.

Scalesville
• 22.2

2305

Witty Rd.

150

• 12.3

150

Yanceyville Rd.

Hillsdale

1001A

2523

Lake Brandt Rd.

9.4 •

2347

Archergate Rd.

Lake
Brandt

Air Harbor Rd.

Townsend
Lake

6.8

Richland
Lake

Lake Brandt Rd.

Old Battleground Rd.

Lawndale Dr.

START/
FINISH

N

220

• 2.7

Guilford Courthouse
National Military Park

Natural Science
Center

Tannenbaum
Historic Park

Greensboro
Country Park

Greensboro

0   1   2 mi
0   1   2   3 km

BIKE SHOPS

♦ Cycles de Oro, 1406 West Northwood Street, Greensboro, NC 27408; (336) 274–5959; www.cyclesdeoro.com.
♦ Friendly Bike, Quaker Village Shopping Center, 5603-D Friendly Avenue, Greensboro, NC 27410-4112; (336) 852–3972; www.friendlybike.com.
♦ Higgins Cycles, 2420 Battleground Avenue, Greensboro, NC 27408; (336) 288–6520.
♦ Paul's Schwinn Cycling and Fitness, 3716-F Battleground Avenue, Greensboro, NC 27410; (336) 286–8006.

REST ROOMS

♦ At the start and finish at the visitor center in Guilford Courthouse National Military Park.
♦ Mile 1.3 near the site of Guilford Courthouse in the park.
♦ Mile 13.9 at a convenience store at the intersection of NC–150 and North Church Street.

MAPS

♦ *DeLorme North Carolina Atlas & Gazetteer,* page 17.
♦ Map from Guilford Courthouse National Military Park.

Chinqua-Penn Plantation Cruise

The cruise to Chinqua-Penn Plantation starts at The Summit, the Episcopal conference center in Browns Summit, North Carolina, and winds along quiet rural roads to Chinqua-Penn Plantation on the western edge of Reidsville. Much of the route follows fairly level roads with some rolling terrain and a few hills. Away from towns and communities, the route has only two convenience stores, so it's best to carry snacks with you or time your trip so you can take advantages of restaurants in northern Greensboro.

This pleasant ride begins in northern Guilford County (north of Greensboro) and travels into southern Rockingham County to the unique and interesting Chinqua-Penn Plantation. The name derives from the combination of the chinquapin tree, a dwarf deciduous tree in the chestnut family, and the name of the family who built it—Penn. Thomas Jefferson Penn and his wife Beatrice (Betsy) Schoellkopf Penn moved from Buffalo, New York, to their 1,000-acre farm in North Carolina in 1923. They both lived in their dream home until their deaths in 1946 and 1965, respectively.

The rustic log construction of this thirty-room mansion makes it unique from an architectural standpoint because flat stones are used between the logs and jut out. But its furnishings and other objects add to the uniqueness. The family collected temple altarpieces from Nepal, rare Chinese terra-cotta sculptures, and a fifteenth-century Byzantine mosaic. The extensive grounds and gardens include thirty landscaped acres and an ornate Chinese pagoda. The foundation that runs the estate has closed it to the public as of this writing, but from the parking lot you can view the large stone clock tower. You can also

The stone clock tower at Chinqua-Penn Plantation dwarfs a lone bike.

glimpse some of the other buildings and gardens through the entrance gate. A small gift shop operates near the entrance.

The area on Wentworth Road is somewhat more densely populated around the plantation, but traffic is still usually light. Even the small country store and roadside stand are rustic and fit naturally into the landscape.

Most of this route traverses rural areas with neatly maintained farms and small communities. You're likely to see open fields, broken by dense pine and hardwood forests. The rolling terrain offers variety and challenge with descents that carry you past small streams and low-lying wetlands. While the road surfaces are generally smooth and well maintained, they are rather narrow with many curves. It's wise to position yourself on the roadway so that motorists can see you before they are too far into the curve.

A few historic farmhouses dot the countryside along with the old-style log tobacco barns. In the past the tobacco was tied in bundles and hung in these barns for curing. Farmers kept a vigil to be sure the fires were kept burning during the curing process. The cured tobacco was then sold at market.

A historic Presbyterian church organized in 1759 stands by a National Historic Site marker that describes a bit of the history. The white frame building is typical of many churches across the country in rural areas and small towns. Because much of this area was settled by Scots-Irish immigrants, Presbyterian churches are a common site in many parts of North Carolina.

The Summit, the Episcopal conference center where the ride begins and ends, hosts religious and secular meetings for groups of up to 200 people. Nestled in the woods, its grounds include beautiful native plants, walking trails, tennis courts, and a scenic lake with a wooden deck overlooking it all.

LOCAL INFORMATION

♦ Reidsville Chamber of Commerce, 321 Southeast Market Street (at Governor Reid's house), P.O. Box 1020, Reidsville, NC 27323–1020; (336) 349–8481.
♦ Western Rockingham Chamber of Commerce, 112 West Murphy Street, Madison, NC 27025; (336) 548–6248; wrcc@library.rcpl.org.

LOCAL EVENTS/ATTRACTIONS

♦ Chinqua-Penn Plantation is an unusual mansion, gardens, and estate built by Thomas Jefferson Penn and his wife Beatrice (Betsy) Schoellkopf Penn; although not currently open to the public, visitors can see the entrance to the estate and the large stone clock tower; work is under way to try to reopen it to the public; Wentworth Road near Reidsville, North Carolina.

RESTAURANTS

♦ Talk of the Town Café, 2130-B New Garden Road, Greensboro, NC 27410; (336) 286–6481. Breakfast and lunch Sunday through Tuesday; brunch, lunch, and dinner Wednesday through Saturday. American cuisine; midrange.
♦ Stuzzico Antica Pizzeria, 2109-E New Garden Road, Greensboro, NC 27410; (336) 282–9660. Lunch and dinner Monday through Sunday; pizza, Italian dishes, sandwiches; midrange.

THE BASICS

Start: Parking lot at The Summit, the Episcopal conference center at Browns Summit, North Carolina.
Length: 34.4 miles.
Terrain: Mainly level to rolling with a few hills.
Traffic and hazards: Traffic is very light on most of these roads, but take care when crossing U.S. Highway 158 and for the quick turns on North Carolina Highway 65/87. North Carolina Highway 150 has slightly more traffic, especially at peak hours of the day, but traffic is not usually heavy and the distance is fairly short.
Getting there: Take US 220 north out of Greensboro. Go right (east) onto NC–150, then turn left on Spearman Road about 2.1 miles after you pass the intersection with North Church Street (SR 1001). A volunteer fire station is situated on the left at the intersection. The Episcopal conference center is on the left about 1.3 miles from the intersection with NC–150. See the *Delorme North Carolina Atlas & Gazetteer,* page 17 D7.

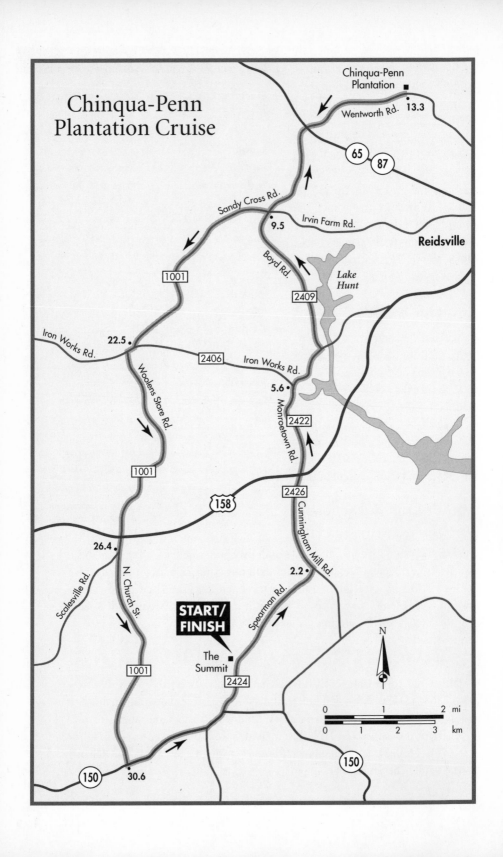

Chinqua-Penn
Plantation Cruise

Chinqua-Penn
Plantation ■

Wentworth Rd. ● 13.3

65 87

Sandy Cross Rd.

Irvin Farm Rd.

● 9.5

Reidsville

Boyd Rd.

1001

2409

Lake
Hunt

Iron Works Rd.

22.5 ●

2406   Iron Works Rd.

Woolens Store Rd.

5.6 ●

Monroetown Rd.

2422

1001

158   2426

Cunningham Mill Rd.

26.4 ●

Scalesville Rd.

N. Church St.

2.2 ●

**START/
FINISH**

Spearman Rd.

The
Summit ■

1001   2424

N

0   1   2 mi

0   1   2   3 km

150   30.6 ●

150

0.0 From the parking lot at The Summit, the Episcopal conference center at Browns Summit, North Carolina, return to the entrance at Spearman Road.

0.5 Turn left onto Spearman Road (SR 2424).

2.2 Turn left onto Cunningham Mill Road (SR 2426).

3.9 At a stop sign at the intersection with US 158, go straight on Monroeton Road (SR 2422).

5.6 Turn right onto Iron Works Road (SR 2406).

6.6 Turn left onto Boyd Road (SR 2409).

9.4 Cross Irvin Farm Road. Tim's Country store is on the left.

9.5 Turn right onto Sandy Cross Road (SR 1001).

11.1 Turn left onto NC–65/87 and then make an immediate right turn onto Wentworth Road.

13.3 Turn left into the entrance to Chinqua-Penn Plantation. After your visit, return to the entrance and turn right onto Wentworth Road.

15.5 Turn left onto NC–65/87 and then right onto Sandy Cross Road (SR 1001).

17.1 At the Intersection with Boyd Road, bear right to stay on Sandy Cross Road (SR 1001).

22.5 Turn right onto Iron Works Road (SR 1001), then watch for signs for a left turn onto SR 1001, the name of which is Woolens Store Road for this section.

26.1 Cross US 158 and continue on Woolens Store Road (SR 1001).

26.4 At the intersection with Scalesville Road, the main road name changes to North Church Street.

30.6 Watch for rumble strips just before the intersection with US 150. Turn left onto US 150.

32.5 Turn left onto Spearman Road (SR 2424).

33.9 Turn left at the entrance to the conference center.

34.4 Arrive at the parking lot.

♦ Danny's Restaurant, 2109-A New Garden Road, Greensboro, NC 27410; (336) 545–0055. Breakfast and lunch Monday through Friday; breakfast Saturday; southern food; low range.

ACCOMMODATIONS

♦ Battleground Inn, 1517 Westover Terrace (just off Battleground Avenue), Greensboro, NC 27408; (336) 272–4737. Midrange.

BIKE SHOPS

♦ Cycles de Oro, 1406 West Northwood Street, Greensboro, NC 27408; (336) 274–5959; www.cyclesdeoro.com.

- Friendly Bike, Quaker Village Shopping Center, 5603-D Friendly Avenue, Greensboro, NC 27410-4112; (336) 852–3972; www.friendlybike.com.
- Higgins Cycles, 2420 Battleground Avenue, Greensboro, NC 27408; (336) 288–6520.
- Paul's Schwinn Cycling and Fitness, 3716-F Battleground Avenue, Greensboro, NC 27410; (336) 286–8006.

REST ROOMS

- At the start and finish at the Episcopal conference center when it is open. They frequently hold conferences and meetings on weekends. The lodge/main building is 0.1 mile from the parking lots.
- Mile 9.4 at Tim's Country Store.
- Mile 30.6 at a convenience store at the intersection of North Church Street and US 150.

MAPS

- *DeLorme North Carolina Atlas & Gazetteer,* pages 17–18.

Old Salem to Bethabara Ramble

The Old Salem to Bethabara Ramble is one of my favorite hometown tours. The 18.3-mile distance can be deceiving because Winston-Salem is quite hilly, but the interesting and varied sights make it worthwhile. The ride begins in the restored eighteenth-century village of Old Salem and skirts the edge of downtown Winston-Salem as it moves through the historic West End neighborhood. The next section travels through Buena Vista, one of the city's most desirable neighborhoods. The route then passes through the grounds of the elegant Graylyn International Conference Center and Reynolda, with its quaint village of shops and restaurants—a great place for a break. From there you take Reynolda Road, past Wake Forest University to Historic Bethabara Park. The route then winds past the site of the old polo grounds, through Sherwood Forest and Buena Vista, on its way back to Old Salem.

Following this route will give you a wonderful insider's historical perspective on Winston-Salem and this part of the Piedmont of North Carolina. The ride starts in Old Salem, a Moravian community established in 1766 when Moravian brethren moved here from Pennsylvania and purchased a large tract of land. Many of the eighteenth-century buildings have been restored or reconstructed according to the Moravians' meticulous records. Costumed guides conduct tours of the historic buildings while others ply trades such as weaving, shoemaking, blacksmithing, and baking, much as the original inhabitants must have.

Start: At the Old Salem Visitor Center on Old Salem Road.
Length: 18.3 miles.
Terrain: Mostly hilly with a few level stretches.
Traffic and hazards: While the route travels mostly neighborhood streets—hence the large number of turns—one portion uses Reynolda Road, a fairly busy four-lane road that is best avoided at rush hour. At other times, traffic can easily pass in the left lane.
Getting there: From eastbound Business 40/U.S. Highway 421 through downtown Winston-Salem, take the Liberty Street exit to Old Salem Road. From westbound Business 40/US 421, take the Main Street exit, turning left onto First Street and then left onto Liberty Street, which becomes Old Salem Road. The visitor center is on the right just past the intersection with Academy Street. Park in the visitor center lot. See the *DeLorme North Carolina Atlas & Gazetteer*, page 36 A4.

Among the buildings and exhibits to see here are the Single Brothers House, Salem Tavern, Miksch Tobacco Shop, the Museum of Early Southern Decorative Arts, and the Winkler Bakery, which still produces fresh breads, cookies, and pastries using the original brick ovens. Riding north on Main Street, you'll pass handsome homes built in a variety of styles from the eighteenth and nineteenth centuries close to the street with tree-lined brick sidewalks.

At about Mile 0.7 you pass the Brookstown Mill, which used to produce textiles but is now home to an inn and offices. At Mile 1.7 you'll see the gazebo for Grace Court Park as the route curves through the West End with its elegant houses from the late nineteenth and early twentieth centuries. West End was Winston-Salem's first "suburb," made possible by the trolley service that ran along Fourth Street until well into the twentieth century.

As you climb the curving hill on Hawthorne (at Mile 2.6), turn into the drive for R. J. Reynolds High School—named for the tobacco magnate who founded the company that bears his name. The end of the drive, in front of the wonderful auditorium in the classical style, offers a fantastic view of the downtown skyline and West End. The school nestles in the heart of Buena Vista (pronounced BEW-nah VIH-sta by natives), one of Winston-Salem's premier neighborhoods.

At Mile 4.3, as you cross Coliseum Drive, you'll enter the Graylyn International Conference Center grounds. The main building as well as the other outbuildings are built with stone in the style of a French chateau. The estate was built by Bowman Gray and his wife on land purchased from R. J. Reynolds, whose country estate is across the street. Unfortunately Gray died a short time after the house was finished in the late 1920s, and his family gave the estate to Wake Forest University, which converted it into this elegant conference center.

Across Reynolda Road from Graylyn is Reynolda, Reynolds's country estate, which now is in the midst of the city. The Reynolds heirs, too, gave this estate to Wake Forest University. The estate represented very innovative approaches to farming and self-sufficiency when it was first built. The manor house has since been converted into the Reynolda House Museum of American Art, while the farm buildings have been transformed into Reynolda Village, a fascinating complex of shops, restaurants, and offices.

The main entrance to Wake Forest University is located at Mile 5.8 and provides an optional side trip. The next point of interest is Historic Bethabara (pronounced buh-THAB-bra), the 1753 site of the first Moravian settlement in the state. The Moravians lived here while they were building Salem. Costumed guides here also conduct tours of the historic buildings. A reconstructed 1756 fort anchors one end of the settlement. Nature and history trails lead visitors to excavation sites.

The return leg of the trip travels along Polo Road, named for the polo grounds that were located here, and then winds through another prime neighborhood called Sherwood Forest and then back through Buena Vista to downtown and Old Salem.

LOCAL INFORMATION

♦ Greater Winston-Salem Chamber of Commerce, 601 West Fourth Street, Winston-Salem, NC 27101; (336) 728–9200; www.winstonsalem.com.

♦ Winston-Salem Convention & Visitors Bureau, 200 Brookstown Avenue, Winston-Salem, NC 27101; (336) 728–4200; www.visitwinstonsalem.com.

Thirsty cyclists try out the old-fashioned water pump in Old Salem.

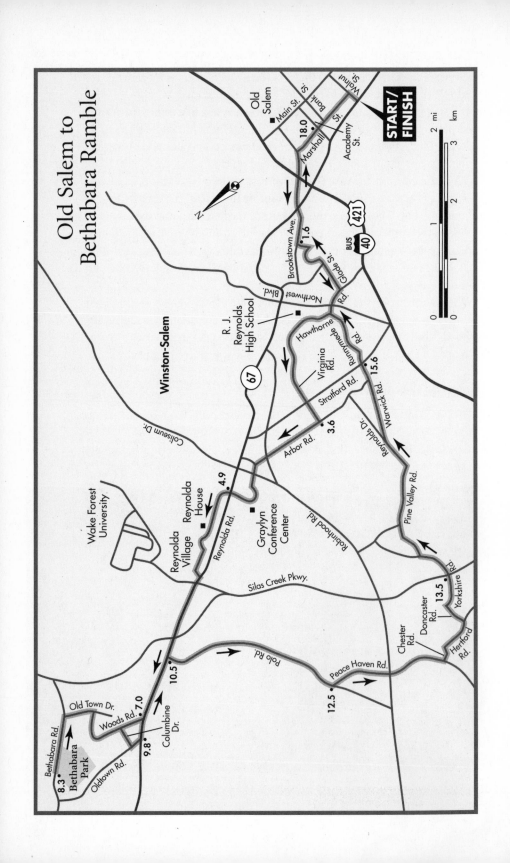

Old Salem to Bethabara Ramble

Winston-Salem

Wake Forest University

Reynolda Village

Reynolda House

Graylyn Conference Center

R. J. Reynolds High School

Old Salem

START/FINISH

Bethabara Park

Coliseum Dr.

Silas Creek Pkwy.

Reynolda Rd.

Robinhood Rd.

Polo Rd.

Peace Haven Rd.

Arbor Rd.

Stratford Rd.

Virginia Rd.

Hawthorne Rd.

Runnymede Rd.

Northwest Blvd.

Brookstown Ave.

Gladde St.

Warwick Rd.

Reynolds Dr.

Pine Valley Rd.

Yorkshire Rd.

Hertford Rd.

Chester Rd.

Doncaster Rd.

Columbine Dr.

Woods Rd.

Old Town Dr.

Oldtown Rd.

Bethabara Rd.

Main St.

Bank St.

Walnut St.

Marshall St.

Academy St.

67

421

BUS 40

1.6

3.6

4.9

7.0

8.3

9.8

10.5

12.5

13.5

15.6

18.0

N

2 mi

km

1 2 3

0 1 2

0 1

0.0 From the Old Salem Visitor Center, cross Old Salem Road onto Walnut Street.

0.1 Turn left at stop sign onto Marshall Street.

0.6 Turn left onto Brookstown Avenue.

0.8 Bear right on Brookstown. (Wachovia Street goes to the left.)

1.3 Cross Broad Street.

1.6 Turn left onto Fourth Street.

1.7 Bear right around the park onto Glade Street (S-curves), then bear left and right around the YWCA, staying on Glade Street.

2.2 Turn right onto Hawthorne Road and cross Northwest Boulevard.

2.4 Bear right going up the hill on Hawthorne after you pass under the railroad trestle.

2.6 Turn right into R. J. Reynolds High School. At end of drive (in front of auditorium) is a great view of downtown Winston-Salem. Continue around the one-way drive.

2.9 Turn right onto Hawthorne Road at entrance columns.

3.0 Bear left onto Virginia Road and cross Buena Vista Road; continue on Virginia Road.

3.4 Cross Stratford Road on Virginia Road.

3.6 Turn right onto Arbor Road.

4.1 Cross Robinhood Road.

4.2 Turn left onto Oaklawn Avenue.

4.3 Cross Coliseum Drive into the road through the Graylyn International Conference Center.

4.4 Bear right toward the main building of the conference center. Stay on the main road until the gate at the entrance.

4.9 Cross Reynolda Road and go through the gates into the Reynolda Estate (one-way road).

5.4 At a stop sign turn right to go through Reynolda Village.

5.5 At a stop sign turn left toward Reynolda Road.

5.6 Turn right onto Reynolda Road.

(continued)

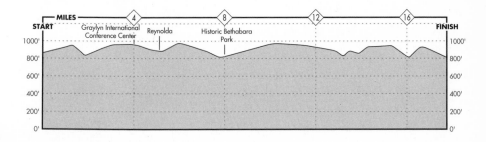

7.0 Turn right onto Woods Road immediately after the intersection with Fairlawn Drive.

7.6 Turn left onto Old Town Drive.

7.8 Turn left onto Bethabara Road. Please note that the road in the historic district is a narrow lane where vehicles must yield to opposing traffic.

8.3 Arrive at the Historic Bethabara Visitors Center. After a tour, take a left onto Bethabara Road from the center.

8.8 Turn right onto Old Town Drive.

9.0 Turn right onto Woods Road.

9.5 Turn right onto Columbine Drive.

9.7 Turn left onto Oldtown Road.

9.8 Turn left at the light onto Reynolda Road.

10.5 Turn right onto Polo Road.

11.9 Turn left onto Peace Haven Road.

12.5 Cross Robinhood Road.

12.9 Turn left onto Chester Road, then immediately bear left onto Hertford Road.

13.1 Turn left onto Doncaster Road.

13.3 Turn right onto Yorkshire Road.

13.5 Cross Silas Creek Parkway (steep hill).

13.8 Turn right onto Pine Valley Road.

14.6 Turn left onto Reynolds Drive.

14.9 Bear right onto Warwick Road.

15.6 Cross Stratford Road. (Warwick Road's name changes to Runnymede Road.)

15.7 Bear left onto Runnymede Road.

16.1 Bear right onto Hawthorne Road.

16.2 Cross Northwest Boulevard.

16.4 Turn left onto Glade Street (an S-curve around the YWCA).

16.9 Bear left onto Fourth Street.

17.0 Turn right onto Brookstown Avenue.

17.3 Cross Broad Street.

17.7 Turn right onto Marshall Street.

18.3 Turn left into the visitor center parking lot.

LOCAL EVENTS/ATTRACTIONS

♦ Old Salem, a living-history restoration of the 1766 Moravian town of Salem; tours are available for fifteen restored buildings; the visitor center is on Old Salem Road south of Academy Street; adults $15.00, ages six through sixteen $8.00; combination ticket with the Museum of Early Southern Decorative Arts $20.00, ages six through sixteen $11.00; (336) 721–3700 or (888) 348–4844.

♦ Reynolda House Museum of American Art, an outstanding collection of American art in the beautiful former home of tobacco magnate R. J. Reynolds; on the grounds of Reynolda, P.O. Box 11765, Winston-Salem, NC 27116; adults $6.00, over fifty-nine $5.00, students with ID $3.00, children under twelve must be accompanied by an adult; (336) 725–5325; reynolda@reynoldahouse.org.

♦ Reynolda Village, a shopping and office complex in the former outbuildings of the Reynolds Estate; no charge.

♦ Historic Bethabara Park, the 1753 site of the first Moravian settlement in the state; tours with costumed guides are available; Bethabara Road west of the intersection with Indiana Avenue, Winston-Salem, NC; no charge to visit the park; tours are $1.00 for adults and 50 cents for children under twelve; (336) 924–8191.

RESTAURANTS

♦ Salem Tavern, 736 South Main Street in Old Salem, Winston-Salem, NC 27108; (336) 748–8585. Upper range for lunch and dinner; reservations suggested.

♦ Village Tavern, 221 Reynolda Village, Winston-Salem, NC 27106; (336) 748–0221. Midrange for lunch and dinner; brunch on Sunday.

♦ Various restaurants at Reynolda Manor Shopping Center at the intersection of Fairlawn Drive and Reynolda Road near Historic Bethabara.

ACCOMMODATIONS

♦ Salem Inn, 127 South Cherry Street (near Old Salem), Winston-Salem, NC 27101; (336) 725–8561; www.saleminn.com. Midrange.

♦ Augustus Zevely Inn, 803 South Main Street in Old Salem, Winston-Salem, NC 27108; (336) 748–9299. Located in a restored house in the historic district. Mid- to upper range.

BIKE SHOPS

♦ Ken's Bike Shop, 114-J Reynolda Village, Winston-Salem, NC 27106; (336) 724–9688.

REST ROOMS

♦ At the start and finish in the visitor center in Old Salem.
♦ Mile 5.4 in Reynolda Village.
♦ Mile 8.3 at the visitor center in Historic Bethabara.

MAPS

♦ Winston-Salem City Map by Quality Maps, Inc., 2000.

Westbend Vineyards Ramble

T he Westbend Ramble, a relatively easy 12.6-mile ride, starts in the small town of Lewisville and, with few turns, takes you to Westbend Vineyards. Located near the west bend in the Yadkin River, the vineyard offers tours and tastings of its award-winning wines. The initial part of the ride has some steep ups and downs but becomes gently rolling around the vineyards. The return trip has more gradual climbs and descents.

Rounding the bend on a rural road in North Carolina and finding acres of well-tended vineyards is something of a surprise. After all, North Carolina has more of a reputation for tobacco and textiles than wine. But Westbend Vineyards—along with the North Carolina Grape Council—has worked hard to change that image. Those efforts have paid off, and now Westbend is the granddaddy of a growing wine industry in the state's Piedmont area. As a bonus, the peaceful country roads around the vineyards make for fantastic cycling.

This tour starts at a small shopping center in Lewisville, which is a popular gathering spot for area cyclists. As the roads closer in to Winston-Salem have grown more congested, cyclists have started meeting here for rides in the western part of Forsyth County and across the Yadkin River into Yadkin and Davie Counties. Especially on weekend mornings, you'll find groups of cyclists gathering here for their regular rides.

Williams Road has very little traffic and offers serene, rolling terrain. The attractive homes along the route are interspersed with hardwood forests and small farms. It's not unusual to see bluebirds perched on the numerous fence posts, although mourning doves and robins are much more common.

Williams Road runs in front of the vineyard property, so you'll pass slopes with trellised grapevines on your way. Open for visitors Tuesday through Sunday, Westbend Vineyards offers guided tours as visitors walk through the actual winery and step out back to see the equipment that's used to harvest the traditional European grape varieties. After the tour, visitors are welcomed to the tasting room, where each of several wines is opened and tasted in turn. Many of Westbend's wines have been awarded gold medals and received critical acclaim.

North Carolina's experience with wine goes back to the earliest settlement on Roanoke Island in the sixteenth century. According to the North Carolina Grape Council, "Sir Walter Raleigh is credited with giving birth to commercial grape production when his men discovered a bronze muscadine vine growing wild." Most of the native North Carolina wines are made from this type of grape. And in the early nineteenth century, North Carolina became the leading wine-producing state in America. Prohibition ended wine production in North Carolina, as elsewhere. The rebirth of this industry in North Carolina began in 1970.

THE BASICS

Start: The Oaks Shopping Center in Lewisville.

Length: 12.6 miles.

Terrain: Steep ups and downs at the beginning of the ride, and rolling in the middle; the ups and downs are more gradual on the return trip.

Traffic and hazards: Traffic is busy around The Oaks Shopping Center and along Williams Road to the south side of U.S. Highway 421. Traffic is light along Williams Road between Concord Church Road and Westbend Vineyards; Shallowford Road has more traffic between Conrad Road and The Oaks Shopping Center. Many of the roads are narrow and curvy.

Getting there: Take US 421 to Lewisville (not the Clemmons/Lewisville exit) and go east on Williams Road. The Oaks Shopping Center is about 0.2 mile on the left. See the *DeLorme North Carolina Atlas & Gazetteer*, p. 36 A2.

The first vineyard with traditional European varieties at Westbend was planted in 1972, against the advice of several authorities on agriculture in North Carolina (despite the state's past success with wine). Going against all the odds given by the agricultural experts, the vinifera varieties have thrived on the slopes near the Yadkin River. As the vines flourished, more acreage was planted, producing a seventy-ton harvest in 1986. Westbend became a bonded winery in 1988, and the first Westbend wines were released in the summer of 1990.

Williams Road ends at its intersection with Shallowford Road, so named because it crosses the Yadkin River at a shallow point that wagons used to ford. A quick side trip to the river is possible by taking Shallowford to the west (go left at the stop sign on Williams Road). But be forewarned that the wonderful

0.0 Start at the Oaks Shopping Center in Lewisville. Exiting from the south end of the parking lot, turn right onto Williams Road (SR 1173).

0.3 At the traffic circle, turn right onto Williams Road (which shares the exit ramp for US 421), then turn left to stay on Williams Road. (You will stay on this road, which has some curves, until you reach Westbend Vineyards.)

2.0 Pass the intersection with Concord Church Road (SR 1171), which goes off to the left.

2.7 Pass Hauser Road (SR 1175), which goes off to the right.

3.9 Pass Double Springs Road, which goes off to the right.

6.9 Turn right into Westbend Vineyards property.

7.4 After your winery tour, turn right onto Williams Road (SR 1173).

7.7 Turn right onto Shallowford Road (SR 1001). Williams Road ends here.

12.6 Turn right into the parking lot at The Oaks Shopping Center.

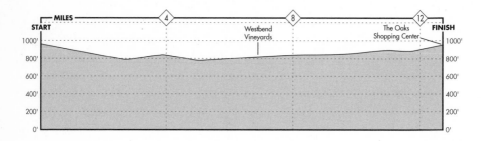

downhill ride to the river only means a long climb coming back. However, a dip in the river may make it all worthwhile.

The route returns along Shallowford Road, which dips and turns as it winds its way back to The Oaks Shopping Center.

LOCAL INFORMATION

♦ Greater Winston-Salem Chamber of Commerce, 601 West. Fourth Street, Winston-Salem, NC 27101; (336) 728–9200; www.winstonsalem.com.

♦ Winston-Salem Convention & Visitors Bureau, 200 Brookstown Avenue, Winston-Salem, NC 27101; (336) 728–4200; www.visitwinstonsalem.com.

LOCAL EVENTS/ATTRACTIONS

♦ Westbend Vineyards, an award-winning winery and vineyards; 5394 Williams Road, Lewisville, NC 27023; tours and tastings from 11:00 A.M.–6:00 P.M. Tuesday through Saturday and 1:00–6:00 P.M. on Sunday; no charge; (336) 945–5032.

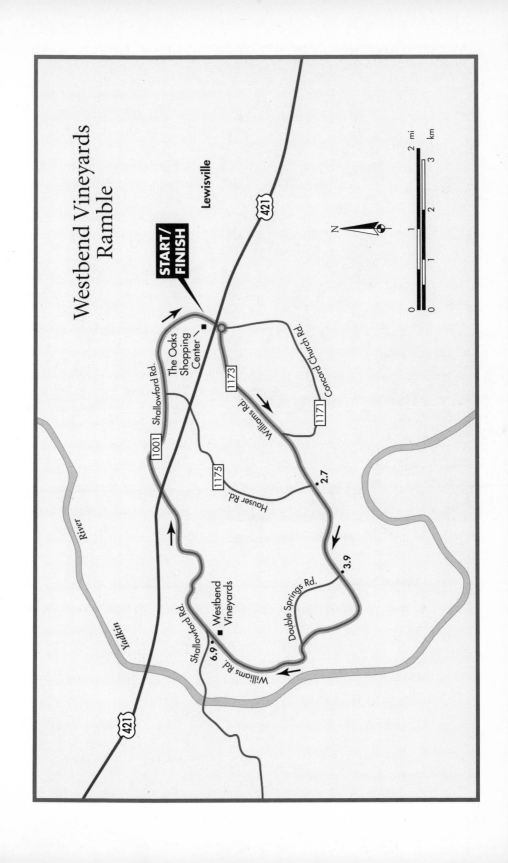

Westbend Vineyards Ramble

Lewisville

START/
FINISH

The Oaks
Shopping
Center

Shallowford Rd.

1001

Shallowford Rd.

1173

Concord Church Rd.

1171

Williams Rd.

1175

Hauser Rd.

2.7

3.9

Double Springs Rd.

Westbend
Vineyards

6.9

Williams Rd.

River

Yadkin

421

421

N

0   1   2 mi

0   1   2   3 km

A cyclist pauses to check out Westbend grapes that are almost ready to harvest.

RESTAURANTS

♦ Subway, The Oaks Shopping Center, 6794 Shallowford Road, Lewisville, NC 27023; (336) 945–6445. Subs and sandwiches; low range.

♦ Liberty Family Restaurant, 7970 Concord Church Road, Lewisville, NC 27023; (336) 945–4409. Traditional Southern cooking; midrange.

ACCOMMODATIONS

♦ Holiday Inn Express, 6320 Amp Drive, Clemmons, NC 27012; (336) 778–1500. Midrange.

BIKE SHOPS

♦ The Bicycle Shop, Clemmons Center, Lewisville-Clemmons Road, Clemmons, NC 27012; (336) 766–5564; www.clemmonsbicycle.com.

♦ Ken's Bike Shop, 114-J Reynolda Village, Winston-Salem, NC 27106; (336) 724–9688.

♦ Paceline Bicycles, 5059 Country Club Road, Winston-Salem, NC 27104; (336) 768–6408.

REST ROOMS

♦ At the start and finish at Subway or Food Lion in The Oaks Shopping Center.

♦ Mile 4.5 at Westbend Vineyards.

MAPS

♦ *DeLorme North Carolina Atlas & Gazetteer,* page 36.

Hanging Rock Challenge

The Hanging Rock Challenge lives up to its name but also offers gorgeous views of the area's mountains and lush valleys. Starting in the small town of Pilot Mountain, this route takes you on curvy and hilly back roads, first around Sauratown Mountain and then on a clockwise tour of Hanging Rock. The first part of the route covers remote areas with no services, so be advised to carry water and snacks. Halfway around Hanging Rock is the town of Danbury, which has several restaurants and a park where you can rest and replenish your energy. Although the route has a lot of climbs, most are short but steep; however, the downhills and fabulous vistas make the climbing well worthwhile.

This beautiful ride starts in the quaint downtown of Pilot Mountain, whose name was transposed to Mount Pilot in the popular Andy Griffith television series. As you leave Pilot Mountain, the curvy back roads wind around Sauratown Mountain, which is easily identified by the transmission towers that grace its summit. On the east side of Sauratown Mountain, you arrive at North Carolina Highway 66 and Moores Springs Road, where you begin the clockwise tour of Hanging Rock.

Highway 66 can be very busy at times, so be cautious. It's shady in summer, which can mean that a cyclist is hard to see, especially with the curves. Moores Springs Road at Mile 14.2 is a North Carolina Scenic Byway, perfect for cycling. A sign points the way to Hanging Rock Park.

As you study the map and see that you can stay on Moores Springs Road all the way to the park entrance, you may wonder why the directions say to take Mickey Road at Mile 14.6. The big payoff comes on this part of the route. Right after you turn, you'll start a climb and then, right in front of you, looms the majestic rocky face of Hanging Rock. This view is one that only the locals are likely to see because it's not visible from the main highways.

In addition to Hanging Rock, you'll have a spectacular view of mountain ridges to your left separated from you by a broad valley. Enjoy! But also watch for horseback riders, who like to frequent this area. At Mile 16.6 you again join Moores Springs Road with its smooth surface. At Mile 19.8 the route turns left onto Hanging Rock Park Road. If you'd like more miles and a strenuous challenge, you can take a right here into the park and climb to the lake area. You'll feel like Lance Armstrong if you tackle this one.

A cyclist takes a break with Hanging Rock in the background.

Your next turn is onto NC–8/89, which leads into Danbury's National Historic District, called the Gateway to the Mountains. You won't have to worry about getting lost in Danbury, the seat of Stokes County and home to one hundred residents. Highway 8/89 is the one main street through town, and the hilly terrain minimizes the number of roads that sprout off the main route. Moratock Park, located on Sheppard Mill Road just off Highway 8/89, makes a nice place for a rest with picnic tables and rest rooms. Be sure to check out the Dan River, which flows through the park and attracts lots of tubers—and maybe hot cyclists—in warm summer months.

The park takes its name from Moratock Furnace, a smelting furnace built by Nathaniel Moody in 1843 that supplied iron to the Confederacy from 1862 to 1865. Danbury itself was an important landmark during the war because General George Stoneman of the Union army set up his headquarters here on April 9, 1865, the day General Robert E. Lee surrendered at Appomattox. Stoneman's name was popularized by a Joan Baez folk song in the 1970s.

As you leave Danbury on NC–8/89, the road climbs and twists around the side of the hills. It levels out a bit after you turn onto Mountain Road. You'll feel as though you've stepped back in time when you see the rustic log house on your right and the old log tobacco barns. In the first mile on this road, you'll have Flat Shoals Mountain on your left. Only a few houses break the forests that stretch along this part of the route. Enjoy the minimal traffic, but watch out for the curves, which aren't always banked right for you to take them fast.

You get a nice payoff when you reach Sizemore Road and have a great view of Hanging Rock to the right. You can understand how it got its name when you see the masses of rock that appear to be hanging from the side of the mountain.

After you turn onto Flat Shoals Road (Mile 32.6), you'll arrive in the small community of Quaker Gap. Straight ahead is Sauratown Mountain. Flat Shoals Road takes you back to NC–66 and Taylor Road for the trip back to Pilot Mountain. Along Taylor Road, you'll have fantastic views of the surrounding mountains and lush valleys of the region. You'll take a slightly different return route following NC–268 all the way into Pilot Mountain, coming into town from the north.

LOCAL INFORMATION

♦ Surry County Economic Development Partnership, Inc., P.O. Box 1282, Dobson, NC 27017; (336) 386–4781; surryedp@surry.net.

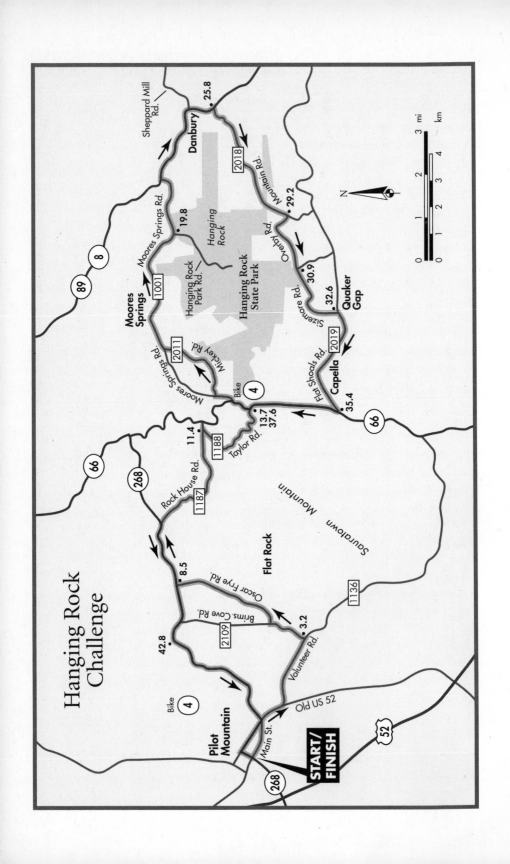

Hanging Rock Challenge

0.0 From the Pilot Mountain Town Hall parking lot, turn right onto Main Street, heading east.

0.9 Turn right onto Old U.S. Highway 52.

1.3 Turn left onto Volunteer Road (SR 1136).

3.2 Turn left onto Brims Cove Road (SR 2109).

4.2 Turn right onto Oscar Frye Road (SR 1182).

6.8 Turn right onto NC–268.

8.5 Turn right onto Rock House Road (SR 1187).

11.4 Turn right onto Taylor Road (SR 1188).

13.7 Turn left onto NC–66 (Bike Route 4).

14.2 Turn right onto Moores Springs Road (SR 1001). *Note:* This road is a North Carolina Scenic Byway.

14.6 Turn right onto Mickey Road (SR 2011). *Note:* You can't miss Hanging Rock, which will be directly in front of you.

16.6 Turn right onto Moores Springs Road (SR 1001).

19.8 Turn left onto Hanging Rock Park Road (SR 2015). The entrance to the park is to the right. *Option:* Turn right to climb the curvy road to the lake.

21.3 Turn right onto NC–8/89, toward Danbury.

23.2 Pass Sheppard Mill Road on the left which leads to Moratock Park.

25.8 Turn right onto Mountain Road (SR 2018).

27.5 Pass Orrell Road on the right.

28.5 Pass Chilton Road on the right.

29.2 Turn right onto Overby Road (SR 1993).

30.9 Go straight onto Sizemore Road (SR 1997). Overby Road ends; Sizemore Road also goes to the left. *Note:* There's a great view of Hanging Rock to the right.

32.6 Turn right onto Flat Shoals Road (SR 2019).

35.4 Turn right onto NC–66.

37.6 Turn left onto Taylor Road (SR 1188).

39.9 Turn left onto Rock House Road (SR 1187).

(continued)

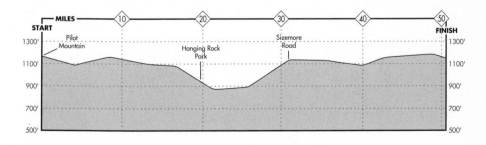

42.8 Turn left onto NC–268 (Bike Route 4).

48.9 Turn right to follow NC–268, which is also Old U.S. Highway 52.

49.8 Turn left onto NC–268 (Bike Route 4).

50.1 Turn left onto Main Street in Pilot Mountain.

50.3 Arrive at Pilot Mountain Town Hall.

LOCAL EVENTS/ATTRACTIONS

♦ Hanging Rock State Park features hiking, picnicking, rock climbing, and swimming in a twelve-acre lake, educational and interpretive programs, snack bar; Hanging Rock Park Road, P.O. Box 278, Danbury, NC 27016; no charge to enter the park; (336) 593–8480; www.ils.unc.edu/parkproject/visit/haro/home.html.

♦ Moratock Park offers picnic tables under tall shade trees next to the Dan River, rest rooms, and swimming in the Dan River (at your own risk); Sheppard Mill Road (0.2 mile from Highway 8), Danbury, NC 27016; no charge.

♦ Hanging Rock Outdoor Center, offering canoe and kayak trips in the area as well as rest rooms, drinks and PowerBars, rocking chairs on the front porch; Moores Springs Road, Danbury, NC 27016; no charge except for canoeing or kayaking; (336) 593–8283; www.hroconline.com.

RESTAURANTS

♦ Artist's Way Café, 508 Main Street, Danbury, NC 27016; (336) 593–2900. Open Tuesday through Friday 7:00 A.M.–5:30 P.M., Saturday 9:30 A.M.–2:00 P.M.; closed Sunday and Monday; box lunches, deli sandwiches, salads; low range.

♦ Dan River Family Restaurant, 1214 North Carolina Highway 8/89, Danbury, NC 27016; (336) 593–2110. Breakfast, lunch, dinner Monday through Sunday; homestyle food; low range.

ACCOMMODATIONS

♦ Best Western Royal Inn & Suites, 711 South Key Street (Highway 268), Pilot Mountain, NC 27041; (336) 368–2237; pmtnc@aol.com. Midrange.

♦ Pilot Mountain Inn Bed and Breakfast, 436 New Pilot Knob Lane, Pilot Mountain, NC 27041; (336) 325–2502; www.pilotknobinn.com. Individual log cabins; upper range.

BIKE SHOPS

♦ None.

REST ROOMS

♦ At the start and finish in Hardee's on Main Street in Pilot Mountain.
♦ At about Mile 19.0 at Hanging Rock Outdoor Center.
♦ Mile 23.2 at Moratock Park on Sheppard Mill Road (rest rooms are in the back of the covered shelter).
♦ Mile 25.8 at a convenience store on NC–8/89 just before Mountain Road.
♦ Mile 33.0 at Quaker Gap Country Store.
♦ Mile 35.4 at Sauratown Country Store.
♦ Mile 48.9 at a convenience store at intersection of NC–268 and Old U.S. Highway 52.

MAPS

♦ *DeLorme North Carolina Atlas & Gazetteer,* page 16.

Pilot Mountain Challenge

*P*ilot Mountain Challenge takes you from The Oaks Shopping Center in Lewisville 53.5 miles on a loop around Pilot Knob, one of the major geographic formations in northwest North Carolina. Fairly long stretches on rolling rural roads are punctuated by curvy and hilly sections in Surry County as you ride around the mountain. The ride covers parts of four counties and several small towns in northwestern North Carolina before looping back to the starting point in Lewisville by a different route.

Our starting point at The Oaks is the most popular gathering spot for cyclists in Forsyth County, so you're likely to see lots of fellow cyclists there on weekend mornings. East Bend, our first town, has long been a popular destination for area cyclists. It's very common in the warm months to see cyclists lounging on the wooden steps or old benches on the front porch of the country store (now a Hispanic grocery) on Main Street, just across from the town hall, as they cool off while sipping their favorite cold drink. The regulars at the store, long accustomed to seeing us cycling enthusiasts in our strange garb, will nod in greeting and sometimes strike up a conversation.

The area around East Bend makes for relaxing cycling because the peaceful farmland and pastures produce nothing noisier than a mooing cow or tractor during plowing. Fall, spring, and summer bring a profusion of colorful wildflowers along the roads and in pastures, the colors and types changing with the seasons.

At Mile 15.6 as you climb Siloam Road (SR 1003) you have some great views of Pilot Mountain while you pass white farmhouses, neat gardens, and green fields. The Indians called this mountain Jomeokee, which meant "great guide" or "pilot," hence its name in English. Composed of two pinnacles of quartzite monadnock, the mountain's larger pinnacle rises 1,400 feet with the knob jutting skyward more than 200 feet from the base. This National Natural Landmark, so designated in 1976, has survived millions of years while natural elements eroded the ground around it. This route takes you fully around the mountain so you see it from all sides during the course of the ride.

There's also a tremendous vista of the distant mountains over the nearby hills to your left. You'll wonder what stories the leaning barn and vacant houses could tell about the history of the area and the families who peopled it. Appreciate the relatively new bridge across the Yadkin River at Siloam (Mile 11.5).

THE BASICS

Start: The Oaks Shopping Center in Lewisville, North Carolina.
Length: 53.5 miles.
Terrain: Rolling to very hilly.
Traffic and hazards: Traffic is light on most of the roads, but you do have to ride short distances on North Carolina Highway 67, which is a major east–west road. In Pilot Mountain you must travel NC–268 for 1.4 miles; however, the road is four to five lanes, so motorists have ample room to pass on the left. Watch out for rough railroad tracks on Donnaha Road.
Getting there: Take U.S. Highway 421 to Lewisville (not the Clemmons/Lewisville exit) and go east on Williams Road. The Oaks Shopping Center is about 0.2 mile on the left. See the *DeLorme North Carolina Atlas & Gazetteer*, page 36 A2.

The old bridge collapsed many years ago with cars on it, killing a number of people, a major tragedy for this lovely rural area.

Hardy Road (SR 2081) just north of the Yadkin River takes off with a curvy climb before you reach a stretch that presents almost a textbook portfolio of all the variations on white frame farmhouses with front porches, typical of an earlier era. Quaker Church Road (SR 2080) offers an eclectic mix of mobile homes guarded by large satellite dishes interspersed with neat brick ranch houses. At Mile 21.0 you cross a small stream, then the road becomes curvier and the surface turns to tar and gravel for a bumpier ride.

Pilot Church Road (SR 2057) displays a grand view of Pilot Knob on the right, and you realize how much closer you are to the mountain. An old log tobacco barn and fields of tobacco bear witness to the important role tobacco has played in the North Carolina economy. Along Shoals Road (SR 2048) a colony of purple martin houses illustrates a successful strategy for battling summer insects that bite people and damage crops.

After Mile 27.8, as you enter the town of Pilot Mountain on NC–268, you'll experience a good hill while you share the four lanes with more traffic. This stretch of road is part of Bike Route 3. Main Street in Pilot Mountain is a wide street that leads you through downtown, known to Andy Griffith and Mayberry fans as Mount Pilot. On the other side of town, you'll take Old Winston Road (SR 2051) off Old U.S. Highway 52 for a view of the north side of Pilot Knob, the view most often seen from the major highways. To your left is Sauratown Mountain with its crown of transmission towers.

After you cross US 52 on Perch Road (SR 1147) at Mile 35.0, you'll see the Bear Shoals Canal. Horne Creek Farm, a historical site, is to your right. At Mile 38.4 continue left on Perch Road where Hauser Road goes off to the right. This section of road winds its way into Forsyth County with several good climbs and rewarding downhills.

The tour returns to Lewisville by a different route, winding through sleepy communities and rural areas to enter town from the north. When you finish, you'll have crossed parts of four counties in northwestern North Carolina.

LOCAL INFORMATION

♦ Yadkin County Chamber of Commerce, 205 South Jackson Street, P.O. Box 1840, Yadkinville, NC 27055; (336) 679–2200; www.yadkinchamber.org.

LOCAL EVENTS/ATTRACTIONS

♦ Horne Creek Farm is a living-history site including home tours, picnic facilities, and rest rooms; 308 Horne Creek Farm Road (off Perch Road), Pinnacle, NC 27043; no charge; open 9:00 A.M.–5:00 P.M. Tuesday through Saturday, closed Sunday and Monday; (336) 325–2298.
♦ Pilot Mountain State Park surrounds 1,400-foot Pilot Mountain, which was dedicated as a National Natural Landmark in 1976; 1792 Pilot Knob Park Road, Pinnacle, NC 27043; no charge; open 8:00 A.M.–9:00 P.M. June through August; until 8:00 P.M. in April, May, and September; (336) 325–2355; www.ils.unc.edu/parkproject/visit/pimo/home.html.

RESTAURANTS

♦ Our Place Family and Seafood Restaurant, North Carolina Highway 67 at the intersection with Smithtown Road, East Bend, NC 27018 (336) 699–5320. Dinner Tuesday through Saturday; Sunday brunch and dinner; chicken, steak, pasta, and sandwiches; midrange.
♦ Mountain View Family Restaurant, 701 South Key Street (off NC–268), Pilot Mountain, NC 27041; (336) 368–9180. Sandwiches, southern dishes; midrange.
♦ Cousin Gary's Family Restaurant, 606 South Key Street, Pilot Mountain, NC 27041; (336) 368–1488. Sandwiches, southern dishes; midrange.

Pilot Mountain stands as a sentinel over the surrounding countryside.

ACCOMMODATIONS

♦ Holiday Inn Express, 6320 Amp Drive, Clemmons, NC 27012; (336) 778–1500. Midrange.
♦ Pilot Knob Bed & Breakfast, P.O. Box 1280, Pilot Mountain, NC 27041; (336) 325–2502; info@pilotknobinn.com. Mid- to upper range.

BIKE SHOPS

♦ The Bicycle Shop, Clemmons Center, Lewisville-Clemmons Road, Clemmons, NC 27012; (336) 766–5564; www.clemmonsbicycle.com.
♦ Ken's Bike Shop, 114-J Reynolda Village, Winston-Salem, NC 27106; (336) 724–9688.
♦ Paceline Bicycles, 5059 Country Club Road, Winston-Salem, NC 27104; (336) 768–6408.

0.0 From The Oaks Shopping Center in Lewisville, turn left onto Shallowford Road (away from Lewisville).

0.9 Turn right onto Conrad Road.

2.9 Turn left onto Yadkinville Road and cross the Yadkin River into Yadkin County.

3.6 Turn right onto Taylor Road (SR 1567).

5.6 Turn right onto Flint Hill Road (SR 1549).

11.1 Cross NC–67 as you enter East Bend.

11.2 Turn left onto Main Street in East Bend.

11.4 Turn right onto Fairground Road (SR 1541).

12.3 Cross NC–67. Fairground Road's name changes to Pride's Road (SR 1541).

13.6 Turn left onto NC–67 then make an immediate right onto Smithtown Road (SR 1003).

15.6 Turn right onto Siloam Road (SR 1003). *Note:* Enjoy the great views of Pilot Mountain.

19.3 After crossing the Yadkin River into the town of Siloam, turn right just past the bridge onto Hardy Road (SR 2081).

20.8 Turn right onto Quaker Church Road (SR 2080).

22.5 Turn left onto Pilot Church Road (SR 2057). *Note:* Notice the much closer view of Pilot Knob.

25.3 Turn left onto Shoals Road (SR 2048).

27.8 Turn right onto NC–268 (part of North Carolina Bike Route 3) into Pilot Mountain, crossing over US 52.

29.2 Turn right onto Main Street in Pilot Mountain.

30.2 Turn right at yield sign onto Old U.S. Highway 52 (SR 1855).

30.3 Turn right onto Old Winston Road (SR 2051). *Note:* Watch for a view of Pilot Mountain from the north.

33.7 Turn right onto Old U.S. Highway 52 (SR 1855) into the town of Pinnacle.

34.2 Turn right onto Perch Road (SR 1147).

35.0 Cross US 52. *Note:* Look for the entrance to Horne Creek Farm.

(continued)

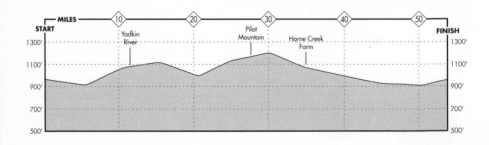

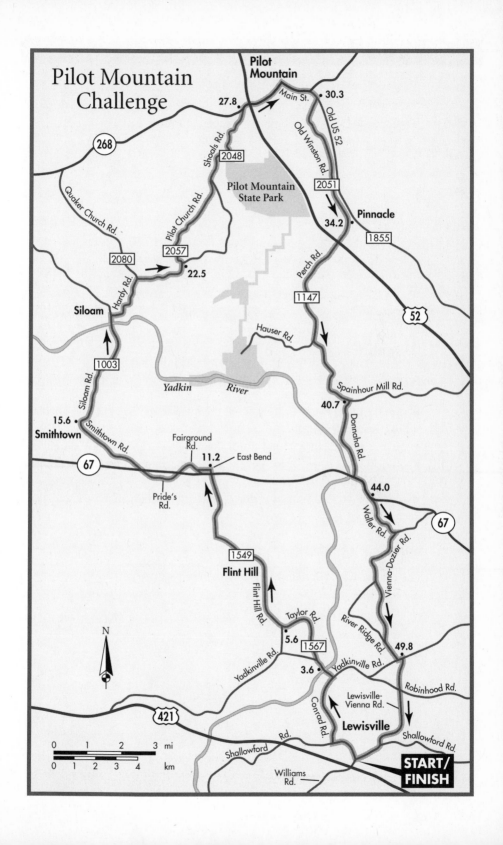

Pilot Mountain Challenge

Pilot Mountain

27.8 •   Main St.   • 30.3

268

Shoals Rd.

2048

Old Winston Rd.

Old US 52

2051

Pilot Mountain State Park

34.2 •   **Pinnacle**

Quaker Church Rd.

Pilot Church Rd.

2080   2057

Perch Rd.

1855

• 22.5

Hardy Rd.

1147

52

Siloam

Hauser Rd.

1003

Yadkin   River

Spainhour Mill Rd.

40.7 •

15.6 •
Smithtown

Smithtown Rd.

Donnaha Rd.

Fairground Rd.

11.2 • — East Bend

44.0 •

67

Pride's Rd.

Waller Rd.

67

1549

Vienna-Dozier Rd.

Flint Hill

Flint Hill Rd.

Taylor Rd.

River Ridge Rd.

49.8 •

N

5.6 •

1567

3.6 •   Yadkinville Rd.

Yadkinville Rd.

Robinhood Rd.

Lewisville-Vienna Rd.

Conrad Rd.

Lewisville

421

Shallowford Rd.

0   1   2   3 mi
0   1   2   3   4 km

Shallowford Rd.

Williams Rd.

START/ FINISH

38.4 Continue left on Perch Road (SR 1147). Hauser Road goes off to the right. As you cross into Forsyth County, the road name changes to Spainhour Mill Road.

40.7 Turn right onto Donnaha Road. Watch for rough railroad tracks.

43.1 Turn left onto NC–67, which is Reynolda Road in Forsyth County.

44.0 Turn right onto Waller Road.

45.4 Turn right onto Vienna-Dozier Road.

49.0 At the stop sign, turn left to stay on Vienna-Dozier Road. River Ridge Road goes off to the right.

49.6 Turn left onto Yadkinville Road.

49.8 Turn right onto Lewisville-Vienna Road.

50.7 Cross Robinhood Road. Continue straight on Lewisville-Vienna Road.

52.7 Turn right onto Shallowford Road in Lewisville.

53.5 Turn right into The Oaks Shopping Center.

REST ROOMS

♦ At the start and finish at Food Lion in The Oaks Shopping Center in Lewisville.

♦ Mile 11.1 at a convenience store at the intersection of Flint Hill Road and NC–67 in East Bend.

♦ Mile 27.8 at restaurants and stores along Highway 268 in Pilot Mountain.

♦ Mile 30.3 at a convenience store at the intersection of Old U.S. Highway 52 and Old Winston Road.

♦ Mile 35.0 at a convenience store at the intersection of US 52 and Perch Road.

MAPS

♦ *DeLorme North Carolina Atlas & Gazetteer*, pages 16 and 36.

Historic Salisbury Ramble

The Historic Salisbury Ramble is an easy, leisurely 11.6-mile ride, designed to introduce you to the historic district in Salisbury and lead you to the North Carolina Transportation Museum in Spencer. The first part of the route involves short distances and quick turns past numerous notable residences in the historic district. At Mile 1.9 the route straightens out on the way to the museum. From there a few turns lead you out into the country for a brief respite before Bringle Ferry Road brings you back into the heart of Salisbury's downtown.

Named for the cathedral town in England, Salisbury was chartered in 1755 as the seat of Rowan County. Its location at the convergence of the Trading Path from eastern Virginia and the Great Pennsylvania Wagon Road spurred economic development in the area, which was further increased by the coming of the railroad in the mid–nineteenth century. Salisbury's thirty-block historic district encompasses all styles of elegant homes from times past. Fortunately the town, its courthouse, and private residences were spared the wrath of Union General George Stoneman during the Civil War, supposedly because both he and the mayor of Salisbury were Masons.

The first part of this tour winds past historic residences. The Wilson-Crawford House at 207 South Ellis was built in 1853 in the Federal style by a local silversmith. The Heilig House (507 South Fulton Street, at the corner of West Monroe Street) was built in 1865 by a partner in the Gold Hill gold mine. The original detached kitchen remains on the site, believed to be the oak grove where General Stoneman's troops camped.

The Josephus Hall House at 226 South Jackson Street was once home to Chief Surgeon Hall of the Salisbury Confederate Prison during the Civil War.

Start: At the intersection of South Church Street and West Fisher Street in downtown Salisbury.

Length: 11.6 miles.

Terrain: Fairly level with a few gradual climbs.

Traffic and hazards: Traffic is fairly light, although there is more traffic along Innes Street and Main Street/Salisbury Avenue. Jefferson Avenue, which leads to I–85, has one of the few bridges across the railroad tracks and so has more traffic. This is railroad country, so there are many railroad crossings, some of which are rough.

Getting there: From I–85, take the U.S. Highway 52 exit at Salisbury. Take Innes Street, the main east–west street, toward downtown Salisbury. Cross over Main Street and turn left onto Church Street. Parking is available in municipal lots and on the street. See the *DeLorme North Carolina Atlas & Gazetteer*, page 36 D2.

Built in 1820 in the Federal style, additions in 1859—including the cast-iron verandas—and in 1900 gave the house Greek Revival and Victorian features. Housed in the building is an important collection of Victorian furnishings and accessories as well as the house's original fixtures.

The Craige House at 329 West Bank Street, constructed in 1877 in the Italianate style, remains in the Craige family to this day. It was built by Kerr Craige, assistant postmaster general, whose father introduced the Ordinance of Secession that took North Carolina out of the Union. The houses at 201 South Fulton and 301 West Fisher represent two outstanding examples of the Spanish Mission style in residential architecture.

In the block before you reach West Innes Street, you'll see the Salisbury Female Academy building at 115 South Jackson. Built in 1839, it's one of the oldest academy buildings in North Carolina. The 1892 Presbyterian Bell Tower near the intersection with Innes is all that remains of the Richardsonian Romanesque First Presbyterian Church. It now symbolizes preservation efforts in Salisbury and Rowan County.

When you turn to cross Main Street on Innes Street (no left turns allowed here), the Kluttz Drug Store Building will be on your left. This three-story structure was the tallest commercial building in North Carolina when it was built in 1858. Lee Street takes you past the visitor center before you turn left on East Liberty Street to get back to Main Street.

Salisbury's spacious Main Street takes you past all sorts of shops, restaurants, and businesses before it turns into Salisbury Avenue in Spencer. This town, once the site of Southern Railway's largest steam locomotive repair shops, is now home to the North Carolina Transportation Museum as well as numerous other businesses and shops.

The museum pays tribute to the golden years of the railroad with displays of elegant private railcars, a massive locomotive on a turntable, its 1924 Bob Julian Roundhouse, and the volunteer railroad buffs who work to preserve

America's steam locomotives. But there's also much more there. You can examine the Original North Carolina Highway Patrol car—a convertible, no less—along with other antique automobile displays. Other forms of transportation —including bicycles and dugout canoes—are also on display. Train rides from the museum start at three or four designated times each day. A fee is charged for the rides, but admission to the museum is free.

The return route loops through the countryside on the outskirts of Salisbury before following Bringle Ferry Road back into Salisbury.

LOCAL INFORMATION

♦ Rowan County Convention & Visitors Bureau, 106 North Lee Street, P.O. Box 4044, Salisbury, NC 28145-4044; (704) 638–3100 or (800) 332–2343; www.visitsalisburync.com.

LOCAL EVENTS/ATTRACTIONS

♦ North Carolina Transportation Museum includes a traditional railway roundhouse, train rides, antique autos, and other transportation exhibits; Samuel Spencer Drive off Salisbury Avenue, Spencer, North Carolina; no charge for admission; fee for train rides; (704) 636–2889 or (877) NCTM–FUN; www.ah.dcr.state.nc.us/sections/hs/spencer/spencer.htm.

A downtown mural of historic Salisbury includes a cyclist.

0.0 From the intersection of South Church Street and West Fisher Street in downtown Salisbury, turn right onto West Fisher Street.

0.3 Turn left onto South Ellis Street.

0.5 Turn left onto West Monroe Street.

0.6 Turn left onto South Fulton Street.

0.7 Turn right onto West Horah Street.

0.8 Turn left onto South Jackson Street (a one-way street).

0.9 Turn left onto West Bank Street.

1.0 Turn right onto South Fulton Street.

1.1 Turn right on to West Fisher Street.

1.2 Turn left onto South Jackson Street.

1.3 Turn right onto West Innes Street.

1.6 Turn left onto Lee Street. The tourist information office will be on your right.

1.8 Turn left onto East Liberty Street.

1.9 Turn right onto North Main Street. Watch out for the rough railroad tracks. North Main Street's name changes to Salisbury Avenue when you enter Spencer.

4.5 Turn right into the North Carolina Transportation Museum on Samuel Spencer Drive.

4.8 Arrive at the visitor center. After a tour, take Samuel Spencer Drive back to Salisbury Avenue.

5.1 Exit the museum, turning right onto Salisbury Avenue.

5.6 Turn right onto Jefferson Street.

5.8 Turn right onto North Long Street.

7.0 Turn left onto Correll Street, the name of which changes to McCanless Road after you cross the one-lane bridge.

8.5 Turn right onto Bringle Ferry Road (SR 1002). Watch out for several rough railroad tracks.

10.6 Turn right onto Railroad Avenue, then left onto Henderson Street.

10.8 Turn left onto North Main Street. Watch out for several rough railroad tracks.

11.4 Turn right onto West Innes Street.

11.6 Turn left onto South Church Street and return to the West Fisher Street intersection.

♦ Historic Homes Tour, an annual walking tour held on the second weekend in October and sponsored by the Historic Salisbury Foundation, P.O. Box 4221, Salisbury, NC 28145-4221; adults $15 in advance or $18 the day of the tour; (704) 636–0103; www.historicsalisbury.org.

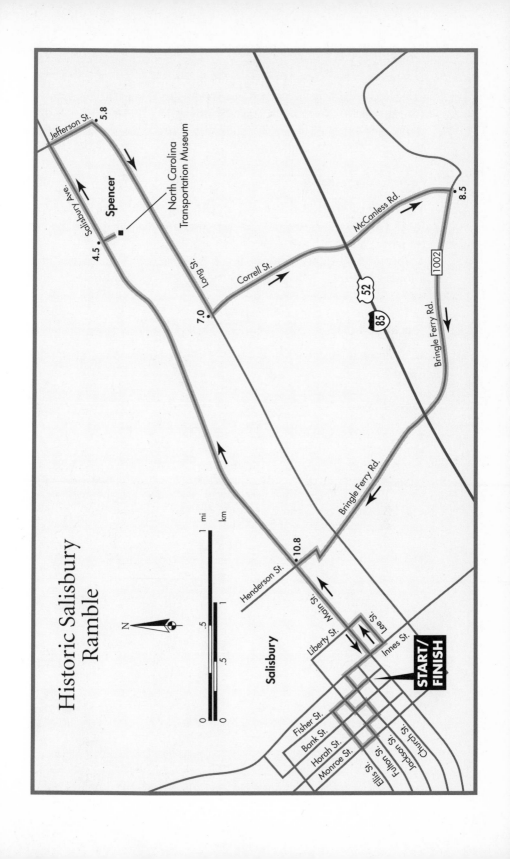

Historic Salisbury Ramble

N

.5   1 mi

.5   1 km

0

0   .5   1

Salisbury

Spencer

North Carolina
Transportation Museum

Jefferson St.   • 5.8

Salisbury Ave.

4.5. •

Long St.

7.0 •

Correll St.

McCanless Rd.

• 8.5

1002

52

85

Bringle Ferry Rd.

Bringle Ferry Rd.

Henderson St.

10.8

Main St.

Liberty St.

Lee St.

Innes St.

**START/
FINISH**

Fisher St.

Bank St.

Horah St.

Monroe St.

Ellis St.

Fulton St.

Jackson St.

Church St.

RESTAURANTS

♦ Sweet Meadow Café, 118 West Innes Street, Salisbury, NC 28144; (704) 637–8715. Open daily for lunch; dinner Wednesday through Saturday.
♦ Spanky's, 101 North Main Street, Salisbury, NC 28144; (704) 638–0780. Soups, sandwiches, salads; open Monday through Saturday for a late breakfast and lunch.

ACCOMMODATIONS

♦ Rowan Oak House Bed & Breakfast, 208 South Fulton Street, Salisbury, NC 28144; (704) 633–2086 or (800) 786–0437; www.rowanoakbb.com. Mid- to upper range.
♦ Turn of the Century Victorian Bed & Breakfast, 529 South Fulton Street, Salisbury, NC 28144; (704) 642–1660 or (800) 250–5349; www.turnofthecenturybb. com. Mid- to upper range.

BIKE SHOPS

♦ The Windsong, 206 South Main Street, Salisbury, NC 28144; (704) 637–6955.

REST ROOMS

♦ At restaurants in the downtown Salisbury area.
♦ Mile 4.8 at the North Carolina Transportation Museum.

MAPS

♦ Salisbury/Rowan County Map by Quality Map Company, 1992.

Cabarrus County Challenge

The 55.7-mile *Cabarrus County Challenge* leads you from the quiet streets of downtown Concord, the county seat, south into the rolling countryside before sweeping east across the southern part of the county to Reed Gold Mine. The terrain is rolling but most hospitable to cyclists, with only a few serious climbs. Historic churches bear witness to the religious commitment of the county's earliest settlers, who sought religious freedom here. Numerous parks are available in the towns, but services are limited otherwise; you should carry ample water and snacks with you.

Concord, the starting place for this route, offers numerous restaurants and shops in its downtown, where many buildings have been restored to their earlier splendor. The Concord Historic District was established along Union Street, with its huge old trees and stately homes. Here you'll see the Concord Hotel, the original downtown hotel for the city; the Historic Cabarrus County Courthouse Museum with its unique architectural style; and the city's oldest churches. The Logan Recreation Center on Lincoln Street in an area called "The Bottoms" has rest rooms and vending machines. Nearby Daniel Pharr Community Center in spacious Caldwell Park offers rest rooms and water plus athletic facilities. Breathe deeply and enjoy the scenic vistas along Zion Church Road, but be aware that traffic can be heavy during peak hours. W.W. Flowe Park gives cyclists yet another rest area with rest rooms and water, trails, horseshoes, and picnic areas.

You'll find country estates and beautiful vistas in the rural areas surrounding these small Cabarrus towns as the rolling hills give way to curvy and hilly sections of road. Nestled among these rolling hills in eastern Cabarrus is Reed

The interesting architecture of the historic Cabarrus County Courthouse and Museum stands out against the sky.

Gold Mine, which set off a gold rush in the early nineteenth century. Reed Gold Mine is the site of the first documented gold find in the United States in 1799 on the farm of John Reed. Reed, whose actual name was Johannes Rieth, was a Hessian soldier who left the British army near the conclusion of the Revolutionary War and came to settle near fellow Germans in the area. Reed's life as a farmer would have long been forgotten but for the chance event one Sunday in 1799. On that day his son Conrad found in Little Meadow Creek a large yellow rock that was later determined to be gold. This discovery helped create a new industry to the extent that North Carolina led the nation in gold production until 1848, when it was eclipsed by the rush to California.

THE BASICS

Start: At the intersection of Union Street and Buffalo Avenue in downtown Concord.
Length: 55.7 miles.
Terrain: Rolling to hilly.
Traffic and hazards: Watch out for the dangerous crossing at U.S. Highway 601 Bypass/Warren Coleman Road. There is poor visibility at the intersection of Morrison Road and Pioneer Mill Road.
Getting there: From I–85 in Cabarrus County, take North Carolina Highway 73 east toward Concord. Follow NC–73 and then the signs for downtown Concord. There is on-street parking along Union Street. See the *DeLorme North Carolina Atlas & Gazetteer*, page 58 B1.

Historic Rocky River Presbyterian Church is situated along this route, offering a shaded and grassy resting spot. A nearby country store sells refreshments for the thirsty. The route wends its way through narrow and curvy country lanes, where you'll need to be alert for tractors on the road. The sweeping countryside and green fields make the ride well worth the effort.

The future Cabarrus County was first settled in the 1730s by Scots-Irish Presbyterians, who had traveled the Great Wagon Road from Pennsylvania and Maryland to settle in the lovely rolling hills of the Carolina backcountry. In the next decade German immigrants of the Lutheran and Reformed faiths followed and settled in the eastern part of this area. Both groups had come to the New World to seek refuge from European wars, famine, and religious intolerance. In Carolina they built log homes, planted crops, and organized congregations. Those early settlers, seeing education as the path to self-government and independence, established the earliest schools in their churches.

In 1771 nine Scots-Irish young men blackened their faces and blew up gunpowder and supplies destined for the king's troops. They are known in the history of the time as the Cabarrus Black Boys. In 1775 settlers from the region of Mecklenburg, which became part of Cabarrus County, participated in a meeting in Charlotte that produced the document known as the Mecklenburg Declaration of Independence. These fiercely independent Scots-Irishmen and their German neighbors so strongly supported the American cause in the Revolutionary War that the region was called the Hornet's Nest by the British.

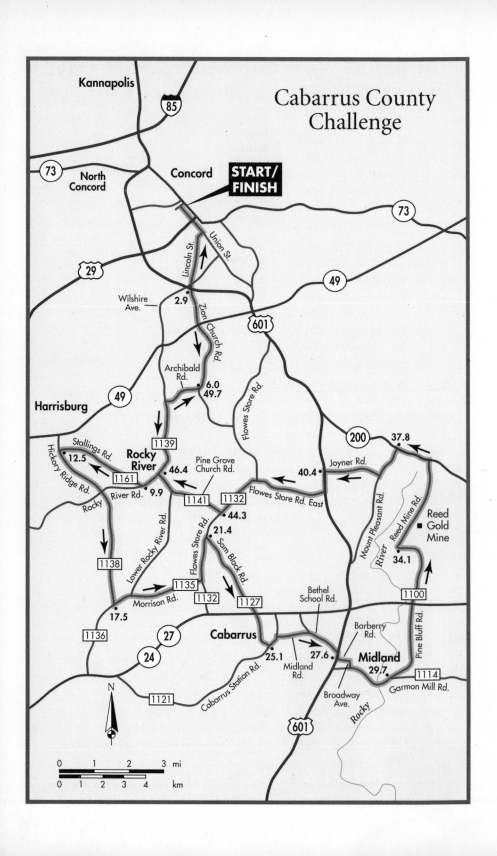

0.0 From the intersection of Union Street and Buffalo Avenue, go south on Union Street toward the main downtown area of Concord.

1.2 Turn right onto Chestnut Drive.

1.4 Turn left onto Lincoln Street. *Note:* Logan Recreation Center is located here.

2.4 Cross the stream at the bottom of the hill. The road's name changes to Rutherford Road.

2.8 Cross Wilshire Avenue.

2.9 Cross US 601 Bypass/Warren Coleman Boulevard. The road's name changes to Zion Church Road. Continue straight onto Zion Church Road.

4.0 Cross NC–49/Central Heights Road.

6.0 Turn right onto Archibald Road (SR 1153). Watch out for the sharp curve.

7.1 Turn left onto Rocky River Road (SR 1139).

9.9 Turn right onto Stallings Road (SR 1161).

12.5 Turn left onto Hickory Ridge Road (SR 1138).

14.2 Cross Rocky River Road.

17.5 Turn left onto Lower Rocky River Road (SR 1136).

18.0 Turn right onto Morrison Road (SR 1135).

19.4 Cross Pioneer Mill Road (SR 1134).

20.1 Turn left onto Flowes Store Road (SR 1132).

21.4 Turn right onto Sam Black Road (SR 1127).

24.1 Cross NC–24/27.

25.1 Turn left onto Cabarrus Station Road (SR 1121).

25.4 Turn right onto Midland Road (SR 1121).

26.4 Turn right onto Bethel School Road (SR 1120).

27.5 Turn right onto US 601.

27.6 Turn left onto Barberry Road (SR 1109).

27.9 Turn right onto Broadway Avenue (SR 1110). Watch out for the rough railroad tracks.

28.1 Turn left on Garmon Mill Road (SR 1114) and cross the Rocky River.

(continued)

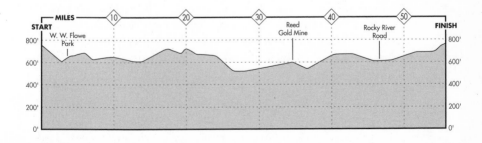

29.7 Turn left onto Pine Bluff Road (SR 1146) then cross into Stanly County. When you reenter Cabarrus County the road number changes to SR 1100.

31.9 Cross NC–24/27. Pine Bluff Road's name changes to Reed Mine Road (SR 1100); it crosses a narrow bridge over Little Meadow Creek.

34.1 The road makes a ninety-degree turn.

34.8 Turn right into Reed Gold Mine. After your tour, return to the Reed Mine Road entrance.

36.8 Turn left onto NC–200.

37.8 Turn left onto Mount Pleasant Road (SR 1006).

38.7 Turn right onto Joyner Road (SR 1105).

40.4 Turn left onto US 601, which has a narrow paved shoulder.

40.9 Turn right onto Flowes Store Road—the eastern leg of it (SR 1132).

43.0 Turn left onto Flowes Store Road (SR 1132). Flowes Store Road actually has three branches at this intersection.

44.3 Turn right onto Pine Grove Church Road (SR 1141).

45.8 Turn right onto Lower Rocky River Road (SR 1136).

46.4 Turn right onto Rocky River Road (SR 1139). *Note:* Look for Rocky River Presbyterian Church on the right.

48.6 Turn right onto Archibald Road (SR 1153).

49.7 Turn left onto Zion Church Road (SR 1153).

51.7 Cross NC–49.

52.8 Cross US 601/Warren Coleman Boulevard and go straight onto Rutherford Street.

52.9 Cross Wilshire Avenue. Rutherford Road's name changes to Lincoln Street after the stream.

54.3 Turn right onto Chestnut Street.

54.5 Turn left onto Union Street.

55.7 Arrive at the intersection with Buffalo Street.

In 1792 Cabarrus County became separate from Mecklenburg County and was named in honor of Stephen Cabarrus, the speaker of the House of Commons who had cast the deciding vote in favor of the county's creation. By 1796 citizens had agreed to the location of the county seat and the town named Concord, or "harmony," was established with the county courthouse built at the intersection of its two main streets. You, too, will experience harmony as you pedal along the tree-lined, welcoming streets in downtown Concord on your return to the starting point.

LOCAL INFORMATION

♦ Cabarrus County Tourism Development Authority, 2391 Dale Earnhardt Boulevard, Kannapolis, NC 28033; (704) 782–4340 or (800) 848–3740; www.cabarruscvb.com.

LOCAL EVENTS/ATTRACTIONS

♦ Reed Gold Mine State Historic Site includes stamp mill and panning operations, exhibits, and guided tours hourly; 9621 Reed Mine Road, Midland, NC 28107; no charge except for panning; (704) 721–4653; www.ah.dcr.state.nc.us/sections/hs/reed/reed.htm.

♦ Historic Concord's beautifully restored Victorian homes, unique shops, restaurants, and coffeehouses blend with historic buildings and a beautiful Memorial Garden; seasonal tours are available for the historic homes; for more information (704) 784–4208.

♦ Memorial Garden in Concord is a beautiful three-acre 1804 garden that boasts enormous oaks, magnolias, dogwoods, and twisted crepe myrtles plus 14,000 tulips, seasonal flowers, and azaleas; open Monday through Saturday 9:00 A.M.–5:00 P.M. and Sunday 1:00–5:30 P.M. For more information (704) 782–6106 or (704) 786–8009.

♦ Historic Courthouse Museum, erected in 1876, is an architecturally unique courthouse listed on the National Register of Historic Places that houses an extensive library used for genealogical and historical research; 65 Union Street South, Concord, NC 28025; open Monday through Friday 9:00 A.M.–noon; no charge; (704) 786–8515.

♦ Rocky River Presbyterian Church, founded in the early 1750s, includes lovely old buildings and cemeteries where Revolutionary War patriots are buried; 7940 Rocky River Road, Concord, NC 28025; no charge; (704) 455–2479.

RESTAURANTS

♦ Union Street Bistro, 48 Union Street, Concord, NC 28025; (704) 795–4902. Sandwiches and salads; closed on Sunday.

♦ Red Pig Café, 24 Corban Avenue, just east of Union Street, Concord, NC 28025; (704) 782–1263. Sandwiches and salads; closed on Sunday.

♦ You'll find a variety of fast-food restaurants along Highway 73 coming into Concord, most of which are open on Sunday.

ACCOMMODATIONS

♦ Odell House Bed & Breakfast, 288 Union Street, Concord, NC 28025; (704) 262–7900. Mid- to upper range; continental breakfast.

◆ Sleep Inn, 1120 Copperfield Road, I–85 at exit 60, Concord, NC 28027; (704) 788–2150 or (800) SLEEP–INN.

BIKE SHOPS

◆ The Right Gear, 863 Cloverleaf Plaza, Kannapolis, NC 28033; (704) 786–2453.
◆ Spokes and Pedals, 912 Brantley Road, Kannapolis, NC 28083; (704) 938–3550.

REST ROOMS

◆ At about Mile 1.4 and Mile 52.9 at the Daniel Pharr Community Center and Park. The Logan Recreation Center is in the same area.
◆ Mile 4.0 at W. W. Flowe Park on Central Heights Avenue, 0.7 mile to the right on Central Heights from where the route intersects.
◆ Mile 12.5 at Harrisburg Park in the town of Harrisburg, to the right on Hickory Ridge Road where Stallings Road intersects. The route goes to the left.
◆ Mile 27.5 at a service station on U.S. Highway 601.
◆ About Mile 45.8 at a country store at the intersection of Rocky River Road and Lower Rocky River Road.

MAPS

◆ *DeLorme North Carolina Atlas & Gazetteer,* pages 57–58.

Queen City Ramble

The Queen City Ramble leads you on a challenging tour of North Carolina's largest city, Charlotte, and is recommended for experienced cyclists. Beginning at the chic shopping area called Southpark Mall, the route winds through some of the city's oldest and most elegant neighborhoods on its way to Uptown Charlotte. There you'll tour the central business district with its impressive skyline, pass by Ericsson Stadium, and see Charlotte's heart at the intersection of Tryon and Trade Streets, distinguished by four large sculptures on each of the corners. The Mint Museum of Craft and Design, along with Discovery Place, are located just two blocks north. From there the route heads east to the Mint Museum of Art before circling through Myers Park neighborhoods on the way back to Southpark Mall. Charlotte is a fast-growing city with traffic to match, requiring cyclists to assert their right to the road while sharing the pavement defensively with motorists.

Charlotte, the largest city in the Carolinas, was named in honor of Queen Charlotte of Mecklenburg-Strelitz, wife of George III of England, also the source of its nickname—the Queen City. As these names indicate, Charlotte initially had very strong ties to England and the British Crown. But these ties were broken in 1775 with the signing of the Mecklenburg Resolves, which invalidated the authority of the English king and Parliament.

Lord Cornwallis, who occupied the town for several days in 1780, called it a "hornet's nest of rebellion" because of the intense activity by the patriots. The story and the name have held through the years and inspired the name for the professional basketball team.

Charlotte is also known as the City of Trees, and you will still see why as you enjoy this tour through many of its loveliest tree-shaded neighborhoods. The Southpark area where the ride starts has become the chic shopping district, so you'll see many interesting boutiques and restaurants mixed with the usual chain stores and restaurants.

After you turn onto Barclay Downs Drive, you'll traverse lovely residential areas, many with stately older homes. At Mile 3.9, you turn onto Queens Road East. With its partner Queens Road West, this street forms a large oval through this lovely Myers Park neighborhood. Queens Road is a divided four-lane with a tree-lined median and very large homes gracing its sides.

At Mile 5.5, Providence Road curves left and becomes Third Street as you head into "Uptown Charlotte"—the heart of the city. You'll have a great view at Mile 5.9 of the Charlotte skyline, which is dominated by the Bank of America building with its choir of reflective spires at the top. Several new skyscrapers now challenge its dominance as Charlotte's tallest building. At Mile 6.2 you can admire the large Corinthian columns and classical architecture of the Mecklenburg County Courthouse.

Skyscrapers at the busy intersection of Tryon and Trade Streets in Uptown Charlotte.

As you turn right onto Stonewall Street, the *Charlotte Observer* newspaper building is to your left. Straight ahead looms Ericsson Stadium, home of the Charlotte football team. South Mint Street becomes one-way south within the next couple of blocks, so you'll take a diagonal to Poplar Street to get to Trade Street, the principal east–west street in Uptown. Riding along Trade Street will help you understand why Charlotte is becoming one of the nation's largest financial centers as you encounter the towers of Bank of America and Wachovia, two major banks headquartered here.

The Bank of America Tower and Corporate Center are located at the intersection of Trade and Tryon Streets, which is called The Square. It's the historic crossroads of the city and the site of its founding more than 250 years ago. This intersection, one of the loveliest anywhere, stands out because of its many varied fountains and large outdoor sculptures. Although the sixty-story Bank of America Tower has no observation deck, you should take a few minutes to visit the magnificent lobby and view the three huge frescoes by Ben Long, which were commissioned especially for this building. Each measures 23 feet by 18 feet.

THE BASICS

Start: Southpark Mall on Morrison Boulevard at the intersection with Roxborough Road.
Length: 19.4 miles.
Terrain: Rolling with some fairly level stretches downtown and some challenging hills.
Traffic and hazards: While much of this ride is on quiet neighborhood roadways, a good portion has to be on fairly busy streets because Charlotte's street system features such a large number of cul-de-sacs. Therefore, this tour is best suited to experienced riders. Most of the busy streets have two lanes in each direction so that cyclists can claim one lane and give motorists ample room to pass. Fortunately, speed limits are only 25 to 35 miles per hour. Travel on weekends is recommended; avoid peak rush hours.
Getting there: From I-77 through Charlotte, exit at Tyvola Road and take Tyvola east toward the city. Tyvola Road's name changes to Fairview after you pass Park Road. Turn left onto Sharon Road and then left onto Morrison Boulevard to park at Southpark Mall. See the *DeLorme North Carolina Atlas & Gazetteer,* page 57 D6.

The Museum of the New South is located one block east of this intersection, and the Mint Museum of Craft and Design is located two blocks north on Tryon Street with Discovery Place diagonally across Tryon Street. The original Mint Museum, the next major stop, is located east on Fourth Street/Randolph Road. The museum is housed in a building constructed from materials used in the original Charlotte Mint, formerly located on Mint Street in Uptown. Opened in 1837 and producing more than $5 million in coins—many using gold from area mines—until the Civil War, the original building was purchased, measured, and demolished. It became the Mint Museum after it was moved to the lovely park where it now stands.

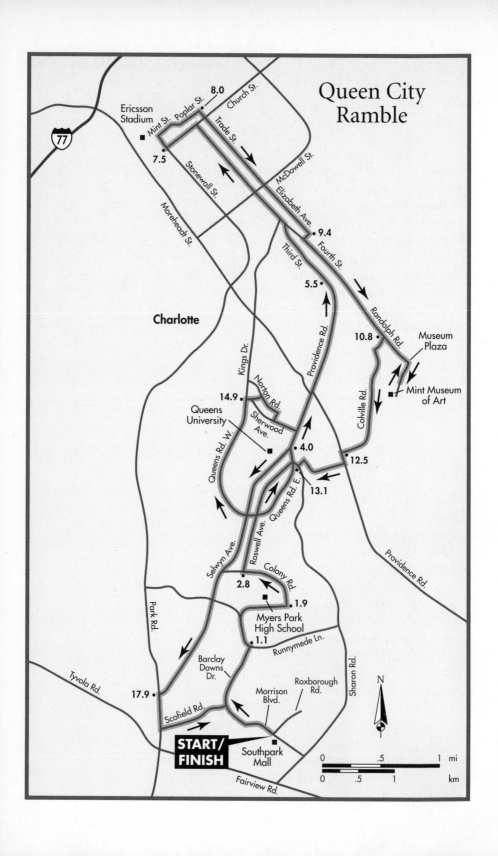

Queen City Ramble

77

Ericsson
Stadium

8.0

Mint St. Poplar St.

Church St.

Trade St.

7.5

Stonewall St.

McDowell St.

Morehead St.

Elizabeth Ave.

9.4

Charlotte

Third St.

Fourth St.

5.5

Providence Rd.

Randolph Rd.

10.8

Museum
Plaza

Kings Dr.

Norton Rd.

14.9

Queens
University

Sherwood
Ave.

Colville Rd.

Mint Museum
of Art

4.0

12.5

Queens Rd. W.

Queens Rd. E.

13.1

Roswell Ave.

Selwyn Ave.

Colony Rd.

2.8

1.9

Myers Park
High School

Providence Rd.

1.1

Runnymede Ln.

Park Rd.

Barclay
Downs
Dr.

Roxborough
Rd.

Sharon Rd.

Tyvola Rd.

17.9

Scofield Rd.

Morrison
Blvd.

N

**START/
FINISH**

Southpark
Mall

Fairview Rd.

0   .5   1 mi

0   .5   1 km

0.0 From Southpark Mall on Morrison Boulevard at its intersection with Roxborough Road, turn left onto Morrison Boulevard.

0.3 Turn right onto Barclay Downs Drive.

1.1 Turn left onto Runnymede Lane.

1.3 Turn right into Myers Park High School property, bear right, and then follow the main drive to the school's main entrance on Colony Road.

1.9 Turn left onto Colony Road.

2.8 Turn right onto Roswell Avenue.

3.4 Cross one intersection of Queens Road East and West—but stay on Roswell Avenue to the stop sign.

3.9 Turn left onto Queens Road East.

4.0 Bear right on Queens Road at five-point intersection.

4.5 Go straight on Providence Road. (Queens Road goes off to the left.)

5.5 Providence Road curves to the left and becomes Third Street at the intersection with Caswell Street.

5.9 Third Street becomes one-way after the intersection with Independence Boulevard. Westbound traffic is routed onto Fourth Street.

7.2 Turn left onto Church Street.

7.5 Turn right onto Stonewall Street. *Option:* For a quick side trip around Ericsson Stadium, you can turn left onto South Mint Street, turn right onto Morehead Street, turn right onto South Cedar Street, then right onto Stonewall Street back to the intersection with South Mint Street.

7.6 Turn right onto South Mint Street. Bear right onto South Poplar Street. (South Mint becomes one-way at this point.)

8.0 Turn right onto West Trade Street.

8.9 West Trade Street's name changes to Elizabeth Avenue at the intersection with McDowell Street.

9.4 Turn right onto Torrence Street.

9.5 Turn left onto East Fourth Street. East Fourth Street's name changes to Randolph Road at the intersection with Caswell Street at Mile 9.8.

10.8 Turn right onto Museum Plaza into the Mint Museum. After your tour, return to the entrance.

11.1 At the Mint Museum entrance, turn left onto Randolph Road.

11.4 Turn left onto Dotger Avenue.

11.5 Turn left onto Colville Road.

12.5 Turn left onto Providence Road.

(continued)

12.6 Turn right onto Beverly Drive.

13.0 Turn left onto Rensford Avenue.

13.1 Turn right onto Sharon Road, then make an immediate sharp left onto Queens Road East, which curves around and becomes Queens Road West after the intersection with Selwyn Avenue.

14.9 Turn right onto Queens Road West at the intersection with East Boulevard. Kings Drive is straight ahead.

15.0 Turn right onto Norton Road.

15.3 Turn right onto Hertford Road and then left onto Sherwood Avenue.

15.5 Turn right onto Queens Road, then bear right on Selwyn Avenue at the traffic signal. Queens University is on the right.

17.9 Turn left onto Park Road.

18.1 Turn left onto Scofield Road.

18.7 Turn right onto Barclay Downs Drive.

18.9 Turn left onto Morrison Boulevard. Carnegie Boulevard goes to the right.

19.4 Arrive at the intersection with Roxborough Road at Southpark Mall.

From the Mint Museum, the route winds back through the Myers Park neighborhoods before returning to Southpark Mall on Morrison Boulevard.

LOCAL INFORMATION

♦ Visit Charlotte , 122 East Stonewall Street, Charlotte, NC 28202; (704) 334–2282 or (800) 231–4636.

LOCAL EVENTS/ATTRACTIONS

♦ Bank of America Corporate Center features three large, 18-by-23-foot murals depicting *Making/Building, Chaos/Creativity,* and *Planning/Knowledge;* 100 North Tryon at the intersection with Trade Street, Charlotte, NC 28202; no charge.

♦ Mint Museum of Craft and Design showcases exhibits of ceramics, fiber, glass, metal, and wood; 220 North Tryon Street, Charlotte, NC 28202; adults $6.00, seniors (sixty-two-plus) and college students $5.00, students six through seventeen $3.00, children five and under free; admission is free on Tuesday from 5:00–10:00 P.M.; closed Monday; a paid ticket is good for same-day admission to the Mint Museum of Art; (704) 337–2000; www.mintmuseum.org.

♦ Mint Museum of Art, permanent and temporary exhibitions on art in the Americas; 2730 Randolph Road, Charlotte, NC 28207; adults $6:00, seniors (sixty-two-plus) and college students $5.00, students six through seventeen $3.00, children five and under free; admission is free on Tuesday from 5:00 to 10:00 P.M.; closed Monday; a paid ticket is good for same-day admission to the Mint Museum of Craft and Design; (704) 337–2000; www.mintmuseum.org.

♦ Discovery Place, one of the top hands-on science museums in the nation; 301 North Tryon Street, Charlotte, NC 28202; ages thirteen through fifty-nine $6.50, ages six through twelve and sixty-plus $5.00, ages three through five $2.75; (704) 372–6261; www.discoveryplace.org.

RESTAURANTS

♦ Cino Grille, 6401 Morrison Boulevard, Charlotte, NC 28211; (704) 365–8226; www.cinogrille.com. Upscale café open for lunch and dinner.

♦ Market Café, Southpark Suite Hotel, 6300 Morrison Boulevard, Charlotte, NC 28211; (704) 364–2400. Upscale cafe serving American food.

♦ Food court at Southpark Mall, Morrison Boulevard.

ACCOMMODATIONS

♦ Southpark Suite Hotel, 6300 Morrison Boulevard, Charlotte, NC 28211; (704) 364–2400. Upper range.

♦ Residence Inn by Marriott Southpark, 6030 J.A. Jones Drive, Charlotte, NC 28287; (704) 554–7001. Mid- to upper range

BIKE SHOPS

♦ Bicycle Sport, 2902 Selwyn Avenue, Charlotte, NC 28209; (704) 335–0323; www.bicycle-sport.com/.

♦ Bike Gallery, 2500 Park Road, Charlotte, NC 28203; (704) 332–2165.

REST ROOMS

♦ At the start and finish in Southpark Mall.

♦ At Mint Museum of Craft and Design, two blocks north of Trade Street, Mile 8.4 on the route, or at Discovery Place, diagonally across Tryon Street.

♦ Mile 10.9 at the Mint Museum of Art.

MAPS

♦ Universal Map of Charlotte, 1998.

Lincoln County Challenge

The Lincoln County Challenge, 41.0 miles in length, begins on the banks of Lake Norman at the Energy Explorium and then loops through resort neighborhoods on the lake's edge before passing traditional houses and into the countryside. Sections of the ride use the area's main highways, but most of the route is on quiet secondary roads. The loop passes through historic Iron Station and then winds its way back toward the Energy Explorium.

This route, which overlaps with part of the North Carolina Mountains to Sea Bicycle Route 6 along North Carolina Highway 73, provides an interesting juxtaposition of rural and resort/residential development as you ride west from Lake Norman. This body of water, 8 miles wide and 30 miles long, is the largest inland and human-made lake in North Carolina, offering 520 miles of shoreline. Its proximity to Charlotte has made it an attractive location for Charlotte commuters and those seeking a weekend retreat. Its development started on the east side, close to I–77, but has since spread to all other parts of the lake as well.

This tour gives you an excellent vantage point of the lake, away from the higher-traffic areas. Duke Energy's Energy Explorium is the starting point. After you turn onto Club Drive (SR 1395), you have a great view of Cowans Ford Dam, which created the lake, and Duke Power's McGuire Nuclear Power Plant. Cowans Ford Country Club is to your left. After Mile 3.7, the lake is bordered by large homes. A quick side trip down Waterford Road gives you a good view of one of the many coves with sailboats tied up at family docks.

After you rejoin it, NC–73 provides some nice ups and downs, especially a nice downhill around Mile 9. Take care, because the shoulderless road has heavier traffic than is desirable for cycling. Ingleside Farm Road (SR 1383) at Mile 10.9 takes you past old farmhouses and pastures. The Ingleside properties once belonged to a family prominent in the iron industry in Lincoln County. The Ingleside home, located west of SR 1383 a slight distance off the road, is listed in the National Register of Historic Places.

At Mile 14.2 along Bethhaven Church Road are two unusual sites: a round barn and a wooden shanty-town built around a quadrangle. You arrive in Iron Station at Mile 22.6, so named because of the successful iron industry that flourished in the county in the early nineteenth century. In 1823 ten forges and four furnaces were producing bar iron and castings in the form of skillets, pots, pans, dog-irons, and ovens for local trade. The isolation of the area at that time made the industry necessary, but it declined as better and cheaper products became more readily available from the North.

THE BASICS

Start: The visitor center at Duke Energy's Energy Explorium.
Length: 41.0 miles.
Terrain: Rolling with a few climbs.
Traffic and hazards: Traffic can be busy along North Carolina Highways 73, 27, and 16, which are necessary connectors along this route.
Getting there: From I–77, take exit 25 to NC–73. Continue west on NC–73, following the signs to the Energy Explorium, located in Building 7414. Park in the visitors parking lot. See the *DeLorme North Carolina Atlas & Gazetteer*, page 57 B5.

Great view of Lake Norman from the park at the Energy Explorium.

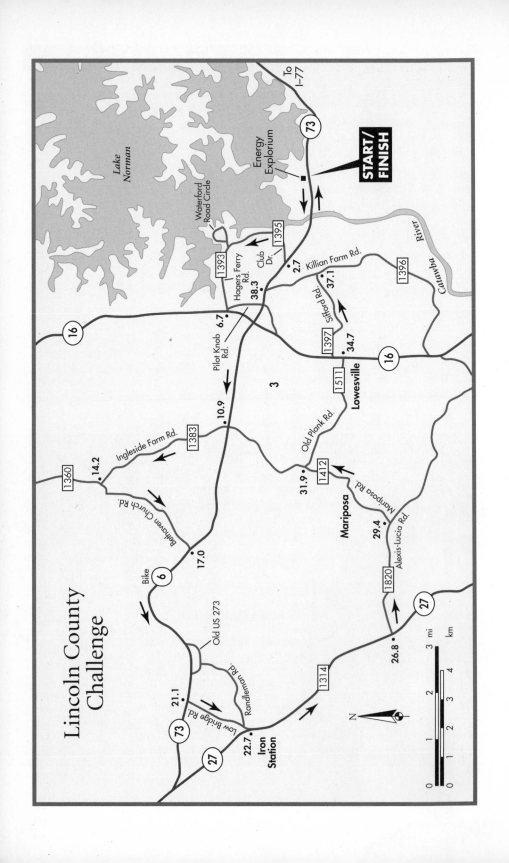

Lincoln County Challenge

Lake Norman

Waterford Road Circle

To I-77

73

Energy Explorium

START/ FINISH

Hagers Ferry Rd.
1393
38.3
Club Dr.
1395

2.7
Killian Farm Rd.
37.1
Sifford Rd.
1396

Catawba River

6.7
Pilot Knob Rd.

16

1397
34.7

16

1511
Old Plank Rd.
Lowesville

3

10.9

Ingleside Farm Rd.
1383

1412
31.9

14.2
1360

Bethlehem Church Rd.

Mariposa Rd.
Mariposa
29.4

Bike **6**
17.0

1820
Alexis-Lucia Rd.

27

Old US 273

26.8

21.1
73

Randleman Rd.

Low Bridge Rd.

1314

27

22.7
Iron Station

N

3 mi
km

0 1 2 3 4

0 1 2 3

0.0 From the visitors parking lot at the Energy Explorium, follow the main road back to NC–73.

0.7 Turn right onto NC–73.

2.7 Turn right onto Club Drive (SR 1395).

5.4 *Option:* Turn right onto Waterford Road. Circle around, return to Club Drive, and turn right.

6.0 Bear left on Hagers Ferry Road (SR 1393).

6.7 After you cross Pilot Knob Road (SR 1394), turn left onto NC–16.

8.4 Turn right onto NC–73.

10.9 Turn right onto Ingleside Farm Road (SR 1383).

14.2 Turn left onto Bethhaven Church Road (SR 1360).

17.0 Turn right onto NC–73 (sign for Bike Route 6). *Note:* Look for a historic home on NC–73 at about mile 18.5.

21.1 Turn left onto Low Bridge Road (SR 1314).

22.5 Turn right at a stop sign where Randleman Road comes in from the left.

22.7 Turn left onto NC–27 into Iron Station.

26.8 Turn left onto Alexis-Lucia Road (SR 1820). Secondary Road 1404 goes off to the left.

27.3 Bear right on Alexis-Lucia Road.

29.4 Turn left onto Mariposa Road (SR 1412).

31.9 Turn right onto Old Plank Road (SR 1511). There's no name sign at the turn.

34.7 Turn left onto NC–16 in Lowesville.

34.9 Turn right onto Sifford Road (SR 1397).

37.1 Turn left at a stop sign onto Killian Farm Road (SR 1396).

38.3 Turn right onto NC–73.

40.3 Turn left into Duke Power's Energy Explorium.

41.0 Return to the visitor center.

Old Plank Road (SR 1511) at Mile 31.9 recalls the plank roads that eventually connected this area with settlements and towns to the east. Duke Power's Lincoln Turbine Station is to the left. At Mile 38.3 you rejoin Highway 73 to return to the Energy Explorium. You again see Cowans Ford Dam from a different vantage point to your left just before you cross the Catawba River. Lake Norman is visible through the trees, as is the McGuire Nuclear Power Plant.

LOCAL INFORMATION

♦ Lincoln County Chamber of Commerce, P.O. Box 1617, Lincolnton, NC 28093-1617; (704) 735–3096; www.lincolnchambernc.org.

LOCAL EVENTS/ATTRACTIONS

♦ Energy Explorium offers interactive games and activities plus a virtual-reality tour of McGuire Nuclear Station. It also has picnic tables and a mile-long nature trail along the shore of Lake Norman; Monday through Friday 9:00 A.M.–5:00 P.M., Saturday and Sunday noon–5:00 P.M.; 13339 Hagers Ferry Road, Huntersville, NC 28078; no charge; (704) 875–5600 or (800) 777–0003; www.dukepower.com/ee.

RESTAURANTS

♦ Lynn's Stop & Shop, 5161 East NC–27, Iron Station, NC 28080; (704) 732–1618. Sandwiches; low range.
♦ Max & Erma's Restaurant & Gathering Place, 8700 Sam Furr Road (at Burkhead off Highway 73), Huntersville, NC 28078; (704) 895–9994. Sandwiches and salads; midrange.

ACCOMMODATIONS

♦ Sleep Inn, 16508 Northcross Drive, Huntersville, NC 28078; (704) 766–2500. Midrange.
♦ Country Suites, 16617 Statesville Road, Huntersville, NC 28078; (704) 895–6565.

BIKE SHOPS

♦ Lake Norman Bicycles, NC–21 and Gilead Road (I–77, exit 23), Huntersville, NC 28078; (704) 875–2522.

REST ROOMS

♦ At the start and finish at Energy Explorium.
♦ Mile 17.6 at a convenience store on the left on NC–73 just after Bethhaven Church Road.
♦ At about Mile 27.0 at a convenience store at the intersection of Low Bridge Road and NC–27.
♦ Mile 38.3 at Beach's Grocery at the intersection of Killian Farm Road and NC–73.

MAPS

♦ *DeLorme North Carolina Atlas & Gazetteer,* pages 56–57.
♦ Lincoln County Map by Quality Maps, 2000.

Kings Mountain Ramble

Kings Mountain Ramble connects two state parks and a national military park on a pleasant but hilly ride from southern North Carolina into northern South Carolina. From Crowders Mountain State Park in Gaston County, North Carolina, the route dips and rises through forests and farm country before it crosses the South Carolina line. Just over the line you enter Kings Mountain State Park and travel through that park to the Kings Mountain National Military Park, which is adjacent. There are limited sources of food on this route, so it's recommended that you carry provisions with you.

This tour, which starts in Crowders Mountain State Park in Gaston County, connects three parks and travels one Scenic Byway through southernmost North Carolina, dipping slightly into South Carolina. Sparrow Springs Road, the Scenic Byway, climbs slightly through the woods of the park, then passes through a residential area. Lewis Road is curvy with all styles of homes tucked into the woods on either side.

The part of Unity Church Road we're traveling is paved, although you'll see where the pavement ends. Battleground Road curves through farmland and woods as it leads to Kings Mountain. You'll know when you've crossed the South Carolina line because the road surface becomes more uneven and nar-rower. When you cross South Carolina Highway 161, the road name changes to Park Road.

Kings Mountain State Park, consisting of 6,471 acres of land, offers a broad range of activities from boating and swimming to hiking and fishing. You can get more information at the visitor center. Also in the park is a restored 1840s homestead called the Living History Farm.

Start: Visitor center in Crowders Mountain State Park.

Length: 21.5 miles.

Terrain: Rolling to hilly.

Traffic and hazards: Traffic is light until you enter the parks, which can be quite busy in the summer months. Take care crossing South Carolina Highway 161.

Getting there: From I-85 west of Gastonia, take the exit for U.S. Highway 29/74 East toward Gastonia. Turn right onto Sparrow Springs Road and follow the signs to Crowders Mountain State Park. You can park in the visitor center parking lot, which is where the ride starts. See the *DeLorme North Carolina Atlas & Gazetteer*, page 56 D2.

The destination of this ride is Kings Mountain National Military Park, one of the largest military parks in the United States. Kings Mountain is a rocky, wooded, outlying spur of the Blue Ridge Mountains, rising some 60 feet above the surrounding plain. A plateau at its summit about 600 yards long provided an excellent campsite and defensive position for Major Patrick Ferguson, leader of the British and Loyalist forces during the Revolutionary War.

Under the command of General Cornwallis, who had easily overrun South Carolina after his resounding win in Charleston, Ferguson was ordered to invade the upcountry of South Carolina. He succeeded in recruiting several thousand Carolinians of loyal British persuasion. He threatened "to lay their country waste with fire and sword." Ferguson's opponents were the "Over-Mountain Men" who hailed from the mountainous areas of Virginia, North Carolina, and South Carolina, remote country that had been little affected by the five-year-old war. Once threatened, however, they proved their mettle by hiking through deep snow and pouring rain to finally catch up with Ferguson at Kings Mountain.

Although outnumbered by the better-trained loyalists, the Over-Mountain Men remained undaunted by the odds and the weather, joining forces and forming a horseshoe around the base of the mountain. The loyalists were taken completely by surprise. The mountain men steadily advanced up the mountain against repeated bayonet charges and eventually captured the summit. Ferguson, conspicuous in his checkered hunting shirt, was fatally shot from his horse. The loyalists surrendered, flagging the spirits of their comrades and leading to Cornwallis' defeat at Guilford Courthouse the next year.

Ferguson was buried on the summit. A Scotsman, Ferguson's remains are marked with a Scottish cairn, a pile of rocks. Local legend has it that American visitors to the site should carry a rock to the summit to place on this cairn, to ensure that Ferguson has no chance to do further harm to the Carolinas. The visitor center has an audiovisual presentation on the battle, and a self-guided

Cyclist at Visitors Center in Kings Mountain Military Park. (Photo by R. Bruce Heye)

walking tour shows different aspects of the battle as well as various monuments to those who died here.

At the end of the tour, Crowders Mountain provides the perfect spot to cool off and recover from the ride.

LOCAL INFORMATION

♦ The Gaston Chamber of Commerce, 601 West Franklin Boulevard, Gastonia, NC 28052; (704) 864–2621 or (800) 348–8461; www.gastonchamber.com.
♦ Cherokee Chamber of Commerce, 225 South Limestone Street, Gaffney, SC 29340; (864) 489–5721.

LOCAL EVENTS/ATTRACTIONS

♦ Crowder Mountain State Park, a natural heritage area of 2,586 acres around the 1,625-foot mountain featuring sheer cliffs composed of quartzite, offers nature programs, hiking trails, backcountry camping, canoeing, picnic shelters, and rest rooms; 522 Park Office Lane, Kings Mountain, NC 28086; no charge; (704) 853–5375; www.ncparks.net/crmo.html.

0.0 From the visitor center parking lot on Park Office Lane in Crowders Mountain State Park, turn left onto State Park Lane.

0.2 Turn right onto Sparrow Springs Road (SR 1125).

2.4 Turn right onto Lewis Road (SR 1126).

4.1 Turn left onto Unity Church Road (SR 1102).

4.2 Turn right onto Battleground Road (SR 1100).

5.3 Cross the South Carolina state line.

6.0 Cross South Carolina Highway 161 into Kings Mountain State Park.

9.8 Turn right into the visitor center for Kings Mountain National Military Park. When you exit, turn left onto Park Road. Return back through Kings Mountain State Park.

13.6 Cross South Carolina Highway 161.

14.3 Stay on Battleground Road as you cross the North Carolina state line.

15.4 Turn right onto Unity Church Road (SR 1102).

16.2 Turn left onto Crowders Creek Road (SR 1103).

17.2 Turn left onto Sparrow Springs Road (SR 1125).

19.9 Stay on Sparrow Springs. Pinnacle Road goes off to the left.

20.4 There's a view of Crowders Mountain to the left.

21.3 Turn left onto State Park Lane.

21.5 Turn right onto Park Office Lane to the visitor center.

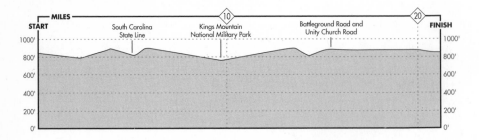

♦ Kings Mountain State Park contains a campground, picnic areas, hiking trails, and a Living History Farm with a collection of nineteenth-century long and timber structures; 1277 Park Road, Blacksburg, SC 29702; adults $1.50, children fifteen and under free, seniors sixty-five and older free; (803) 222–3209.

♦ Kings Mountain National Military Park contains a visitor center and exhibits commemorating the Battle of Kings Mountain during the Revolutionary War; 2625 Park Road, Blacksburg, SC 29702; no charge; open 9:00 A.M.–5:00 P.M. daily, until 6:00 P.M. on weekends during the summer; (864) 936–7921.

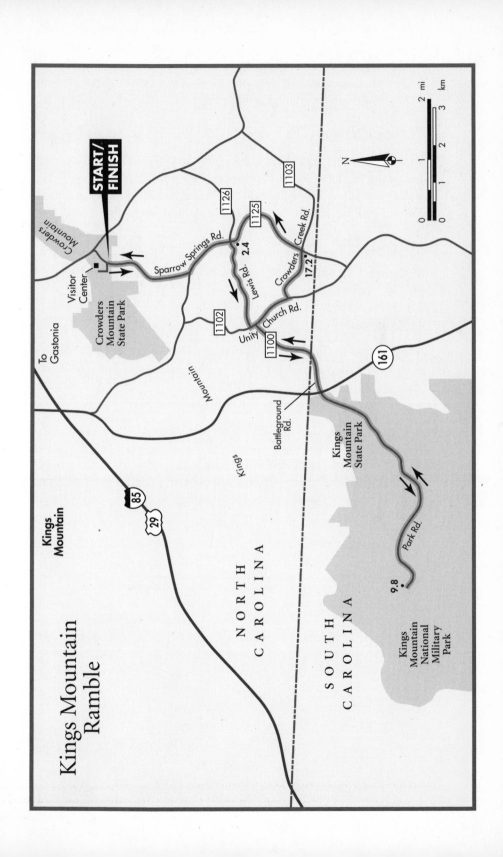

Kings Mountain Ramble

START/FINISH

Crowder's Mountain

Visitor Center

Crowders Mountain State Park

To Gastonia

Sparrow Springs Rd.

1126

1125

2.4

Lewis Rd.

Crowders Creek Rd.

1103

17.2

1102

Unity Church Rd.

1100

161

Battleground Rd.

Kings Mountain State Park

Mountain

Kings

85

29

Kings Mountain

Park Rd.

9.8

Kings Mountain National Military Park

NORTH CAROLINA

SOUTH CAROLINA

N

2 mi

km

3

2

1

1

0

0

RESTAURANTS

♦ The Captain's Cap, 3140 Linwood Road, Gastonia, NC 28052; (704) 865–7433. All-you-can-eat seafood and salad bar.

ACCOMMODATIONS

♦ Holiday Inn Express, 100 Woodlake Parkway (I–85 and Highway 161), Kings Mountain, NC 28086; (704) 734–0014 or (800) HOLIDAY. Midrange.
♦ Comfort Inn, 722 York Road (I–85 and Highway 161), Kings Mountain, NC 28086; (704) 739–7070 or (800) 228–5150. Midrange.

BIKE SHOPS

♦ Cycling & Fitness, 411 East Franklin Boulevard, Gastonia, NC 28054; (704) 865–5471 or (800) 955–RIDE.

REST ROOMS

♦ At the start and finish at the visitor center in Crowders Mountain State Park.
♦ At about Mile 7 and 12.6 at Lake Crawford Bath House in Kings Mountain State Park.
♦ Mile 9.8 at the visitor center in Kings Mountain National Military Park.

MAPS

♦ Map of Gaston County from Map Supply, Inc., 1994.
♦ North Carolina Department of Transportation Highway Map, 1997–98.
♦ *DeLorme North Carolina Atlas & Gazetteer,* page 56.

Polk County Cruise

The Polk County Cruise takes you on a 39.8-mile tour of horse country and the small towns of Columbus, Tryon, and Saluda. The rolling ups and downs of the roads in hunting country give way to steep hills as you enter Tryon. From there U.S. Highway 176 ascends a steady 6 miles up the Saluda Grade into the historic town of Saluda, where you turn around and enjoy the downhill ride. The route follows back roads to the starting point at the historic courthouse in Columbus, North Carolina.

Polk County, situated in the Carolina foothills, serves as a gateway to Asheville and the mountains to the west. Before you begin riding, take a moment to study the historic Polk County Courthouse. Built by slaves in 1857, it holds a place in the National Register of Historic Places and still has its original slave block out front.

Much of this route traverses horse country, as you can tell by the names. The hardwood forests along Peniel Road break to present the first large horse farms as you turn onto Red Fox Road (SR 1519). Immaculate white horse fences line this section of the route punctuated with yellow caution signs warning about horses and carriages in the area. Along Hunting Country Road (SR 1501) after Mile 4.9 you're rewarded with a great vista to your left before you cross the creek.

Amazing blankets of kudzu encroach on the road; you can almost see it spreading before your very eyes. Farms in the area sport names like Red Fox and Breezy Hill. Half a mile after you turn onto Hunting Country Road (SR 1501) at Mile 6.8, the road curves sharply and leads to FENCE, the Foothills Equestrian Nature Center. This 300-acre nature preserve incorporates hiking

Start: From the front of the courthouse in downtown Columbus, North Carolina.
Length: 39.8 miles.
Terrain: Rolling to hilly with some very long and/or steep climbs.
Traffic and hazards: Because of the mountainous terrain, US 176 is the main road connecting Tryon to Saluda; traffic can be heavy at times. Fortunately there's a climbing lane as you ascend the mountain into Saluda.
Getting there: From US 74 or I–26 in western North Carolina, take North Carolina Highway 108 into Columbus. NC–108 is the main street, which is called East Mills Street. The courthouse is to the right as you head into town. There is a parking lot south of the courthouse as well as on-street parking in the area. The ride begins in front of the courthouse. See the *DeLorme North Carolina Atlas & Gazetteer*, page 54 C2.

and riding trails, picnic areas, and a pond with boardwalk. Open to the public year-round, the facility hosts equestrian events, concerts, and private gatherings in its lodge. Its large and natural setting makes it perfect for bird-watching.

At Mile 8.5, after you cross I–26 for the third time, Chinquapin Farm spreads out against a glorious mountain backdrop. New Market Road's curvy and somewhat rough surface looks down on cornfields in the valley before climbing through a residential area into Tryon. The town's Thermal Belt—an unusual microclimate that is usually free of dew and frost—ensures an enjoyable climate, whatever the season, although the surrounding hills change colors to mark time's passing.

A North Carolina Scenic Byway, US 176 keeps pace with the Pacolet River as it rolls past lovely mountain retreats, dense forests barely eclipsing the mountains that lie behind. At the intersection of US 176 and Warrior Road, you begin the climb into Saluda. Don't let the flat stretch at the beginning fool you. But if your legs and lungs can handle it, Saluda is well worth the effort.

Called a "town the railroad built," Saluda nestles at the crest of the Saluda Grade, the steepest mainline railroad grade in the United States. Fortunately a climbing lane provides extra space for cyclists going into Saluda, and signs along the route encourage motorists to share the road with bicycles. About halfway up the grade, if you need to rest for a moment, a perfect stopping point overlooks Pearson's Falls on the Pacolet River.

Other visual respites along the way come from tiny waterfalls tumbling over massive rocks to the road's edge and streams that crisscross the highway. Log houses and artisans' shops such as Fig Falls Pottery and Valhalla Hand Weavers pique your curiosity. Your strenuous efforts are rewarded when you arrive at the Wildflour Bakery or one of the fine restaurants in Saluda. However, the Wildflour Bakery is the favorite stopping point for cyclists from a broad area around Polk County. Operated as a cooperative run by a few dozen women, the shop tempts you with freshly baked sticky buns and other

A long unused slave block still stands in front of the historic Polk County Courthouse.

0.0 Facing the front of the courthouse, go to the right to the stop sign in front of the jail. Turn right at the stop sign onto West Ward Street.

0.1 Turn left at the next stop sign (no street sign there) onto Walker Street.

0.2 Turn right onto Peniel Road (SR 1521).

1.5 Bear left to stay on Peniel.

2.9 Turn right onto Red Fox Road (SR 1519).

4.9 Turn right onto Hunting Country Road (SR 1501). *Note:* Great vista to the left.

5.6 Cross the creek and bear left around a ninety-degree curve.

6.0 Cross over I-26.

6.8 Turn right to stay on Hunting Country Road (SR 1501). East Prince Road goes straight ahead.

7.3 Follow the sharp right curve.

7.7 Cross under I-26.

8.5 Cross I-26 for the third time. *Note:* There's a glorious view across Chinquapin Farm.

12.8 Turn right onto New Market Road (SR 1502), which passes through Tryon. Watch out for the steep hills.

14.7 Turn right onto South Trade Street (US 176).

15.2 Veer left onto US 176 West toward Saluda.

16.2 Cross the Pacolet River.

21.0 Pass Pearson's Falls Overlook.

24.1 Enter downtown Saluda. *Note:* Look for the Wildflour Bakery on the left. After a visit, turn around and go east on US 176.

31.9 Turn left onto Warrior Road (SR 1125).

34.4 Turn left onto Howard Gap Road (SR 1122), which is a sharp turn.

34.6 Turn right onto Old Howard Gap Road (SR 1122).

35.4 Turn left onto NC-108, which is also called Lynn Road.

35.7 Turn left onto Skyuka Road (SR 1135).

39.7 Turn left onto East Mills Street in Columbus.

39.8 Turn right into the courthouse parking lot.

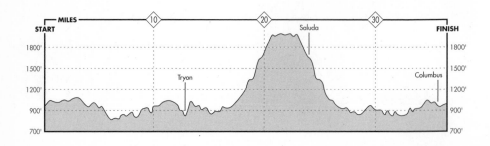

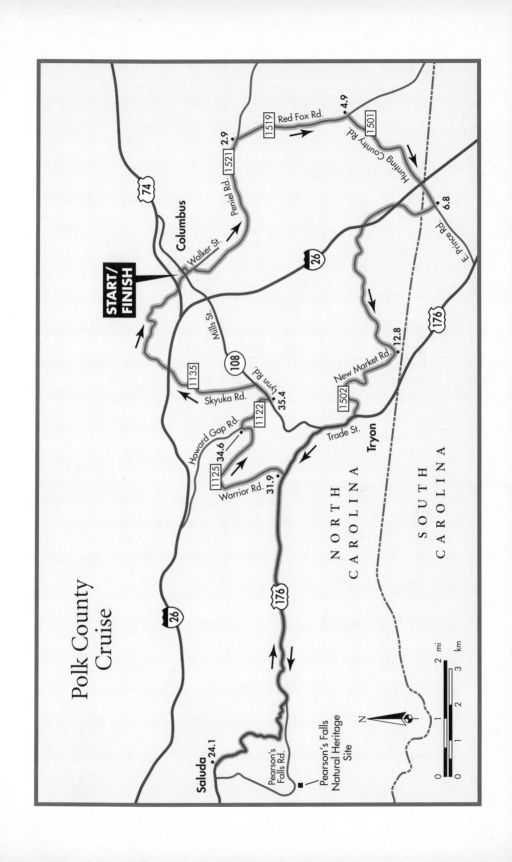

Polk County
Cruise

START/
FINISH

Columbus

Walker St.

74

1521 Peniel Rd.
• 2.9

1519 Red Fox Rd. →
• 4.9

1501

Hunting Country Rd.

E. Prince Rd.
• 6.8

26

176

Mills St.

108

1135

Skyuka Rd. ←

Lynn Rd.
35.4

New Market Rd.

12.8

1502

1122

Trade St.

Tryon

Howard Gap Rd.

34.6

1125

Warrior Rd.
31.9

NORTH
CAROLINA

SOUTH
CAROLINA

26

176

Saluda
• 24.1

Pearson's
Falls Rd.

Pearson's Falls
Natural Heritage
Site

N

0   1   2 mi
0   1   2   3 km

delicious offerings. Outside tables allow you to enjoy both the goodies and the view when the weather's nice.

Saluda's downtown area remains much as it looked in the past and is honored with a listing on the National Register of Historic Places. Two walking tours are mapped out—or you can just stroll around before you head down the mountain and wind your way back to Columbus.

LOCAL INFORMATION

♦ Polk County Department of Travel and Tourism, 425 North Trade Street, Tryon, NC 28782; (828) 859–8300 or (800) 440–7848; visitpolk@teleplex.net.

LOCAL EVENTS/ATTRACTIONS

♦ Historic Polk County Courthouse was completed in 1859, four years after the county was permanently established. Built by slaves using native clay bricks, the two-story Greek Revival structure has recently been restored. Listed on the National Register of Historic Places, the courthouse is the only permanent courthouse in Polk County's history; no charge.

♦ Blue Ridge BBQ Festival, an annual event held in June in Tryon, no charge; (828) 859–RIBS; www.blueridgebbqfestival.com.

♦ Rockhouse Vineyards, offering tastings of its award-winning wines; 1525 Turner Road, Tryon, NC 28782; no charge; (828) 863–2784; www.rockhouse vineyards.com.

♦ Foothills Equestrian Nature Center (FENCE), a 320-acre nature preserve offering concerts and other events, hiking trails, picnic areas; Hunting Country Road, Tryon, NC 28782; charges for some events; (828) 859–9021.

♦ Pacolet Scenic Byway, a 10-mile scenic drive on US 176 from Tryon to Saluda with views of the Pacolet River, waterfalls, and scenic vistas; no charge.

♦ Pearson's Falls Natural Heritage Site, a privately owned retreat with picnic areas, hiking trails, a 90-foot waterfall; Pearson's Falls Road, Saluda, closed Monday, and closed Tuesday from November through March; admission charged; (828) 749–3031.

RESTAURANTS

♦ The Purple Onion Café & Coffeehouse, 16 Main Street, Saluda, NC 28773; (828) 749–1179. Creative sandwiches, salads, pizza; lunch and dinner daily except Wednesday and Sunday; midrange.

♦ Preston's Pub & Grill, 218 North Trade Street, Tryon, NC 28782; (828) 859–9615. Lunch and dinner daily; sandwiches and ribs; midrange.

♦ The Brick Pizzeria, 311 Mills Street, Columbus, NC 28722; (828) 894–2299; lunch and dinner Tuesday through Friday; dinner only Saturday through Monday; Italian; midrange.

ACCOMMODATIONS

♦ Mimosa Inn, Mimosa Inn Drive, off NC–108, Tryon, NC 28782; (828) 859–7688 or (877) 646–6724; www.carolina-foothills.com. Restored historic landmark between Tryon and Columbus; mid- to upper range.
♦ Days Inn, 501 West Mills Street, Columbus, NC 28722; (828) 894–3303 or (800) 325–2525; midrange.

BIKE SHOPS

♦ None.

REST ROOMS

♦ At the start and finish in government buildings in Columbus during weekdays.
♦ At about Mile 7.0 at the Foothills Equestrian Nature Center (FENCE).
♦ At about Mile 15.1 at the Polk County Visitors Center.
♦ Mile 15.2 at the convenience store at the intersection of South Trade Street and US 176.
♦ Mile 24.1 in restaurants in downtown Saluda.

MAPS

♦ Polk County Map by Southern Engineering GPP, Inc., 2002.

Hendersonville—Flat Rock Challenge

The Hendersonville–Flat Rock Challenge will try your skills not only at distance but also at climbing. This 44.4-mile ride takes you from downtown Hendersonville past apple orchards to the east side of the county then south to Flat Rock. From there the route loops through the southwestern corner then curves around Davis Mountain on the way back into Hendersonville. While many of the roads are gentle ups and downs, there are some serious hills. Few services are available from Flat Rock west, so plan accordingly for your water and snack needs.

Historic downtown Hendersonville, the starting point for this ride, has managed to maintain the charm and advantages of a traditional downtown. Main Street, with its many trees and planters overflowing with colorful flowers, is clearly designed for pedestrians, although some on-street parking is provided. Main Street is lined with an eclectic mix of antiques and gift shops, clothing stores and restaurants. Sidewalks are always busy, and you'll see lots of out-of-town license plates, a testament to the town's appeal. Take some time to stroll through the area either before or after your ride. In summer you'll be tempted by the ice cream and lemonade stands on the sidewalk.

The route takes you from downtown through Jackson Park and toward the east side of Henderson County. You'll pass the Henderson County airport and the Western North Carolina Air Museum on Airport Road. You'll find that Tracy Grove and Orchard Roads are aptly named for the rolling hills covered with apple trees of all varieties. You'll see why Hendersonville hosts the North Carolina Apple Festival each September.

On Upward Road the route turns south toward the communities of Flat Rock and East Flat Rock. Flat Rock was established in the mid–nineteenth century by wealthy Charlestonians, Europeans, and prominent plantation owners of South Carolina's Low Country, who built large summer estates in the English manner. These families came to the North Carolina mountains to escape the sweltering heat, yellow fever, and malaria that plagued the Low Country in summer. The entire district of Flat Rock is included in the National Register of Historic Places. Besides being the site of Carl Sandburg's home, Flat Rock features several attractions such as St. John in the Wilderness Episcopal Church, Historic Woodfield Inn, and the Singleton Centre art studios as well as many unique specialty shops and enterprises.

THE BASICS

Start: At the intersection of Church Street and Fourth Avenue in downtown Hendersonville.
Length: 44.4 miles.
Terrain: Rolling to very hilly with some steep climbs.
Traffic and hazards: Watch out for rough railroad tracks on Fourth Avenue as you leave downtown. On Jeter Mountain Road there's a steep downhill with sharp curves that you shouldn't take too fast.
Getting there: Take U.S. Highway 64 to Hendersonville and turn left onto Church Street, which is one-way south. A public parking lot is available at the intersection of Church Street and Fourth Avenue, where the route begins. See the *DeLorme North Carolina Atlas & Gazetteer*, page 53 C7.

Carl Sandburg's house at Connemara stands on a hilltop overlooking the farm.

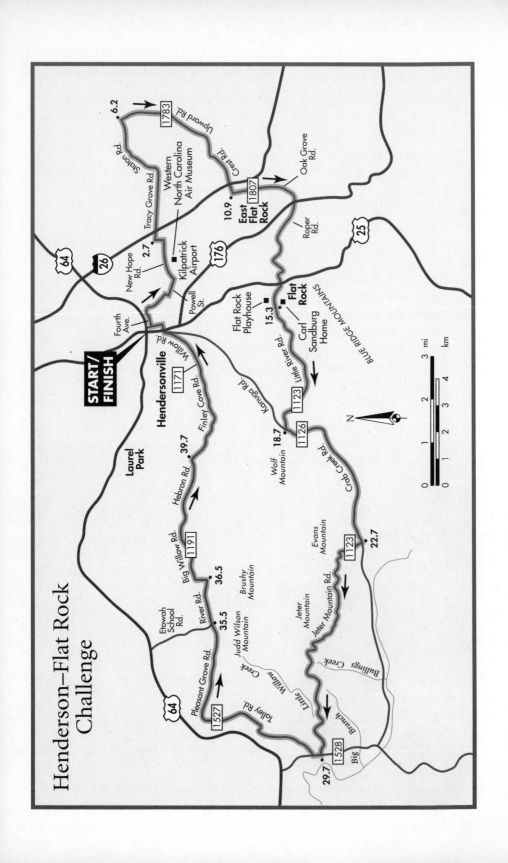

Henderson–Flat Rock Challenge

0.0 At the intersection of Fourth Avenue and Church Street in downtown Hendersonville, go east on Fourth Avenue (toward Main Street). *Note:* The Mineral and Lapidary Museum is on the corner of Fourth Avenue and Main Street.

0.5 Enter Jackson Park on Fourth Avenue; the road's name changes to Glover Street (SR 1758) in the park.

1.4 Turn left onto Powell Street (SR 1763).

1.7 Turn left onto New Hope Road (SR 1757) then continue straight on Airport Road at the stop sign where Airport Road goes to the right. *Note:* Check out the Western North Carolina Air Museum.

2.5 Turn left to stay on Airport Road (SR 1755).

2.7 Turn right onto Tracy Grove Road (SR 1793).

4.3 Cross Howard Gap Road. Tracy Grove Road's name changes to Staton Road (SR 1795).

6.0 Turn left onto Orchard Road (SR 1796).

6.2 Turn right onto Upward Road (SR 1783).

8.9 Turn left onto Crest Road (SR 1804).

9.8 Cross over I–26.

10.9 Turn left onto Oak Grove Road (SR 1807).

12.6 Cross Spartanburg Highway/US 176 onto Roper Road (SR 1807), where you pick up North Carolina Bike Route 8.

13.6 Turn left onto West Blue Ridge Road (SR 1812).

14.8 Turn right onto Greenville Highway/US 25 in Flat Rock.

14.9 Turn left onto Little River Road (SR 1123). *Note:* Flat Rock Playhouse is on the right.

15.3 Entrance to the Carl Sandburg Home. After your visit, turn left and continue on Little River Road. *FYI:* Bicycles are not allowed on roads or trails at Connemara. A bike rack is provided in the parking lot.

18.7 Turn left onto Crab Creek Road (SR 1126).

22.7 Turn right onto Jeter Mountain Road (SR 1123).

(continued)

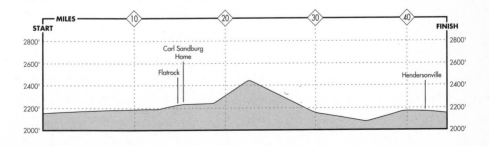

29.7 Turn right onto Crab Creek Road (SR 1528).

29.9 Turn right onto Talley Road (SR 1527). The road's name changes to Pleasant Grove Road when you reenter Henderson County.

35.5 At the intersection with Etowah School Road, continue straight. Pleasant Grove Road's name changes to River Road (SR 1191).

36.5 Turn left onto Big Willow Road (SR 1191).

36.9 Big Willow Road's name changes to Hebron Road.

39.7 Go straight onto Finley Cove Road (SR 1171). Hebron Road goes off to the left.

41.6 Go straight onto Willow Road (SR 1171). Willow Road goes to the right as well.

42.0 At the intersection with Price Street, go straight on Willow Road, which becomes Willow Street when you enter Hendersonville.

43.4 Turn left onto Kanuga Street.

43.8 Turn left onto King Street.

44.2 Turn left onto Fourth Avenue.

44.4 Arrive at the intersection with Church Street.

Carl Sandburg was already famous when he retired at age sixty-seven with his family to Connemara, his quiet 240-acre retreat in the Blue Ridge Mountains near Flat Rock. Here this poet, minstrel, lecturer, biographer, and Pulitzer Prize–winning author spent the last twenty-two years of his long, productive life. While in residence at Connemara, he published a novel, his autobiography, and several volumes of history and poetry, including the *Complete Poems* for which he won the Pulitzer in 1951. Life at Connemara was busy, too, for Mrs. Sandburg and her daughters, who continued to breed and care for a large, prizewinning goat herd and run the farm business. It's well worth a stop to walk about the estate and tour the home. Walking trails crisscross the mountain, and the barn is also open to tourists; however, bicycles are not allowed on the road or trails.

Another attraction here is the Flat Rock Playhouse, considered one of the ten best seasonal theaters in the country. With a fifty-year history, the playhouse presents quality entertainment, rarely found so far from Broadway, such as comedies, American classics, musicals, farces, and whodunits. Matinees and evening performances are given from mid-March to mid-October. You'll want to call ahead to see what's playing and reserve your tickets.

After you leave Flat Rock, be prepared for a narrow road with climbs and blind curves, but fortunately much of this route is shaded, with lots of lakes to cool your spirit if not your body. Appropriately named Jeter Mountain Road will take you up several curvy climbs. Take care not to pick up too much speed on the steep downhill with its sharp curves. You'll get a respite along Pleasant Grove Road, which is fairly level as you meander through the western side of the county.

Hebron Road involves a climb along roads guarded by large clusters of rhododendron that help screen the mountain houses hidden in the dense forests. Finley Cove Road curves around Davis Mountain and the beautiful town of Laurel Park before Willow Road leads you back into Hendersonville.

LOCAL INFORMATION

◆ Henderson County Travel and Tourism, P.O. Box 721, Hendersonville, NC 28793; (828) 693–9708 or (800) 828–4244; www.historichendersonville.com.

LOCAL EVENTS/ATTRACTIONS

◆ North Carolina Apple Festival, an annual event held the first weekend of September with crafts, entertainment, food, and more; downtown Hendersonville; no charge; (828) 697–4557.
◆ Connemara—Carl Sandburg's Home, declared a National Historic Site in 1968, including the main house that dates from 1838; a variety of programs

A bike sculpture has a companion on Main Street in downtown Hendersonville.

(birth of baby goats in spring, poetry readings, musical events, and dramatic performances), numerous hiking trails; bicycles are not allowed on the estate's roads or trails; open daily except for Thanksgiving, Christmas, and New Year's Day; 1928 Little River Road, Flat Rock, NC 28731; no charge except for the home tour; (828) 693–4178; www.nps.gov.carl.

♦ Flat Rock Playhouse, considered one of the ten best seasonal theaters in the country, presents comedies, American classics, musicals, farces, and whodunits; US 25 and Little River Road, Flat Rock; open from late May through mid-October, with matinees and evening performances Wednesday through Sunday; ticket prices vary; (828) 693–0731; www.flatrockplay house.org.

♦ Historic Main Street in Hendersonville, entered into the National Register of Historic Places in 1988, specialty and antiques shops and many activities including the North Carolina Apple Festival during Labor Day weekend, art shows, street dances, and parades throughout the year; no charge; (828) 697–2022; www.historichendersonville.com.

♦ Mineral and Lapidary Museum of Henderson County, established in 1997 to house exhibits from North Carolina and the Smithsonian, English minerals, Indian artifacts, and a special exhibit of fossils, gems, and fluorescent minerals; located at the corner of Fourth Avenue and Main Street on the lower level of the Henderson County Genealogical and Historical Society building in downtown Hendersonville; Monday through Friday 1:00–5:00 P.M. and Saturday 10:00 A.M.–5:00 P.M.; no charge; (828) 698–1977; www.minmuseum.org.

♦ Western North Carolina Air Museum, the first air museum in North Carolina, with award-winning restored and replica antique and vintage airplanes; Hendersonville Airport at 1340 Gilbert Street, Hendersonville, NC 28792; Wednesday, Saturday, and Sunday noon–6:00 P.M. (weather permitting); no charge; (828) 698–2482; www.wncairmuseum.com.

RESTAURANTS

♦ Hannah Flanagan's Pub & Eatery, 300 North Main Street, Hendersonville, NC 28792; (828) 696–1665. Authentic pub food plus sandwiches and salads; lunch and dinner seven days a week; midrange.

♦ The Park Deli Café & Pizza Company, 437 North Main Street, Hendersonville, NC 28792; (828) 696–3663. Creative sandwiches and salads; breakfast Tuesday through Saturday, lunch and dinner Monday through Saturday; Sunday brunch; midrange.

♦ Papa's Dog House, 104 Blue Ridge Road, East Flat Rock, NC 28726; (828) 697–9005. Sandwiches; lunch Monday through Saturday; low range.

ACCOMMODATIONS

♦ Waverly Inn, 783 North Main Street, Hendersonville, NC 28792; (828) 693–9193 or (800) 537–8195; www.waverlyinn.com. Mid- to upper range; in business since 1898.

♦ Best Western Inn, I–26 and U.S. Highway 64 East, Hendersonville, NC 28792; (828) 692–0521. Midrange.

BIKE SHOPS

♦ The Bicycle Company of Hendersonville, 779 North Church Street, Hendersonville, NC 28792; (828) 696–1500; www.thebikecompany.com.

♦ Justice Cycle Sales, 137 Orr's Camp Road, Hendersonville, NC 28792; (828) 693–3952.

REST ROOMS

♦ At the start and finish in restaurants in downtown Hendersonville.

♦ Mile 0.6 in Jackson Park; rest rooms are in the picnic area.

♦ Mile 15.3 at the Carl Sandburg Home; rest rooms are located near the parking lot.

♦ Mile 43.4 at a convenience store on Kanuga Street.

MAPS

♦ *DeLorme North Carolina Atlas & Gazetteer,* pages 53–54.

French Broad River Cruise

The French Broad River Cruise, amazingly enough in light of the surrounding terrain, is not difficult because it wanders through the French Broad River valley, caressing the river along much of its 40.3-mile route. It ranges from tree-shaded lanes to country roads, passing lovely pastures with a profusion of wildflowers blooming along the roadside in the warm months. Throughout, you have wonderful views of the mountains that surround this peaceful valley. The route starts in downtown Brevard then follows country roads into western Henderson County, returning to Transylvania County by Crab Creek Road. The route turns west and then south to follow the river as it meanders through the broad valley south of Brevard and then takes U.S. Highway 276 back into downtown Brevard.

This tour starts in downtown Brevard but quickly reaches quiet country roads as it meanders through the French Broad River valley in Transylvania County, making much of the route relatively flat. As you prepare to begin, be sure to note the impressive stone wall surrounding the Brevard College campus. The wall and arch are listed on the National Register of Historic Places.

Transylvania County was formed from parts of Henderson and Jackson Counties about the time North Carolina seceded from the Union on May 20, 1861. The first order of business was to build a two-story brick courthouse and jail. However, North Carolina had just voted that very day to secede from the Union, so the tax moneys they collected had to be used to send local recruits to the Civil War.

At that time, the area was inhabited by native Indians and white settlers, attracted to the area from the late 1700s by the mild climate, rich soil, abundant wildlife and game, and beautiful setting. This route demonstrates the attractiveness of the area and why settlers and tourists have been drawn here since the earliest European settlements were established.

There's a bit of traffic to contend with at the beginning and very end. US 64/276 is a divided, four-lane highway but not fully controlled access, so cyclists can use it. Fortunately the lanes are wide and the distance along this road is not great. Once you turn onto US 64, the road is two-lane, again with wide lanes and a smooth road surface.

THE BASICS

Start: The parking lot at College Plaza Shopping Center across the street from Brevard College.
Length: 40.3 miles.
Terrain: Amazingly level to rolling with just a few hills.
Traffic and hazards: Broad Street (US 64/276) is five lanes and can be busy, but you're on it for just a short distance.
Getting there: Take US 64 to Brevard in Transylvania County. The College Plaza Shopping Center will be on the right across Broad Street (US 64/276) from Brevard College in downtown Brevard. See the *DeLorme North Carolina Atlas & Gazetteer*, page 53 D5.

At Mile 6.4 you leave the traffic, turning onto Crab Creek Road (SR 1528) for a more rural and peaceful setting. Along Talley Road the road flirts with the French Broad River while Queen Anne's lace, daylilies, dandelions, and wild sweet peas grace the roadside. The river supposedly got its name from Frenchman Jean Couture in 1696. He was a follower of explorer Robert Cavelier LaSalle. The river is noted for its complexity with four major forks: the North Fork, the West Fork, the East Fork, and the Middle Fork. Its valley through the Brevard area is considered one of the most beautiful river valleys in North Carolina, draining approximately 2,800 square miles of mountains and valleys.

You'll see little traffic on this flat to rolling route as you pass a tree nursery and dairy farm and negotiate the sharp curves, necessitated by the whims of the river. The road's name changes to Pleasant Grove Road when you cross into Henderson County. Pleasant Grove Road's name changes to River Road (SR 1191) at the intersection with Etowah School Road.

After you turn onto Big Willow Road, broad bands of corn dress the shoulders of the river in summer and an apple orchard provides a temptation to summer cyclists. After you turn again onto Crab Creek Road, you'll be treated in summer to trees shading the road, the shade broken only by clumps of bright daylilies and pale pink rhododendron flowers.

Along Everett Road (SR 1533) horses graze lazily on the lush green grasses growing in the rich soil of the riverbank. At Mile 31 the road kisses the river-

The dramatic stone wall at Brevard College serves as a backdrop for a cyclist.

bank and you have great views of the gently gurgling river, which isn't very deep but spreads wide in places.

As you swing south of Brevard along Wilson Road (SR 1540) you'll pass the Glen Cannon Golf Course. Bright orange daylilies line the road's edge in summer and buffer the road from the verdant green pastures. The gentle ups and downs of the route appear minor when compared to the steep hillsides all around the valley. Along Elm Bend Road you see neatly tended vegetable gardens in the small communities that periodically people the route.

As you come back into Brevard on US 276, Silvermont Park will be on your left. U.S. Highway 276 joins US 64 in the heart of downtown Brevard, with its tree-shaded streets and inviting front porches. The charming old downtown area is perfect for strolling or lounging in one of the many cafes.

In summer Brevard teems with visitors as musicians from across the country gather for the internationally renowned Brevard Music Festival, which runs from late June through early August. Concurrent with the festival is a summer camp to provide quality music education for talented young people. A steady schedule of more than fifty concerts and operas attracts tens of thousands of visitors from across the country to the festival's covered amphitheater, which seats about 1,500. This influx means that area restaurants stay busy and reservations are advised during the festival. Famous guest musicians such as Mitch Miller and Keith Lockhart attest to the acclaim of the festival and its wide appeal in the musical community.

Founded in 1936 by Dr. James Christian Pfohl, the Music Center began as a summer camp for boys. Dr. Pfohl, a music professor at Davidson College, decided that the college's music facilities should be used during the summer months. Summer sessions were held on the Davidson College campus until World War II began and all the campus was needed for military barracks. The operation moved then to Queens College, a woman's college in Charlotte, and became coeducational. The search for the perfect setting for the program of outdoor recreation and instruction for music and art led to the establishment of the Music Center in Brevard.

LOCAL INFORMATION

♦ Transylvania County Tourism Development Authority, 35 West Main Street, Brevard, NC 28712; (828) 883–3700.

LOCAL EVENTS/ATTRACTIONS

♦ Holmes State Educational Forest includes a Forestry Center with exhibits, Talking Tree Trail, educational classes, hiking trails; located on Crab Creek Road; Route 4, Box 308, Hendersonville, NC 28739; open from mid-March to the Friday before Thanksgiving; closed Monday; call for hours of operation. (828) 692–0100
♦ Brevard College's stone wall and gate are listed on the National Register of Historic Places; Broad Street, Brevard, NC 28712; no charge.
♦ Brevard Music Festival, classical and pops concerts, operas, lectures, recitals from mid-June to early August; Brevard Music Center, Brevard, NC 28712; ticket prices vary; (888) 884–2011; www.brevardmusic.org.
♦ Downtown Brevard has an interesting mix of shops and restaurants.

RESTAURANTS

♦ Pepper Mill Café, 708 North Broad Street, Brevard, NC 28712; (828) 884–7400. Sandwiches and salads; breakfast and lunch Monday through Saturday, Sunday brunch; low range.
♦ Kelly's Family Dining, 306 North Broad Street, Brevard, NC 28712; (828) 884–3725. Sandwiches and plate lunches; breakfast and lunch Tuesday through Sunday; closed Monday; low range.

ACCOMMODATIONS

♦ The Inn at Brevard, 410 East Main Street, Brevard, NC 28712; (828) 884–2105; brevardinn@citcom.net. Mid- to upper range.

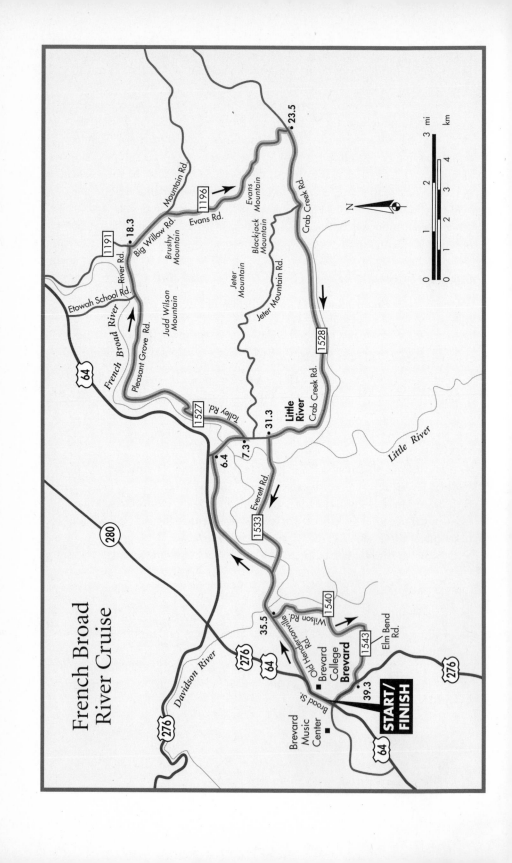

French Broad
River Cruise

0.0 From the College Plaza Shopping Center on Broad Street, across from Brevard College, turn left onto Broad Street (US 64/276). *Note:* The stone wall around the college campus is listed on the National Register of Historic Places.

0.5 Bear right onto Old Hendersonville Road (SR 1533). U.S. Highway 64/276 goes off to the left.

6.4 Turn right onto Crab Creek Road (SR 1528).

7.3 Turn left onto Talley Road (SR 1527). Talley Road's name changes to Pleasant Grove Road when you cross into Henderson County.

11.6 Pleasant Grove Road curves to the right, and its name changes to River Road at the intersection with Etowah School Road.

18.3 Turn right onto Big Willow Road (SR 1191).

19.5 Big Willow Road's name changes to Evans Road (SR 1196) at the intersection with Mountain Road.

23.5 Turn right onto Crab Creek Road (SR 1127).

31.3 Turn left onto Everett Road (SR 1533).

34.4 Turn left onto Old Hendersonville Road (SR 1533).

35.5 Turn left onto Wilson Road (SR 1540), about 0.2 mile after crossing the bridge. The road sign is hidden by a building but it's just past the traffic signal.

38.0 Turn right onto Elm Bend Road (SR 1543).

39.3 Turn right onto US 276.

39.5 Turn right to stay on US 276.

40.0 At the intersection, turn right onto Broad Street (US 64/276).

40.3 Turn left into the parking lot at the College Plaza Shopping Center.

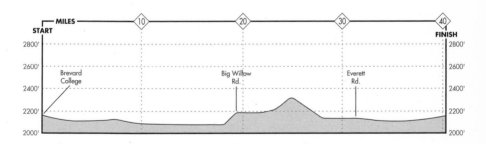

♦ Holiday Inn Express, 1570 Asheville Highway, Brevard, NC 28712; (828) 862–8900 or (800) 465–4329. Midrange.

BIKE SHOPS

♦ None.

♦ At the start and finish in restaurants.

♦ Mile 1.7 at a convenience store on Old Hendersonville Road.

♦ At about Mile 25.0 at Holmes State Educational Forest.

♦ At about Mile 39.5 at Silvermont Park.

♦ Mile 40.0 at public rest rooms located one block north of the intersection of US 276 and Broad Street.

MAPS

♦ *DeLorme North Carolina Atlas & Gazetteer,* page 53.

Whitewater Falls Ramble

T he Whitewater Falls Ramble, although only 17.2 miles, provides quite a challenge in this mountainous area known for its
numerous waterfalls. The ride starts at the intersection of U.S. Highway
64 and North Carolina Highway 281 and travels south along NC–281
to Whitewater Falls, then retraces the same route back to Sapphire. The
route includes several long climbs, eliminating any doubt that you're in
the mountains, but the spectacular falls make the ride worth it.

Whitewater Falls, the highest cascade east of the Mississippi River, forms
the dividing line between Jackson and Transylvania Counties. The water tumbles steeply over large boulders in tiers to the floor 411 feet below. The Indian
name for the falls was Charashilactay, which meant "white water." The spectacular view of the falls from below greets visitors to the scenic area about half a
mile from the parking area. More adventurous souls can hike a steep trail to the
top of the falls. This vantage point gets you closer to the falls, but the view is
not nearly as breathtaking as that from below. These sights make the rather
strenuous trip well worth the effort.

Keep this in mind as you start the ride because the first climb comes at Mile
1.6 and continues for 0.7 mile. At Mile 2.2 you'll cross the Horsepasture River,
which itself hosts numerous waterfalls. Another climb—0.6 mile in length—
awaits you at Mile 3.5.

At Mile 7.2 you enter the Nantahala National Forest and 0.6 mile later cross
the Whitewater River, which feeds the falls. At Mile 8.6 you'll see the sign for
the Nantahala National Forest Whitewater Falls Scenic Area on your left. A
short road brings you to the ranger hut and parking area. There are rest rooms

Whitewater Falls tumbles over rocks to the floor 411 feet below.

and water sources here. You pay a modest user's fee per vehicle to enter the park.

Because the falls are actually situated on the boundary between what are now Jackson and Transylvania Counties, both claim it as a local attraction. This situation amounts to friendly sharing compared to the bitter battle between North Carolina and Georgia over the exact locations of the states' common boundary. The battle started early in the nineteenth century when—given the increasing population in the area—it became more important to establish property lines and state boundaries. In the Transylvania-Jackson region, the matter was complicated because many people held land grants from both North Carolina and Georgia.

The state of Georgia, believing its northern boundary to run along 35 degrees north latitude, created Walton County there, while North Carolina claimed the same area. Both states were performing governmental actions in the same area at the same time. According to historian Martin Skaggs, the opposition became active and violent; administrative officials were beaten and abused, and it was impossible to collect taxes. These chaotic conditions attracted outlaws and violent refugees, who further added to the confusion. There was even an armed confrontation between governmental forces on each side around 1810. The Carolinas won those battles and, as a result, Georgia's northern boundary was moved so far west that it does not even touch Transylvania County today.

The issue was even resurrected in 1971 when Georgia named a legislative commission to study the issue. North Carolina legislators from the area jumped to the defense. Fortunately, both states' proposals died in committee. Otherwise Whitewater Falls might today be in Georgia.

Transylvania County prides itself on being one of the state's most beautiful, with its rugged mountain peaks and gorgeous river valleys. More than half the county is included in either the Pisgah National Forest (83,000 acres) or the Nantahala National Forest (5,000 acres).

The magnificent variations in altitude—from 1,025 feet at the lowest point to 6,045 feet on Tanassee Bald—create more than 250 waterfalls in the county,

0.0 From the parking lot at businesses along US 64 in Sapphire, turn right and head south on NC–281.

0.9 Pass the entrance to Gorges State Park.

2.2 Cross the Horsepasture River.

7.2 Enter the Nantahala National Forest.

7.8 Cross the Whitewater River.

8.6 Turn left into the scenic area for Whitewater Falls. After your visit, turn around and retrace the route.

17.2 Arrive back in Sapphire.

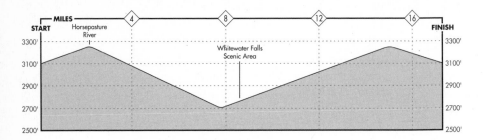

more than any other county in the United States. Waterfall guidebooks are available from both the USDA Forest Service and local bookstores in the area if you're interested in visiting other sites.

LOCAL INFORMATION

♦ Transylvania County Tourism Development Authority, 35 West Main Street, Brevard, NC 28712; (828) 883–3700.

LOCAL EVENTS/ATTRACTIONS

♦ Whitewater Falls Recreation Area, picnic tables, rest rooms, hiking trails; NC–281 near the South Carolina border; $2.00-per-vehicle park fee.

RESTAURANTS

♦ Sapphire Country Store, intersection of US 64 and NC–281, Sapphire, NC 28774. Pizzas, subs, biscuits, salads; low range.

ACCOMMODATIONS

♦ The Inn at Brevard, 410 East Main Street, Brevard, NC 28712; (828) 884–2105; brevardinn@citcom.net. Mid- to upper range.

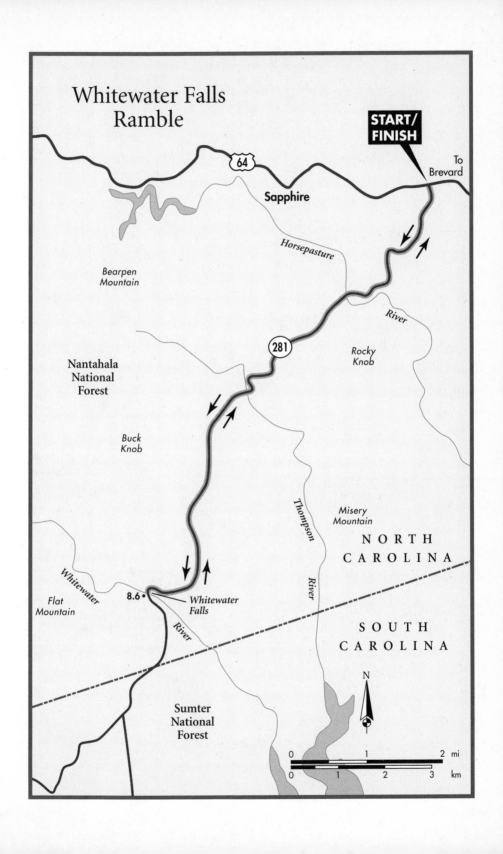

Whitewater Falls
Ramble

START/ FINISH

To Brevard

64

Sapphire

Horsepasture

Bearpen
Mountain

River

281

Rocky
Knob

Nantahala
National
Forest

Buck
Knob

Misery
Mountain

Thompson

NORTH
CAROLINA

River

Whitewater

Flat
Mountain

8.6

Whitewater
Falls

River

SOUTH
CAROLINA

Sumter
National
Forest

N

0   1   2 mi
0   1   2   3 km

♦ Holiday Inn Express, 1570 Asheville Highway, Brevard, NC 28712; (828) 862–8900 or (800) 465–4329. Midrange.

BIKE SHOPS

♦ None.

REST ROOMS

♦ At the start and finish at Sapphire County Store.
♦ Mile 8.6 at Whitewater Falls Recreation Area.

MAPS

♦ *DeLorme North Carolina Atlas & Gazetteer,* page 70.

Cedar Mountain Cruise

The 36.1-mile Cedar Mountain Cruise makes a loop from Brevard through the small communities of Pisgah Forest, Little River, Cedar Mountain, and Connestee before returning to Brevard. Offering great variety, the route winds through the French Broad River valley on fairly level roads. As the route dips into Henderson County, you'll encounter some climbs. After a level stretch along the first section of the Greenville Highway, the roads begin to curve, dip, and climb as you approach Connestee. The section of the route north of U.S. Highway 64 is quite hilly because it lies at the base of the surrounding mountains—but you'll be rewarded with some gorgeous views.

This route offers great variety of terrain and sites from the starting point in downtown Brevard, the county seat as well as the largest town in Transylvania County. Keep your eyes open for the unusual white squirrels that live in the area, even in town. They aren't albinos but true white squirrels with dark eyes. Local legend claims that a pair of rare white squirrels were given to a Brevard resident, who kept them as pets. Since they wouldn't breed in captivity, the squirrels were eventually freed and have flourished in Brevard ever since.

You leave Brevard and travel along fairly level rolling blacktop in the French Broad River valley for the first stretch. Everett Road is fairly level but curvy as it mimics the snakes of the river. Along Hart Road, you have great views of the surrounding mountains as well as a glimpse of llamas on a farm. Cascade Lake Road is framed by thick fields of corn in summer. This route coincides with part of the North Carolina Southern Highlands Bike Route 8 along Crab Creek Road, where the route dips into Henderson County. Dupont Road, part

THE BASICS

Start: The parking lot at College Plaza Shopping Center across the street from Brevard College.

Length: 36.1 miles.

Terrain: Ranges from fairly level to gently rolling in the first half to curvy and hilly with some steep climbs in the last half.

Traffic and hazards: There are a few high-traffic areas along this route: at the beginning along US 64/276 before turning onto Old Hendersonville Road; around the community of Cedar Mountain; and as you approach Connestee. Take special care along the 0.1-mile stretch of US 64 between Illahee Road and Cashiers Valley Road.

Getting there: Take US 64 to Brevard in Transylvania County. The College Plaza Shopping Center will be on the right across Broad Street (US 64/276) from Brevard College in downtown Brevard. See the *DeLorme North Carolina Atlas & Gazetteer,* page 53 D5.

of Transylvania Bike Route 4, challenges with a 1.4-mile climb rewarded by a long downhill.

Forests help shade the road along the next stretch of Cascade Lake Road. Enjoy the fairly level first part of the Greenville Highway/US 276 because you'll encounter switchbacks and climbs as you approach Connestee. You'll pass a sign for Connestee Falls, which is on the left. The 110-foot waterfall is located on Carson Creek on private property. According to Indian lore, the Princess Connestee leapt to her death over the falls after her English husband returned to his people. Dr. F. A. Miles named these falls for the Indian princess in 1882. Look for several of the potteries located in this area, which make a nice stopping place to catch your breath and check out the goods.

The next section along Island Ford Road and South Country Club road is curvy with lots of ups and downs. On Illahee Road you'll climb through a residential area that has great views of the mountains. Take care on the short stretch of US 64 that you have to take to Cashiers Valley Road, where you can follow the Bike Route 6 signs. Probart Road offers a slight climb then a fast downhill before the road starts climbing again. From there it's a question of a few turns and you're back on Broad Street in Brevard.

The town was named for Dr. Ephraim Brevard, a Revolutionary War colonel and surgeon who, incidentally, drafted the Mecklenburg Declaration of Independence. Born in 1744, the socially prominent Brevard resident studied medicine at Princeton College. He joined the fight for independence when the British invaded the South and was taken prisoner at the surrender of Charleston. He was among prisoners who became severely ill from such afflictions as dysentery. Reportedly, Andrew Jackson's mother cared for him at the prison camp.

Brevard never recovered from his illness, despite special medicines and treatment. In 1781, about the time the hostile force trod his native soil, he died

Cyclists cruise along a flat section of the route.

and was buried in an unmarked grave in Hopewell. To honor his memory, his family erected a monument in front of Brevard City Hall with a plaque that reads: FOUGHT BRAVELY AND DIED A MARTYR TO THAT LIBERTY WHICH NONE LOVED BETTER AND FEW UNDERSTOOD SO WELL.

Take some time to enjoy the downtown area, which is perfect for strolling. The Transylvania County Arts Council on Main Street offers art exhibits or you may want to browse in the antiques shops. You might also want to relax with a cup of coffee and a slice of pie at one of the restaurants as you reward yourself for your physical exertion.

LOCAL INFORMATION

◆ Transylvania County Tourism Development Authority, 35 West Main Street, Brevard, NC 28712; (828) 883–3700.

LOCAL EVENTS/ATTRACTIONS

◆ Brevard College's stone wall and gate are listed on the National Register of Historic Places; Broad Street, Brevard, NC 28712; no charge.
◆ Brevard Music Festival, classical and pops concerts, operas, lectures, recitals from mid-June to early August; Brevard Music Center, Brevard, NC 28712; ticket prices vary; (888) 884–2011; www.brevardmusic.org.
◆ Downtown Brevard with its interesting mix of shops and restaurants.

MILES AND DIRECTIONS

0.0 From the parking lot at College Plaza Shopping Center on Broad Street (US 64/276) across the street from Brevard College, turn left onto Broad Street, going east.

0.5 Turn right onto Old Hendersonville Road (SR 1504).

3.2 Turn right onto Everett Road (SR 1533).

5.7 Turn right onto Hart Road (SR 1534). *Note:* Enjoy the great views of the mountains.

8.1 Turn left onto Cascade Lake Road (SR 1536).

9.4 Turn right onto Crab Creek Road (SR 1528).

11.3 Turn right onto Dupont Road (SR 1259).

12.5 Dupont Road's name changes to Staton Road (SR 1593) when you reenter Transylvania County.

16.8 Turn left onto Cascade Lake Road (SR 1536).

19.3 Turn right onto US 276/Greenville Highway.

27.0 Turn left onto Connestee Road (SR 1112).

27.5 Turn left onto Island Ford Road (SR 1110).

28.2 Bear right on Island Ford Road. Walnut Hollow Road goes off to the left.

29.0 Turn right onto South Country Club Road (SR 1113).

30.7 Turn left onto Illahee Road (SR 1114). *Note:* More great mountain vistas.

31.8 Turn left onto US 64.

31.9 Turn right onto Cashiers Valley Road (SR 1344). Follow Bike Route 6 signs.

33.7 Turn left onto Probart Road (SR 1348).

35.4 Turn right onto Oaklawn Avenue.

35.5 Turn left onto Main Street in Brevard.

35.6 Pass public rest rooms on the right.

35.8 Turn left onto West Broad Street (US 64/276).

36.1 Turn left into College Plaza.

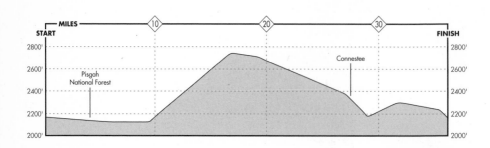

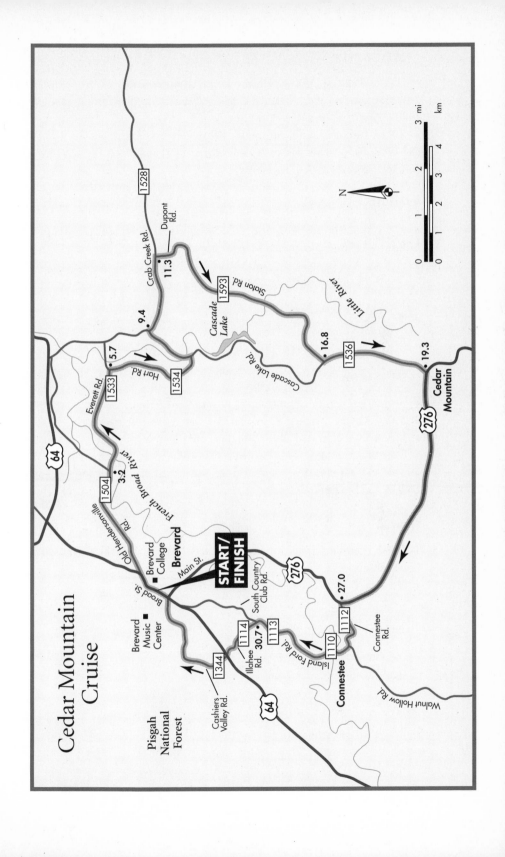

Cedar Mountain Cruise

RESTAURANTS

♦ Pepper Mill Café, 708 North Broad Street, Brevard, NC 28712; (828) 884–7400. Sandwiches and salads; breakfast and lunch Monday through Saturday; Sunday brunch; low range.

♦ Kelly's Family Dining, 306 North Broad Street, Brevard, NC 28712; (828) 884–3725. Sandwiches and plate lunches; breakfast and lunch Tuesday through Sunday; closed Monday; low range.

ACCOMMODATIONS

♦ The Inn at Brevard, 410 East Main Street, Brevard, NC 28712; (828) 884–2105; brevardinn@citcom.net. Mid- to upper range.

♦ Holiday Inn Express, 1570 Asheville Highway, Brevard, NC 28712; (828) 862–8900 or (800) 465–4329. Midrange.

BIKE SHOPS

♦ None.

REST ROOMS

♦ At the start and finish in restaurants on Broad Street.

♦ Mile 2.2 at a convenience store on Old Hendersonville Highway.

♦ Mile 14.4 at Hooper Falls, where there are portable toilets.

♦ Mile 21.3 at a convenience store on US 276/Greenville Highway.

♦ Mile 40.0 at public rest rooms located one block north of the intersection of US 276 and Broad Street.

MAPS

♦ North Carolina Department of Transportation's Bicycling Transylvania County Map, 1998.

♦ *DeLorme North Carolina Atlas & Gazetteer,* page 53.

36

Asheville-Biltmore Ramble

The Asheville-Biltmore Ramble, a delightful but challenging 17.5-mile ride, takes you by many of Asheville's scenic and historically important sights and through architecturally diverse neighborhoods. It begins at the South Forest Shopping Center south of downtown, travels through Biltmore Forest, and passes near the entrance to the famed Biltmore Estate. After a challenging climb to downtown, the route winds past Pack Square and the Thomas Wolfe Memorial to the historic Grove Park Inn Resort & Spa, which offers spectacular views of Asheville and the mountains beyond. After passing the campus of the University of North Carolina at Asheville and the UNC Botanical Gardens, the route diverts through the Montford Historic District before heading back downtown. The route weaves through interesting streets in the heart of downtown, past the Grove Arcade, and then turns south to the starting point.

Cycling in Asheville is not for the fainthearted, but the rewards are well worth the efforts because the city is surrounded by the Great Smoky and Blue Ridge Mountains, with a few mountains in the middle for good measure.

It's easy to see why Asheville is one of the most popular mountain resort areas in the eastern United States. The Blue Ridge Parkway skirts its perimeter, and two rivers divide it: the Swannanoa and the French Broad. No wonder George Washington Vanderbilt chose this area in the late nineteenth century as the site of his fabulous estate.

A cyclist crosses Pack Square in downtown Asheville.

This tour begins in the southern part of Asheville in a premier residential area known as Biltmore Forest because it abuts the Biltmore Estate. The route passes near the entrance to Biltmore at Mile 2.0. Self-guiding tours of the estate include the upstairs and downstairs of the mansion itself, the gardens, greenhouse, and the Biltmore Estate Winery, which offers tastings as well. You should allow a minimum of four hours to complete the tour.

The mansion, built using distinctive architectural features from famous French chateaux, contains 255 rooms. Not all the rooms are open, but the main living areas upstairs give a feel for the life the Vanderbilts enjoyed. The downstairs has the less formal rooms including kitchen, work areas, and servants' quarters. New rooms are opened periodically, and major artworks from the collection are on display throughout the house.

The gardens surrounding the house are comprised of seventy-five acres of formal gardens and grounds designed by Frederick Law Olmsted, who designed Central Park in New York City. Across U.S. Highway 25 from the estate is Biltmore Village, listed on the National Register of Historic Places, an interesting assortment of craft shops and upscale boutiques with many restaurants in the area. From this point the route climbs a half-mile hill toward downtown. Fortunately the right lane widens about halfway up the hill to give cars more room to pass heavily breathing cyclists. A sidewalk also offers an alternative.

At Mile 4.2 is Pack Place, Asheville's arts, education, and science center. The complex combines performance and exhibit spaces with retail shops, bringing arts, science, culture, and entertainment together in one location. The Asheville Art Museum is located here, along with the Colburn Gem and Mineral Museum.

When you turn left onto Market Street, you'll find yourself on brick cobblestones for about a block through one of Asheville's restaurant districts. The Thomas Wolfe Visitor Center is on Market Street, while the large white house that was the author's boyhood home is situated behind the center on Woodfin Street. The house was clearly the model for the boardinghouse in Wolfe's famous novel *Look Homeward, Angel*. Tours of the house take about thirty minutes.

The next point of interest is the Grove Park Inn at the top of Macon Avenue. The short, steady climb starting at Mile 5.6 passes through a residential area with lovely old homes. The Grove Park, one of the South's grand old resorts, was built in 1913 on the hillside overlooking downtown Asheville and the surrounding mountains. The inn's remarkable architecture represents an outstanding engineering feat because of the massive granite boulders used in construction.

As you pass around the side of the inn, you'll see the Homespun Shops, Grovewood Gallery, and museums on your right. The Homespun Museum

THE BASICS

Start: South Forest Shopping Center on US 25/Hendersonville Road south of Asheville.
Length: 17.5 miles.
Terrain: Hilly. There's a long climb up Biltmore Avenue into downtown; a long climb up Macon Avenue to the Grove Park Inn; a slight climb on Chestnut Street; a short climb up Waneta; and a gradual climb up Montford toward downtown. The rest of the route is slightly rolling.
Traffic and hazards: Where possible, the route follows side streets with less traffic. However, some of the direct routes have major traffic. Biltmore Avenue is busy but has four lanes and a sidewalk that can be used for climbing (watch out for low-hanging branches). Charlotte Street and Merrimon Avenue can be very busy, but fortunately the distances are short. A nice bikeway parallels W. T. Weaver Boulevard toward the university to offer some respite.
Getting there: From I–40 exit onto US 25 going south on Hendersonville Road to the South Forest Shopping Center. From I–26 take North Carolina Highway 280 (Long Shoals Road) east to US 25. Go north on US 25 until you see the South Forest Shopping Center on the right. See the *DeLorme North Carolina Atlas & Gazetteer*, page 53 A6.

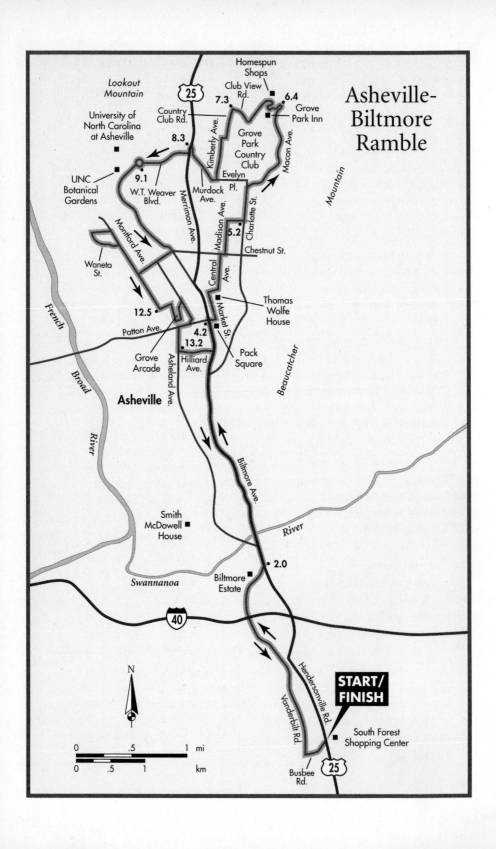

Asheville-Biltmore Ramble

Lookout Mountain

Homespun Shops

Club View Rd.

25

7.3

6.4

Grove Park Inn

University of North Carolina at Asheville

Country Club Rd.

8.3

Kimberly Ave.

Grove Park Country Club

Macon Ave.

Mountain

9.1

UNC Botanical Gardens

W.T. Weaver Blvd.

Evelyn Pl.

Murdock Ave.

Charlotte St.

Merrimon Ave.

Madison Ave.

5.2

Chestnut St.

Monford Ave.

Central Ave.

Waneta St.

French

12.5

Thomas Wolfe House

Patton Ave.

Market St.

4.2

13.2

Broad

River

Grove Arcade

Ashland Ave.

Hilliard Ave.

Pack Square

Beaucatcher

Asheville

Biltmore Ave.

Smith McDowell House

River

2.0

40

Biltmore Estate

Swannanoa

Hendersonville Rd.

START/ FINISH

Vanderbilt Rd.

South Forest Shopping Center

N

0   .5   1 mi

0   .5   1 km

Busbee Rd.

25

0.0 From the South Forest Shopping Center, go straight across US 25/ Hendersonville Road onto Busbee Road.

0.2 Turn right onto Vanderbilt Road.

2.0 Turn left onto Hendersonville Road, which becomes Biltmore Avenue. The entrance to the Biltmore Estate is nearby.

4.2 Turn right onto Patton Avenue at Pack Square in downtown, which is one-way east.

4.3 Turn left onto Market Street (brick surface for one block). The Thomas Wolfe Visitor Center is on the right.

4.5 Turn right onto Woodfin Street. The Thomas Wolfe Homeplace is on the right.

4.6 Turn left onto Central Avenue.

4.9 Turn right onto East Chestnut Street at a stop sign, then make an immediate left onto Madison Avenue.

5.2 Turn right onto Hillside Street.

5.3 Turn left onto Charlotte Street.

5.6 Turn right onto Macon Avenue at the Grove Park Inn sign.

6.4 Turn left into Grove Park Inn. Bear left at the first stop sign, then turn right just in front of the inn and continue to bear right, following the arrows through the parking lot.

6.6 Turn left at the second stop sign, go to the next stop sign, and turn left.

6.7 Turn right into the Grove Park Homespun Shops (allow 0.2 mile to circle the drive).

6.9 Turn right back onto the main road through Grove Park property. Pass the Grove Park Country Club on your left and turn left on Club View Road.

7.3 Turn left onto Country Club Road.

7.6 Turn left onto Kimberly Avenue.

8.0 Turn right onto Evelyn Place, then turn right onto Murdock Avenue.

8.3 At a yield sign bear left on Murdock Avenue to a stoplight at Merrimon Avenue, then turn left onto Merrimon Avenue and immediately right onto

(continued)

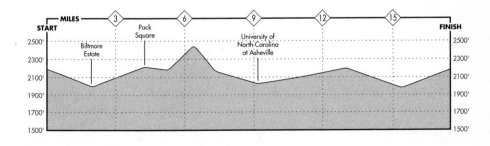

W. T. Weaver Boulevard at the next light. There is a bike path on the right side of Weaver Boulevard.

9.1 *Option:* Side trip through University of North Carolina at Asheville at the traffic circle. Take the circle exit toward Broadway Street.

9.8 Turn left onto Broadway Street toward downtown.

10.5 Turn right onto Chestnut Street.

10.9 Turn right onto Montford Avenue in Historic Montford.

11.2 Turn left onto Waneta Street.

11.3 Turn right onto Danville Street and immediately turn left onto Pearson Street.

11.4 Turn right onto Watauga Street.

11.7 Turn right onto Montford Avenue toward downtown.

12.5 Turn left onto Haywood Street.

12.6 Turn right onto O'Henry Avenue. The Grove Arcade will be on your left.

12.7 Turn left onto Battery Park Avenue then turn left on Page Avenue.

12.8 Turn right onto Haywood Street.

12.9 Turn right onto College Street, which merges into Patton Avenue.

13.0 Turn left onto Asheland Avenue.

13.2 Turn left onto Hilliard Avenue.

13.5 Turn right onto Biltmore Avenue.

15.4 Turn right onto Vanderbilt Road at a stoplight.

17.3 Turn left onto Busbee Road, then bear left at the next fork so that you come out at the traffic signal.

17.5 Continue straight across US 25 (Hendersonville Road) into the South Forest Shopping Center parking lot.

contains implements from a bygone era and is next to the Antique Car Museum. A flute maker, glassblower, weaver, and other artisans share studio space in the building.

At Mile 9.1 is the entrance to the University of North Carolina at Asheville, which could be the starting point for an optional side tour. Immediately past the university entrance are the Botanical Gardens, providing ten acres of native plants.

The route then turns west on Chestnut Street for a brief tour of the Montford Historic District before heading downtown. As you turn the corner onto O'Henry Avenue, you'll see the recently restored Grove Arcade, a magnificent structure that houses shops on the first floor with offices and apartments upstairs. After circling the arcade, you'll pass all sorts of interesting shops and restaurants on Haywood and College/Patton Streets before you turn south for the final stretch. More art deco architecture from the late 1920s and '30s can be found in downtown Asheville than in any other southeastern city except Miami Beach.

After you turn back onto Biltmore Avenue, you'll see St. Joseph's Medical Center and signs for the Smith-McDowell House, another option for a short but hilly side trip. The route concludes with a serene ride past the elegant homes of Biltmore Forest.

LOCAL INFORMATION

♦ Asheville Convention & Visitors Bureau, P.O. Box 1010, Asheville, NC 28802; (828) 258–6101; www.ashevillechamber.org or www.exploreasheville. com.

LOCAL EVENTS/ATTRACTIONS

♦ Bele Chere Festival, an annual event on the last weekend in July, downtown Asheville; largest free outdoor festival in the Southeast, including fine arts and crafts, children's activities, entertainment, 5K race, food from all over the region; no charge; (828) 259–5800.
♦ Craft Fair of the Southern Highlands; annual gathering of the Southern Highlands Crafts Guild, featuring the finest craftsmanship from the mountains of nine states, live regional music, and demonstrations; Asheville Civic Center, Haywood Street, downtown; admission charged; (828) 298–7928.
♦ Mountain Dance and Folk Festival, an annual event held the first weekend in August; oldest continuing celebration in America of traditional folk music, singing, and dancing; Diana Wortham Theatre on Pack Square in downtown; admission charged; (828) 452–0152.
♦ Asheville Historic Trolley Tours, a professionally narrated tour of Asheville's finest sights; adults $16.00, children seventeen and younger $9.00; family pack $42.00 for two adults and their children; AARP members $15.00; (888) 667–3600; www.ashevilletrolleytours.com.
♦ Biltmore Estate, America's largest private home; the 255-room Biltmore House still contains its original collection of 50,000 furnishings, artwork, and antiques. The 8,000-acre estate also features fabulous gardens and a winery that produces award-winning, European-style wine; located on US 25, just north of I–40; adults $34.00; children ages ten through fifteen $25.50; children nine and under admitted free with paying adult; (800) 543–2961.
♦ Folk Art Center, a gallery where works of Southern Highland Crafts Guild members are displayed and sold and artisans frequently demonstrate their craft; Milepost 382 on the Blue Ridge Parkway, Asheville; no charge. (828) 298–7928.
♦ The Grove Park Inn Resort & Spa, one of the most famous hotels in the South, built of massive boulders and overlooking Asheville's skyline, with fabulous

views of the mountains beyond. An engineering marvel, the resort is one of the preeminent landmarks in the city; 290 Macon Avenue, Asheville, NC 28804; no charge; (800) 438–5800 or (828) 252–2711.

♦ Montford Historic Area, listed in the National Register of Historic Places, boasts a variety of architectural styles and fifteen bed-and-breakfasts; no charge; (828) 255–4946.

♦ Pack Place Education, Arts and Science Center, houses the Asheville Art Museum, Colburn Gem and Mineral Museum, The Health Adventure, and the Diana Wortham Theatre, with the affiliated YMI Cultural Center located at the corner of Eagle and Market Streets; located on Pack Square in downtown; admission varies; (828) 257–4500.

♦ Smith-McDowell House, Asheville's oldest house (circa 1840); 283 Victoria Road, Asheville, NC 28801; adults $4.50; senior citizens, students, and children ages five through eighteen $3.50; (828) 253–9231.

RESTAURANTS

♦ Laughing Seed Café, 40 Wall Street (downtown), Asheville, NC 28801; (828) 252–3445; www.laughingseed.com. International gourmet with vegetarian cuisine; open weekdays except Tuesday for lunch and dinner; Sunday brunch.

♦ La Caterina Trattoria, 5 Pack Square, Asheville, NC 28801; (828) 254–1148. Classic southern Italian with outside dining available; open daily Monday through Saturday for lunch and dinner; Sunday brunch.

♦ Left Bank, 90 Patton Avenue, Asheville, NC 28801; (828) 251–5552. French and American fusion; open for dinner Tuesday through Sunday 5:00 P.M.–closing.

ACCOMMODATIONS

♦ The Grove Park Inn Resort and Spa, 290 Macon Avenue, Asheville, NC 28804; (828) 252–2711 or (800) 438–5800; www.groveparkinn.com. Premier accommodations at a famous inn listed on the National Register of Historic Places; high range.

♦ Sleep Inn-Biltmore, 117 Hendersonville Road, Asheville, NC 28803; (828) 277–1800; www.biltmoreinns.com. Midrange with continental breakfast; two blocks from the Biltmore Estate.

♦ The Wright Inn and Carriage House, 235 Pearson Drive, Asheville, NC 28801; (828) 251–0789 or (800) 552–5724; www.wrightinn.com. A three-diamond award winner, listed on the National Register of Historic Places; mid- to high range; includes a full breakfast and afternoon tea.

BIKE SHOPS

♦ Liberty Bicycles, Parkway Center, 1378 Hendersonville Highway, Asheville, NC 28803; (828) 274–2453 or (800) 96–BIKES; www.libertybikes.com.

- Hearn Cycling & Fitness, 34 Broadway Street, Asheville, NC 28801; (828) 253–4800.
- Professional Bicycles, 793 Merrimon Avenue, Asheville, NC 28804; (828) 253–2800.

REST ROOMS

- Mile 2 and Mile 15.4 in the Gate House at the entrance to the Biltmore Estate.
- Mile 4.3 at the Thomas Wolfe Visitor Center.
- Mile 6.8 at the Grove Park Inn.
- At about Mile 9.8 at Citgo convenience store on Broadway Street.
- Mile 12.6 at the Grove Arcade.

MAPS

- North Carolina Department of Transportation Bicycle Map, 1998.

Yancey County River Cruise

This route is testament to the restorative qualities of cycling. In this area called the Heart of the Blue Ridge, steep slopes shelter the roads hugging the banks of Jack's Creek and then the Toe River as they meander through these narrow valleys. With little traffic to contend with, you can content yourself with listening to the sounds of gurgling streams and the birds flitting about and gliding on mountain currents. Don't let yourself be too mesmerized and miss a turn or you'll find that intersecting roads go straight up over the mountains!

Imagine being in the midst of the Blue Ridge Mountains, following streams and rivers with only a couple of minor hills to climb. That's what this route is like. With every turn you follow a stream that then feeds into a river, so that you're always next to water. Burnsville itself feels like a step back in time. This feeling continues as you ride this route where not much has changed over the last fifty years.

The first part of the route takes you along a curvy, narrow road through the mountain valleys filled with tobacco or cornfields. You'll pass the tin-roofed Jack's Creek Presbyterian Church and, in summer, see large round hay bales dotting fields, a sure sign that you're near dairy or cattle farms.

At Mile 4.7 Coxes Creek Road goes off to the left and you see Jack's Creek on the right. Steep mountain pastures climb from roadside to summits perhaps 1,000 feet above. Over the next 4 miles, Jack's Creek gurgles beside the road, creating a moist environment for the profusion of Queen Anne's lace and other colorful wildflowers on the roadside.

At Mile 10.2 Jack's Creek flows into the Toe River. I speculate that it's called that because it's so shallow that it barely wets your toes. The clear, cold water looks inviting on a hot summer's day. At Mile 13.3 the former one-lane bridge has been widened but still recalls earlier times when horse-drawn wagons crossed the river at this point over the low-water bridge.

At Mile 13.6 you turn left onto North Carolina Highway 197, with the railroad tracks up the bank to the right. Although rail usage has continued to decline, the tracks serve as a reminder of how important the railroad was to connecting these remote areas to the rest of North Carolina and the world. The railroad, too, liked to follow rivers and streams when laying tracks because the banks are generally flatter.

At Mile 15.1 our route continues straight as the road becomes Hunt-dale Road (SR 1304). Highway 197 bears off to the right and across the railroad tracks. The Huntdale community is situated at Mile 16.3. At Mile 16.5 you'll cross a one-lane bridge over the Toe River. Take care when crossing because the sight distances on either side of the bridge are not good, and the bridge is so narrow that's there not sufficient room for a car to pass while a cyclist is on the bridge.

Along SR 1417 it's surprising to see the large number of footbridges across the Cane River to the houses on the other bank of the river. All manner of signs warn that crossing these bridges is at your own risk. Be sure to check out all the different types of construction and decide if you'd be willing to cross.

At Miles 27.9 and 29.8 bridges cross the Cane River, which bends and winds its way around the mountains. At Mile 34.9 you'll turn left on Old U.S. Highway 19E, which brings you to the new main road, U.S. Highway 19E. This busy highway may have heavy traffic, including trucks. The speed limit along US 19E is 55 mph, so it's quite a change from the laid-back rural roads to this point. Fortunately this stretch is not very long, and you're soon back to the starting point at the intersection with Jack's Creek Road.

Settled by sturdy and independent Scots, Irish, and English immigrants, Yancey County was named for Bartlett Yancey, a U.S. congressman and president of the North Carolina Senate in the early nineteenth century. Among his many accomplishments that benefited the state was the creation of an education fund that was the beginning of the North Carolina public school system.

LOCAL INFORMATION

♦ Yancey County Visitors Center, 106 West Main Street, Burnsville, NC 28714; (800) 948–1632; www.yanceychamber.com.

LOCAL EVENTS/ATTRACTIONS

♦ Mount Mitchell Crafts Fair, an annual event held on a Friday and Saturday in early August; more than 225 crafters fill Burnsville's historic streets with handmade quilts, pottery, woven baskets, and other crafts; ongoing bandstand entertainment; food court and refreshment vendors; sponsored by the Yancey County Chamber of Commerce; no charge; (828) 682–7413 or (800) 948–1632.

♦ Mount Mitchell State Park, the highest peak east of the Mississippi, is located in Yancey County, 33 miles northeast of Asheville on the Blue Ridge Parkway at Milepost 355; no charge; (828) 675–4611.

♦ Historic Orchard at Altapass on Orchard Road, Milepost 328.4 on the Blue Ridge Parkway. Fresh apples and peaches July to November (pick yourself or already picked), fresh-baked goods, free tours of orchard, music, history, tall tales, and hayrides by request on Saturday. Music, pickin' and singin', Milepost 328.4 on the Blue Ridge Parkway; Route 3, Box 260, Spruce Pine, NC 28777; no charge; (828) 765–9531; bcarson@mitchell.main.nc.us.

♦ Parkway Playhouse presents various plays and musicals; admission charged; 202 Green Mountain Drive, Burnsville, NC; (828) 682–4285.

RESTAURANTS

♦ China Garden, 409 West Main Street, Burnsville, NC 28714; (828) 682–6462.

♦ Garden Deli, Town Square on Main Street, Burnsville, NC 28714; (828) 682–3946.

ACCOMMODATIONS

♦ Nu Wray Inn, Town Square, Burnsville, NC 28714; (800) 368–9729. Midrange.

♦ Wray House Bed & Breakfast, 2 South Main Street, Burnsville, NC 28714; (877) 258–8222. Mid- to upper range.

A footbridge over the Cane River connects the house to the road.

0.0 From the east on US 19E, turn right onto Jack's Creek Road (SR 1336).

4.7 Pass Coxes Creek Road on the left.

6.6 Stay on Jack's Creek Road, which curves sharply to the left. Clearmont School is to the right on SR 1416.

9.4 Stay on Jack's Creek Road, which curves to the right. There's a sign on left for North Bend Church.

10.2 Turn left onto SR 1338. Jack's Creek flows into the Toe River on the right.

13.2 Cross a bridge over the Toe River.

13.3 *Caution:* Very uneven railroad tracks. Cross them, then veer left onto Relief Road Extension (SR 1338).

13.6 Turn left onto NC–197.

15.0 Stay straight on Huntdale Road (SR 1304). NC–197 goes off to the right.

16.4 Turn right onto SR 1417 after crossing a one-lane bridge over the Toe River.

20.1 Turn left onto US 19W South at the stop sign.

21.7 Coxes Creek Road joins US 19W.

26.5 Turn left on US 19W South at the yield sign.

27.9 Cross a bridge over the Cane River.

29.8 Cross a bridge over the Cane River again.

34.9 Turn left onto Old U.S. Highway 19E (SR 1454). U.S. Highway 19W goes off to the right.

36.9 Turn left onto US 19E.

37.4 Arrive at Jack's Creek Road and the parking area on the left.

BIKE SHOPS

♦ None.

REST ROOMS

♦ Mile 16.3 at Phin Peterson's Groceries in Huntdale.
♦ Mile 26.5 at Wells Grocery where U.S. Highway 19W goes to the left.

MAPS

♦ *DeLorme North Carolina Atlas & Gazetteer,* page 32.

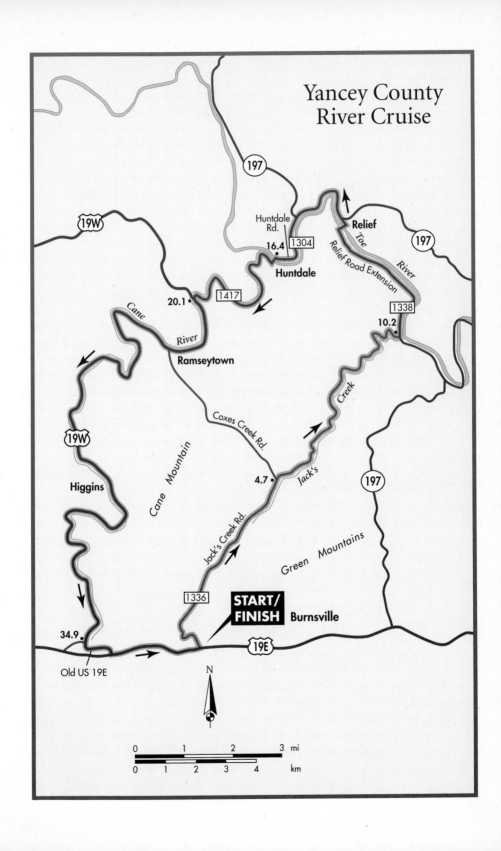

Yancey County River Cruise

197

19W

197

Huntdale Rd.

16.4 • 1304

Relief

Huntdale

Toe River

Relief Road Extension

1417

20.1 •

1338

10.2 •

Cane River

Ramseytown

Creek

Coxes Creek Rd.

197

19W

Higgins

4.7 • Jack's

Cane Mountain

Green Mountains

Jack's Creek Rd.

1336

START/ FINISH

Burnsville

34.9 •

19E

Old US 19E

N

| 0 | 1 | 2 | 3 mi |
| 0 | 1 | 2 | 3 | 4 km |

Blue Ridge Parkway Challenge

The Blue Ridge Parkway Challenge, suited for advanced and in-shape riders, is an out-and-back ride with spectacular views on this parkway built along the crest of the Blue Ridge Mountains in western North Carolina. The ride starts at the Moses Cone Manor House and Craft Center at Milepost 294 with a quick downhill before a 7-mile climb. Following the uppermost contours of these ancient mountains, the route has several climbs that are rewarded with speedy descents. Cyclists are advised to carry snacks and extra water because there are no vendors on this section of the parkway, although two restaurants are located in Pineola just off the parkway.

This ride begins with a breezy downhill followed by a long, gradual climb, about 7 miles in length. Fortunately, there are plenty of overlooks and spectacular views along the way to break up the climb. Of course, the reward is a glorious 7-mile downhill run on the return trip that makes the climb well worth it. The Moses Cone Manor House at the starting point was built at the turn of the twentieth century by textile magnate and businessman Moses H. Cone. He and his wife built this elegant twenty-room manor house on Flat Top Mountain, which afforded them wonderful views of the mountains' natural beauty. The house was used as the setting for the opening and closing scenes of the film *The Green Mile*, starring Tom Hanks.

The manor house is now home to the Parkway Craft Center, which showcases the work of members of the Southern Highland Craft Guild, recognized for excellence in craftsmanship and design. Artistic skills that have passed through several generations are preserved in the lovely pottery, baskets, ironwork, hand-carved wood, and many other distinctive crafts. There is no charge to visit the galleries because almost every craft item is available for purchase.

Across the 3,500 acres Cone purchased spread glorious groves of rhododendron, mountain laurel, and wild azaleas broken only by ridgetop meadows setting the stage for the magnificence of Grandfather Mountain's rocky crest. The 25 miles of trails crisscrossing the property invite horseback riders in summer and cross-country skiers in winter to enjoy the natural setting so appreciated and conserved by the Cones.

Plan to take advantage of all the overlooks along the way and enjoy the variety of mountain scenery. During late June and early July, the rhododendron with its large white and pink blooms can be spectacularly showy. In autumn the brilliance of the fall foliage brings thousands of people to the parkway.

The Blue Ridge Parkway, running through Virginia and North Carolina, is a huge monument to the heroic efforts of the Civilian Conservation Corps, which built much of the parkway on the crest of the Blue Ridge during the 1930s. As one of the highlights, this tour includes the newest section—the Linn Cove Viaduct, completed in 1987.

Begun in 1935 at Cumberland Knob in North Carolina, 462.5 miles of the parkway had been completed by 1967. The last stretch, though, posed one of the greatest challenges: how to build a road at an elevation of 4,100 feet without damaging one of the world's oldest mountains. The resulting Linn Cove Viaduct has been called "the most complicated concrete bridge ever built, snaking around the boulder-strewn Linn Cove in a sweeping 'S' curve." The viaduct is 1,243 feet long and contains 153 segments weighing fifty tons each.

Along much of the parkway carefully crafted stone walls and zigzag split-rail fences—in some cases double split-rail—define the parkway's boundaries. Because no truck traffic is allowed on the parkway and the roadway is not scraped in the winter (sections of the parkway are closed during winter snows), the pavement remains quite smooth and great for cycling. In most places grassy shoulders grace the sides of the road.

The viewing point at Lost Cove Cliffs—elevation 3,500 feet—is the best vantage point for the Brown Mountain Lights of folklore. The lights are first mentioned in Indian lore in the early 1700s and have continued to puzzle observers for centuries. In 1913 the U.S. Geological Survey studied the lights and concluded that they were headlights of locomotives in the valley. However, a flood a few years later stopped the trains—but the lights continued to appear.

Another study in 1922 speculated that the lights from a variety of sources such as autos, towns, and brushfires were refracted and bent skyward by the unstable air currents in the valleys. Phosphorus, UFOs, radium ore deposits, and marsh gas have been put forth as other possible causes of the mysterious lights.

The Linville Gorge and Falls is a popular destination for hikers and for more casual strollers who take the trail from the visitor center to the upper falls. The Linville has been designated a Wild and Scenic River, and the massive gorge it created is home to rare plants and diverse wildlife. The river descends some 1,800 feet over 12 miles in a series of spectacular drops, eventually emptying into Lake James. The 1,200-acre site, part of the National Park System, is a refreshing place to relax and enjoy the views before turning around for the return trip.

LOCAL INFORMATION

♦ North Carolina High Country Host, 1700 Blowing Rock Road, Boone, NC 28607; (800) 438–7500 or (828) 264–1299; www.highcountryhost.com.

LOCAL EVENTS/ATTRACTIONS

♦ Grandfather Mountain is the highest peak in the Blue Ridge Mountains with spectacular views, Mile High Swinging Bridge, hiking trails, wildlife; adults (thirteen through fifty-nine) $12.00, seniors (sixty-plus) $11.00, children (four through twelve) $6.00, children under four free; U.S. Highway 221 and the Blue Ridge Parkway at Milepost 305, Linville, NC 28646; (828) 468–7325; www.grandfather.com.
♦ Grandfather Mountain Highland Games, an annual four-day celebration of traditional highland games and gathering of the clans held on the second full weekend in July; four-day tickets purchased in advance cost $55.00 for adults, $25.00 for children. Tickets for individual events range $5.00–20.00; P.O. Box 1095, Linville, NC 28646; (828) 733–1333; www.gmhg.org.
♦ Linn Cove Viaduct at Mile 10.6 is an engineering marvel with exhibits explaining its construction at the Linn Cove Visitor Center; no charge.

The front porch of the Moses Cone Manor House offers splendid views of the Blue Ridge Mountains.

- Flat Rock Trail at Mile 15.0, a thirty-minute loop trail with impressive views of Linville Valley and Grandfather Mountain; no charge.
- Linville Falls at Mile 24.5, trails start at the visitor center to the upper falls and to other viewpoints overlooking the Linville Gorge and valley; no charge.
- Spectacular views from the numerous scenic overlooks along this stretch of the parkway; no charge.

RESTAURANTS

- Christa's General Store, North Carolina Highway 181, Pineola, NC 28662. Packaged sandwiches, snacks, drinks, ice cream.
- Mountain Top Restaurant, NC–181 at its intersection with Old Pineola Motel Lane (1.3 miles north on NC–181 from Blue Ridge Parkway exit), Pineola, NC 28662; (828) 733–6375. Casual country food for breakfast and lunch Monday through Wednesday plus dinner Thursday through Saturday; closed Sunday.

ACCOMMODATIONS

- Alpen Acres Motel, 318 Old U.S. Highway 321, Blowing Rock, NC 28605; (828) 295–7981 or (888) 297–7981; www.alpenacres.com. Moderately priced; kitchenettes available.

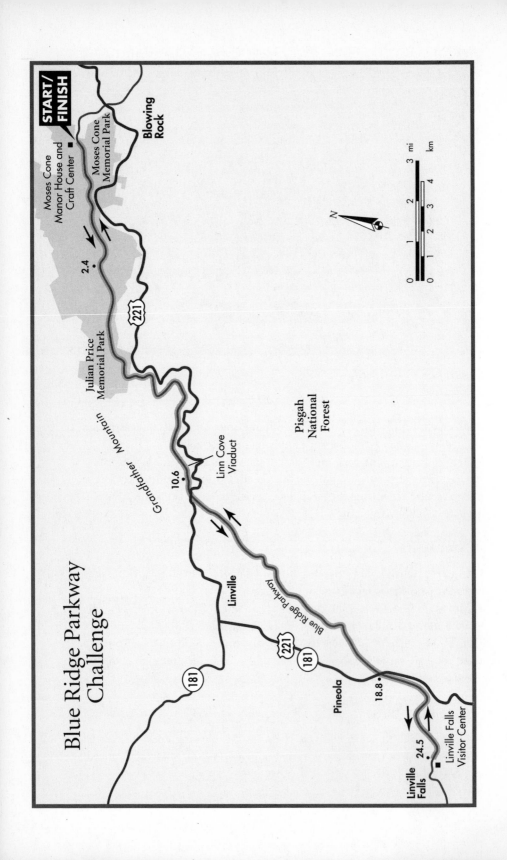

0.0 Start at the entrance to Moses Cone Manor House and Craft Center at Milepost 294 on the Blue Ridge Parkway.

2.4 Pass the parking lot and one of the entrances to Julian Price Park.

6.7 Pass Green Mountain Overlook.

8.7 Pass Raven Rock Overlook.

10.1 Pass Wilson Creek Overlook.

10.5 Pass Yonahlassee Overlook.

10.6 Cross the Linn Cove Viaduct.

11.1 Pass the Linn Cove Visitors Center.

13.3 Pass the Green Mountain Overlook.

15.0 Trailhead for the Flat Rock Trail at beginning of the Pisgah National Forest.

16.8 Pass Lost Cove Viewing Area.

18.8 Cross NC–181 at Pineola.

22.3 Pass Camp Creek Overlook.

23.1 Entrance to Linville Falls Visitors Center.

24.5 Arrive at Linville Falls Visitors Center. Turn around and retrace your route.

49.0 Return to Moses Cone Manor House and Craft Center.

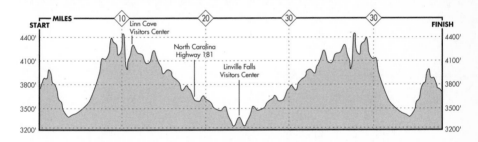

♦ Green Park Inn, U.S. Highway 321 South, Blowing Rock, NC 28605; (828) 295–3141 or (800) 852–2642; www.greenparkinn.com. Moderately priced historic inn.

♦ Days Inn, U.S. Highway 321, Blowing Rock, NC 28605; (828) 295–4422 or (800) DAYS–INN. Moderately priced.

BIKE SHOPS

The nearest bike shops are in Boone.

♦ Boone Bike & Touring, 899 Blowing Rock Road, Boone, NC 28607; (828) 262–5750.

♦ Magic Cycles, 208 Faculty Street, Suite 1, Boone, NC 28607; (828) 265–2211.

♦ Rock N' Roll Sports, 280 East King Street, Boone, NC 28607; (828) 264–0765.

A fly fisherman tries his luck in the Linville River.

REST ROOMS

- ♦ At the start and finish at Moses Cone Manor House and Craft Center.
- ♦ Mile 2.4 in Julian Price Park.
- ♦ Mile 11.1 at Linn Cove Visitor Center.
- ♦ About mile 18.8 at Christa's General Store on NC–181.
- ♦ Mile 24.5 at Linville Falls Visitor Center.

MAPS

- ♦ *DeLorme North Carolina Atlas & Gazetteer,* pages 13 and 33.

Valle Crucis Ramble

The Valle Crucis Ramble is a challenging ride with long climbs in this lovely mountainous area. Fortunately the climbs are off-set by valley sections that are level to rolling. Starting at the Mast General Store in Valle Crucis, the route winds through rustic farming communities almost to the Tennessee border, turning east on U.S. Highway 421. The return route loops back to Old U.S. Highway 421 and then retraces the route to the Mast Store.

The Mast General Store will certainly take you back in time. Set up like the old country store it has been for about a century, the Mast Store carries cast-iron pots and frying pans along with the latest in hiking shoes and Birkenstocks. The renewed popularity of the store in the last decade or so en-couraged the newer owners to establish additional locations in other mountain cities.

From the store, this tour loops through the mountain countryside past farms and small communities. Mast Gap Road at Mile 1.3 begins a fairly steep climb but takes you past dense hardwood forests, acres of Christmas trees in neatly trimmed rows, small white churches, and masses of rhododendron. The route follows part of the Watauga River valley through small mountain crests and lush green valleys.

After you turn right onto Old U.S. Highway 421 (Mile 3.6), you'll see a swiftly running stream and mounds of rocks. It's no surprise, then, that many of the homes and businesses in the area are built of native stone. At Mile 4.6 the route gradually climbs through Henson Hollar—a misspelling of the Southern Appalachian word *holler*. Regional pronunciation dictates that words ending in

Start: From the parking lot behind the Mast General Store on North Carolina Highway 194 in Valle Crucis.

Length: 24.4 miles.

Terrain: Mountainous—long climbs interspersed with level to rolling roads through the valley.

Traffic and hazards: U.S. Highway 321 and US 421 are major highways, but fortunately the distances on these roads are short. U.S. Highway 421 has a climbing lane until the turn-off on Slabtown Road. North Carolina Highway 194 is moderately busy as it connects towns. The other roads are quiet with little traffic. Curvy sections require proper positioning on the road for better visibility to motorists. Some of the roads have uneven surfaces.

Getting there: From US 421 in Boone, turn south on NC–194 to Valle Crucis. The Mast General Store will be on the right. There's a large parking area behind the store. See the *Delorme North Carolina Atlas & Gazetteer,* page 13 D5.

-ow are pronounced like *er.* So *holler* means a hollow or small valley between two mountains.

The roads here are narrow paved ones, somewhat uneven with no shoulders, but there's very little traffic in this area. You'll find most people friendly to cyclists; it doesn't hurt to throw up your hand in greeting either, if they don't beat you to it. This stretch takes you right up to the Tennessee border with North Carolina.

After you turn right on US 421 (Mile 11.7), watch for heavier traffic and a steep climb. Fortunately an extra right climbing lane provides a greater margin of safety. Slabtown Road (SR 1302) is the first paved road to the right. Be on the lookout because you come up on it suddenly, and it begins with a sharp turn. The name changes to Mabel School Road after about 1.4 miles. You'll probably wonder how the residents on this very curvy road manage in winter when the area typically receives about 58 inches of snow!

The return trip along Mast Gap Road offers great views of the valley and rustic log houses with stone fireplaces. This road leads you back to Highway 194 and the Mast General Store.

This ride takes place in Avery County, North Carolina, named for Colonel Waightstill Avery, who served in the Revolutionary War from 1779 until 1781 and later became the first attorney general of North Carolina. All of the county's approximately 15,000 residents live above 3,000 feet in elevation. The highest ski slopes in the South, golf resorts, and Grandfather Mountain attract visitors to the area year-round, making tourism the leading industry in this rural county. The second largest industry is Christmas tree and ornamental shrubbery farming, giving the county its nickname, Fraser Fir Capital of the World.

♦ North Carolina High Country Host, 1700 Blowing Rock Road, Boone, NC 28607; (828) 264–1299 or (800) 438–7500; info@highcountryhost.com or www.highcountryhost.com.

LOCAL EVENTS/ATTRACTIONS

♦ Mast General Store, an old-timey mercantile store with household items, old-fashioned candies, traditional clothing, and rugged outdoor wear and equipment; Highway 194, Valle Crucis, NC 28691; (828) 963–6511; no charge.

♦ Mast General Store Annex offers more items like the main store plus a deli and homemade ice cream; NC–194, Valle Crucis, NC 28691, (828) 963–6511; no charge.

♦ Valle Crucis Park, located behind the Mast General Store Annex, features a stream, walking trail, and picnic shelters; no charge.

The Blue Ridge Mountains loom in the distance ahead of this cyclist.

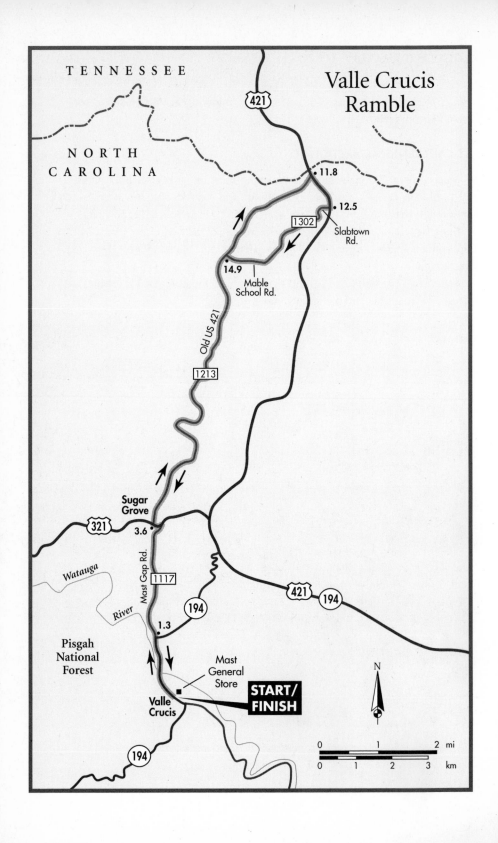

Valle Crucis Ramble

TENNESSEE

NORTH
CAROLINA

421

• 11.8

• 12.5

1302

Slabtown
Rd.

• 14.9

Mable
School Rd.

Old US 421

1213

Sugar
Grove

321

3.6 •

Mast Gap Rd.

Watauga

1117

River

194

Pisgah
National
Forest

1.3 •

421   194

194

Mast
General
Store

START/
FINISH

Valle
Crucis

194

N

0   1   2 mi

0   1   2   3 km

0.0 Turn right out of the Mast General Store parking lot onto Highway 194.

0.6 Cross a bridge over the Watauga River.

1.3 Turn left onto Mast Gap Road (SR 1117).

3.5 Turn left onto US 321.

3.6 Turn right onto Old US Highway 421 (SR 1213).

11.8 Turn right onto US 421 (near Tennessee state line).

12.5 Turn right onto Slabtown Road (SR 1302)—this is the first road to the right.

12.7 Bear left on Slabtown Road. The road's name changes to Mabel School Road.

14.9 Turn left onto Old U.S. Highway 421 (SR 1213).

20.9 Turn left onto US 321.

21.0 Turn right onto Mast Gap Road (SR 1117).

23.2 Turn right onto NC−194 to return to the starting point.

24.4 Turn left into the parking lot at Mast General Store.

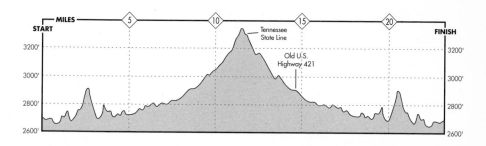

RESTAURANTS

♦ Mast Farm Inn Restaurant, P.O. Box 704, Valle Crucis, NC 28691; (888) 963–5857; www.mastfarminn.com. Upscale new southern cuisine.

♦ Columbine Restaurant in Valle Landing, 3657-4 NC−194 South, Sugar Grove, NC 28679; (828) 963–6037; visitor@columbinerestaurant.com or www. columbinerestaurant.com. Moderately priced Continental cuisine.

ACCOMMODATIONS

♦ Mast Farm Inn, P.O. Box 704, Valle Crucis, NC 28691; (888) 963–5857; www.mastfarminn.com. Upper range but full breakfast included.

♦ Mast Gap Inn, 1914 Mast Gap Road, Sugar Grove, NC 28679; (828) 297–5287; www.mastgapinn.com. Upper range but gourmet breakfast included.

♦ Altavista Bed & Breakfast & Gallery, 2839 Broadstone Road, P.O. Box 756, Valle Crucis, NC 28691; (828) 963–5247; altavista@boone.net or www.altavista gallery.com.

♦ Taylor House Inn, Highway 194, P.O. Box 713, Valle Crucis, NC 28691; (828) 963–5581 or (800) 963–5581; contactus@taylorhouseinn.com or www.taylor houseinn.com.

BIKE SHOPS

The closest bike shops are in Boone.
♦ Boone Bike and Touring, 899 Blowing Rock Road, Boone, NC 28607; (828) 262–5750.
♦ Magic Cycles, 208 Faculty Street, Suite 1, Boone, NC 28607; (828) 265–2211.
♦ Rock N' Roll Sports, 280 East King Street, Boone, NC 28607; (828) 264–0765.

REST ROOMS

♦ At the start and finish at the Mast General Store.
♦ Miles 3.6 and 20.9 at a convenience store at the intersection of US 321 and Old U.S. Highway 421.

MAPS

♦ *DeLorme North Carolina Atlas & Gazetteer,* page 13.

New River Ramble

The New River Ramble is an ideal ride for beginners with its scenic setting and minimal traffic. Following the South Fork of the New River, the route stays in the valley between slopes covered with Christmas tree farms. The ride follows the same road, built on an old railroad bed, from the small town of Fleetwood to the historic general store in Todd, where food and drinks are available as well as benches on the front porch for relaxing. Although this area is becoming popular for vacation homes, the river's protected status as a Wild and Scenic River has curbed rampant development that has overtaken other mountain areas to the south.

This wonderfully easy ride, long popular with North Carolina cyclists, covers a stretch of road that used to be the railroad route to Abingdon, Virginia. Established well before most rail-to-trail conversions, this route connects two small farming communities in Ashe County in the northwesternmost corner of North Carolina. Although motor vehicles must use the very narrow road, most drivers are friendly sorts who wave as they pass.

The road hugs the South Fork of the New River most of the route as it wends its way through these mountain valleys. Most people are amazed to find that they can ride a mountain route that is so flat, "it's downhill both ways," as the local saying about the route goes. In warm weather tubing and canoeing bring many people to the river. The cool, shallow waters flow briskly enough to keep canoes moving while slowly enough that those in the canoes can enjoy the scenery and wave to the many cyclists on their bikes.

The author cycles along the New River on the way to Todd. (photo by R. Bruce Heye)

The quiet of this pastoral setting is good for whatever may trouble your mind. In places, thickets of rhododendron on steep hillsides dip their branches into quickly flowing streams that feed the river. These sections must have inspired those who lobbied diligently in the 1970s for the New to be declared a National Wild and Scenic River.

Lush, green pastures color the roadsides in the sparsely populated areas. Sometimes goats and sheep graze. In others the more familiar cows and horses share space. On one visit to the area, I came upon a woodchuck munching vegetation by the side of the road and was able to get within 3 feet of him before he scurried into the underbrush.

While Ashe County is home to several major businesses, most of the residents rely on farming or tourism for their livelihoods. Some rolling hills along the river sprout with young spruces and Fraser firs destined for Christmas tree markets all over the East Coast.

Other sites to see in the area include two contemporary religious frescoes. One graces Holy Trinity Church in Glendale Springs, while the other is located in St. Mary's Church on Beaver Creek School Road in West Jefferson.

The mineral springs in the area used to attract people who wanted to benefit from their healing qualities. Shatley Springs in northern Ashe County is noted for its southern country cooking, served up family style, but leave your calorie and cholesterol counter behind if you go there.

At the Todd General Store, you can see products from the 1930s and '40s that have long since disappeared from today's supermarket shelves. The store is also a museum of sorts with old farm implements and advertising signs. Homemade goodies and a variety of cold drinks are available for sale. At the back is a small restaurant. You might just want to sip your drink while resting on a bench on the front porch overlooking the New River before heading back to Fleetwood.

THE BASICS

Start: From the parking lot in Fleetwood, North Carolina, across from the post office.

Length: 20.5 miles.

Terrain: So flat that it's downhill both ways.

Traffic and hazards: The road is narrow and unmarked, but most motorists are used to cyclists and very courteous. In some places the pavement is uneven and the roadway slopes a bit.

Getting there: Take U.S. Highway 421 toward Ashe County, North Carolina, and turn north onto US 221. (This turn is a short distance west of the highway's intersection with the Blue Ridge Parkway.) Go 6.1 miles on US 221, then make a sharp left turn onto Railroad Grade Road in Fleetwood. (There's a sign for the Fleetwood Post Office.) The road descends to the river level along a very curvy stretch then straightens and flattens as you enter the town of Fleetwood. There is public parking in the grassy areas across from the church and the post office. See the *DeLorme North Carolina Atlas & Gazetteer*, page 13 C7.

0.0 Turn left from the parking lot onto Railroad Grade Road.

3.5 Stay on Railroad Grade Road. New River Bridge Road (SR 1105) goes off to the left.

5.2 Stay on Railroad Grade Road. Brown Road (SR 1104) goes off to the left.

6.4 Bear right on Railroad Grade Road. Cranberry Springs Road (SR 1100) goes off to the left. The name of the main road changes to Todd Railroad Grade Road (SR 1100) at this intersection.

10.3 Arrive in Todd at Todd General Store. Reverse these directions for your return trip.

20.5 Bear left all the way back to Fleetwood.

LOCAL INFORMATION

♦ North Carolina High Country Host, 1700 Blowing Rock Road, Boone, NC 28607; (828) 264–1299 or (800) 438–7500; www.highcountryhost.com.

♦ Ashe Chamber of Commerce, 6 North Jefferson Avenue, West Jefferson, NC 28694; (888) 343–2743; www.ashechamber.com.

LOCAL EVENTS/ATTRACTIONS

♦ Old-Time Jam Music, every Friday at 7:00 P.M. at the Todd General Store; (336) 877–1067; no charge.

♦ Concerts in the Walter and Annie Cooke Memorial Park, across from the Todd General Store, 3:00–5:00 P.M. every Saturday in summer; (336) 877–1067; no charge.

♦ Todd Fall Festival, an annual event on the second Saturday in October; food, crafts, music; (336) 877–1067; no charge.

♦ The Churches of the Frescoes. Ben Long painted three frescoes at St. Mary's in West Jefferson: *Mary Great with Child* in 1974, *John the Baptist* in 1975, and *The Mystery of Faith* in 1977. In summer 1980 he painted *The Last Supper* at Holy Trinity; P.O. Box 177, Glendale Springs, NC 28629; (336) 982–3076; no charge; visitors are welcome.

RESTAURANTS

♦ Todd General Store (restaurant at the back of the store), Todd-Railroad Grade Road, Todd, NC 28664; (336) 877–1067. Sandwiches, salads, pizza.

♦ Shatley Springs Inn, Highway 16 North, 407 Shatley Springs Road, Crumpler, NC 28617 ; (336) 982–2236; www.shatleysprings.com. Family-style country cooking; midrange.

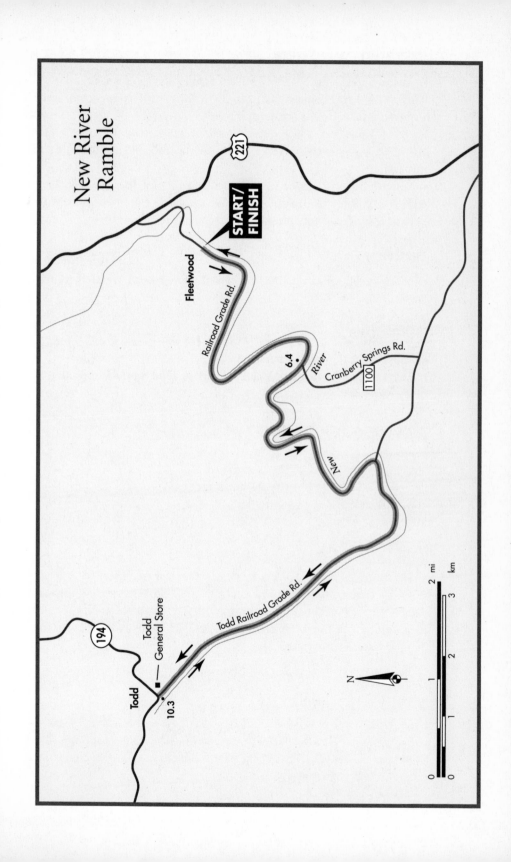

New River Ramble

START/FINISH

221

Fleetwood

Railroad Grade Rd.

6.4

River

Cranberry Springs Rd.

1100

New

Todd Railroad Grade Rd.

194

Todd
General Store

Todd

10.3

N

2 mi

km

3

2

1

1

0

0

ACCOMMODATIONS

♦ Shatley Springs Inn, NC–16 North 407 Shatley Springs Road, Crumpler, NC 28617; (336) 982–2236; fax (336) 246–3999; www.shatleysprings.com. Several rustic cabins along a lake, moderately priced.

♦ French Knob Inn, 133 Ferguson Road, West Jefferson, NC 28694; (336) 246–5177; www.frenchknobinn.com. Prices run $65 and up including full breakfast.

♦ Nation's Inn, 107 Beaver Creek School Road, West Jefferson, NC 28694; (336) 246–2080 or (800) 801–3441; www.nationsinn.com. New modern inn, moderately priced, complimentary continental breakfast.

BIKE SHOPS

♦ Biking Buddies, P.O. Box 758, 137 Blevins Express Road, West Jefferson, NC 28694; (336) 246–7603.

REST ROOMS

♦ Mile 10.3, at the Todd General Store.
♦ At Walter and Annie Cook Memorial Park in Todd (portable toilets).

MAPS

♦ *DeLorme North Carolina Atlas & Gazetteer,* page 13.